'. . . an important—and timely—chronicle of
extraordinary events.'
Adelaide Advertiser

'. . . a compelling picture of a press gallery so afraid of
missing the story that journalists become complicit in
their own manipulations.'
Anne Summers Report

'Anyone wanting to understand the dark art of media
manipulation needs to read this book.'
Mark Latham, *Australian Financial Review*

'A powerful glimpse of powerful people.'
Courier Mail

Kerry-Anne Walsh was born and grew up in Sydney. In 1978 she was lured to country Canberra by the light on the hill and the joys of working for the ALP in Opposition. She worked for eighteen months as a press secretary in the Hawke government before joining the *Daily Telegraph*'s Canberra bureau. Known as 'KA', Kerry-Anne remained in the federal parliamentary press gallery for the next twenty-five years, occupying senior posts in print, radio and TV: as national affairs writer for seven years for the *Bulletin* magazine, for the *Sun-Herald* for just shy of seven years and for News Ltd's *Sunday Telegraph*. KA also worked for the ABC as the political producer on Radio National's flagship *Daybreak* program, and for Channel Ten as associate producer on current affairs program *Face to Face*. She wrote for the *Irish Times*, the *South China Morning Post*, the *Singapore Straits Times* and other international publications, and was a regular on ABC TV's *Insiders* program and a string of radio programs. Disenchanted with political spin and the nature of political reporting, KA left the press gallery in August 2009 to establish her consultancy KA Communications. She remains in Canberra, and tragically continues to watch Question Time and listen to parliamentary debates on the radio. KA remains a political commentator on *Sky Agenda*, and on radio programs.

THE STALKING OF
JULIA
GILLARD

THE STALKING OF
JULIA
GILLARD

KERRY-ANNE WALSH

ALLEN&UNWIN

First published in Australia in 2013
This edition published in 2014

Allen & Unwin

83 Alexander Street
Crows Nest NSW 2065
Australia
Phone: (61 2) 8425 0100
Email: info@allenandunwin.com
Web: www.allenandunwin.com

Cataloguing-in-Publication details are available from the National Library
of Australia
www.trove.nla.gov.au

ISBN 978 1 76011 086 4

Typeset in Adobe Caslon by Midland Typesetters, Australia
Printed and bound in Australia by Griffin Press

10 9 8 7 6 5 4 3 2

The paper in this book is FSC® certified.
FSC® promotes environmentally responsible,
socially beneficial and economically viable
management of the world's forests.

For my mum Trish and late father Brian,
with love and thanks

And for the light of my life, my son Kieran

CONTENTS

PART TWO   THE FAILED AVENGER

AUTHOR'S NOTE

This is my contemporaneous diary of an extraordinary time in Australian politics—that of the Gillard Government from June 2011 to April 2013. From mid-2011 I scribbled notes, conducted interviews, chatted to people informally, and kept media and personal diaries of the rolling events. Initially, my idea was to record the unfolding drama of how the government and Independents handled Australia's first minority parliament since 1939, but it became quickly apparent that while the minority parliament was functioning remarkably well under Gillard's leadership, there was a heaving political undercurrent being generated by a minority within the Labor caucus that kept threatening to derail its success. I noticed that as the months passed, the vast resources of the press gallery became more focused on Rudd's ambitions for a comeback than anything the historic minority parliament had to offer.

So these are my personal observations, focusing on Team Rudd's slow-death destabilisation campaign against Gillard, the media's treatment of it and the combined effect on the government. It's not a defence of Gillard; I didn't talk to her for the book, and I don't gloss over her mistakes. This does not pretend to be a definitive account of her government. It's an expanded personal diary of observations, if you will, about a politician who was never given a fair go: not in the media, not by Rudd, not by some in caucus.

I don't dispute what a tough job it is chasing daily news; I did it for twenty-five years in the federal parliamentary press gallery. I made mistakes and inflicted damage on politicians, and I put my hand up for taking the golden egg-beater to some yarns. I was also on the other side of the fence in the early 1980s, trying to influence how the media portrayed the ministers I worked for in the first Hawke government. I know what a bastard of a business politics and journalism can be.

While there are rigorous, professional and highly competent journalists reporting from the press gallery, what confounded and disturbed me as the months passed was how many more got swept up in Rudd's power play, giving undeserved momentum to his ambitions to reclaim the prime ministership. They became players, not reporters.

There seemed to be a lack of appetite for rigorous assessment of Rudd the man and Rudd the politician, and of his motives, and the devastating impact he was having on the government. I noted how some of the best-paid journalists and commentators at News Ltd and Fairfax became Rudd's mouthpieces in the war he raged against Gillard. He could seldom do any wrong; his antics were generally afforded benign, unquestioning prime-time media coverage. The underhanded work being done by his acolytes was respectfully kept in anonymous shadows while being given headline treatment.

On the other hand Gillard was continually cast as a liar and policy charlatan, and lampooned for her hair, clothes, accent, arse, even the way she walks and talks. If ever the deck was stacked against someone, it was Gillard.

April 2013

PRELUDE

Julia Gillard took the reins of the ALP and with it the prime minister-ship on 24 June 2010 in one of the most abrupt leadership transitions in modern political history. She did so with the goodwill of most of her party, and with a fawning Canberra press gallery at her feet. The man she supplanted, Kevin Rudd, led an isolated band of angry Labor voices at this surprising turn of events; the collective political and media verdict was that his time, short though it had been, was up.

Gillard allies say Rudd started planning for his return to the prime ministership within days of the removalists stacking up the Rudd furniture and trappings and shifting them out of The Lodge. By the time Gillard announced in February 2011 that her government would introduce a carbon pricing scheme, Rudd and his small team of malcontents were in lock-step with key journalists in Canberra and around the country in a drive to push her out of the prime ministerial chair.

A year after her ascent, the undercurrent had become so poisonous that Gillard was forced into fighting a ludicrous battle against a man who had been removed from office because he was incapable of governing, who was despised by the overwhelming majority of his caucus colleagues and whose return many feared would plummet the government into the same chaotic state that had prompted his removal. In the words of a former high-level Rudd government policy adviser who penned a personal, unpublished account of his time in the Rudd Government, the way Rudd operated was 'a powerful warning for future governments . . . The Rudd government was never and could never have been a functional government because of the man who ran it.' This adviser was in a trusted position; he was intimate with the running and functioning of Rudd's cabinet and at the centre of much of its day-to-day mayhem. For those reasons, he will remain anonymous in this book.

Once deposed, Rudd's toxic ambition appears to have been either to return to the leadership, or to destroy both the government that had dumped him and the woman who had replaced him. In this pursuit he was abetted by political journalists who became pawns in his comeback play, channelling the Chinese whispers of his spruikers and giving credibility and substance to exaggerated claims about the pretender's level of support within the parliamentary party for a comeback.

On the morning of 24 June 2010, when a ballot for the leadership was still expected even though most of Rudd's caucus withdrew support for him the previous night, Chris Uhlmann predicted on the ABC website that the Prime Minister probably would not contest because he had such poor numbers. 'Ms Gillard has secured more than 70 votes, while Mr Rudd has just 30,' he wrote. As we know, in the end Rudd bowed out and Gillard assumed the prime ministership without the need for a ballot. Rudd had been deserted by colleagues who only three years previously had been prepared to laud him publicly as a Labor saviour. Privately, however, there had always been deep unease about Rudd—his over-powering personal ambition, his ruthless use of people and power blocs to get the leader's job, his lack of strong policy focus and his uneven temperament.

The oft-quoted fable that his crash in the opinion polls was the reason for his removal by his colleagues is hotly disputed by those central to Rudd's fate. Anybody who had an ear to the ground in Canberra at the time of the leadership change knew that Rudd was in a bad way; that he'd been unravelling since the disaster of the December 2009 climate change summit in Copenhagen; that his office, his department and the wider bureaucracy were paralysed by a prime minister who could not make the big decisions, but who sweated the minutiae of irrelevant tasks and board appointments; that he was so obsessed with his polling numbers and day-to-day politics that months into 2010, with an eye to the election, he was designing ever more extravagant and untenable policies that would provide him with the quick fixes of media limelight he appeared to need.

'For all that the PM could take vast amounts of time to make relatively straightforward decisions, he would all too frequently not tolerate the time for proper policy processes to function,' states the former Rudd government adviser. 'This was in part about a lack of respect for advice . . . but it was principally due to the way he geared the entire government's decision-making process to the media cycle.' As Rudd toyed with possible election dates, his cabinet ministers became increasingly alarmed that the agenda was getting bigger and the announcements more prolific, but there was no follow-through. When Gillard eventually moved into the prime ministerial suite, she inherited a daunting mess of unfinished business and half-baked ideas. 'The incoming Gillard government had an in-tray full to bursting with half-started and half-finished ideas to work its way through,' proclaims the adviser.

Rudd has always displayed erratic work tendencies, plus a Jekyll-and-Hyde personality. His mercurial temper and his appalling treatment of any member of staff or bureaucrat he considered an underling was legendary; these traits were occasionally reported when he was Opposition leader, and again—sporadically—when he became PM. In the lead-up to the events of 23 and 24 June, these tendencies bordered on the manic. Of all his ministers, Gillard and Swan most intimately knew how unhinged Rudd had become in the first half of 2010; so, too, did most of his staff. Perhaps, in his heart of hearts, Rudd knew it about himself as well. He may have possessed an overweening ambition to succeed and slick PR skills, but he did not, and still does not, have that essential mix necessary to lead a political party: a steely and steady personality, the ability to be calm under great pressure and under the weight of extreme criticism, and consistently clear thinking.

It's not as if the many facets of Rudd's personality weren't known to his caucus colleagues and the wider Labor family. Many were deeply uneasy at the remorseless way he had gone about whittling away Beazley's leadership, but their disquiet about Rudd's personality didn't stop them promoting him to the job of Opposition leader. His caucus colleagues, and the factional and union bosses he duchessed, primarily chose to support a man whose fitness for office they questioned for one reason: the perception, fuelled by the ever-present omniscient opinion polls, that he was more popular in the electorate than Beazley. To them, Rudd represented a guarantee they would plonk their bums on government seats, whereas

Beazley was an each-way bet. Those in the federal parliamentary Labor Party who voted for Rudd in 2006, and those outside it who wielded their factional muscle to help install him, bear as much responsibility for the lurching disasters of the last five years as Gillard or Rudd.

As Rudd's grip on the realities of day-to-day governing slipped dangerously, his close colleagues saw it as their duty to restore good government by taking the unprecedented step of removing him. Their intent was matched by the wider caucus: MPs who had propelled Rudd into the Opposition leader's chair had wised up about his unfitness for the job of Prime Minister. On the night of 23 June and into the wee hours of 24 June, faced with the surprising choice of either dumping a first term Labor prime minister or keeping someone who only a few years before had been one of the party's great success stories, Rudd's colleagues didn't hesitate to cut him adrift. But in the political shorthand of media reporting, the extraordinary circumstances that forced such an outcome were boiled down to winner and loser, victor and vanquished. The deeper reasons became too hard for many journalists to explore.

It has been confirmed to me by impeccable sources who were at the centre of the action on the night of 23 June that Gillard was deeply reluctant to take the job. Even former Hawke government minister Graham Richardson—no friend of Gillard's and for most of the last few years a fierce critic, who still talks to the 'right' Labor people in the faction of the same description—has debunked conspiracy theories that Gillard was either the architect or complicit in a planned attack on Rudd's prime ministership. She was a most reluctant draftee; despite the media perception to the contrary, no credible evidence has ever been offered to suggest otherwise.

Yet the story that she was an active plotter dogs the prime minister. It doesn't matter what Gillard says, she is disbelieved. The mythology is now stamped as part of her political DNA: she is disloyal, treacherous, a liar. It wasn't the only picture painted of Gillard early on in her first term; the other was that she was a politically manipulative, compassionless (single, childless) woman lacking basic integrity. Opposition leader Tony Abbott also promptly set his tone about her, taunting her as an untrustworthy political assassin—a rich description from a man who had ambushed his own leader, Malcolm Turnbull, and snatched his party's leadership by just one vote on 1 December 2009.

The white-anting against Gillard started almost as soon as she'd stepped up as prime minister. The first 'exclusives' about what had been promised to Rudd and what dastardly acts were perpetrated by Gillard against him bobbed up in the *Australian* and other News Ltd publications within weeks of Rudd's departure from the prime ministerial suite.

Once the election was called in July, the dams burst. There was speculation that Rudd had been sounded out for a top United Nations job; there was the allegation that Gillard had sent her bodyguard in her place to highly sensitive meetings of Cabinet's National Security Committee; she was also alleged to have opposed Rudd's parental leave scheme.

In a devastating blow to Gillard's credibility, which haunted her for months despite her protestations that the accusations were wrong, it was claimed that she had questioned cash handouts to pensioners because they were Coalition voters. It was Channel Nine's veteran political editor, doyen of the press gallery and Rudd favourite, Laurie Oakes, who 'broke' the killer stories about Gillard's alleged harsh attitude to pensioners and the parental leave scheme. He also delivered a crushing question at the National Press Club to Gillard about the events of the night of 23 June that portrayed Rudd sympathetically. Channelling Rudd, Oakes asked whether, in a private meeting with Rudd that fateful night, Gillard had agreed to Rudd's plea to be given until October to improve the government's standing, and if he couldn't he would stand aside voluntarily. Futhermore, he asked if Gillard then left the room, consulted colleagues, returned and told Rudd he didn't have the numbers and would challenge anyway. Demurring, she tried to make light of the question by referring to Oakes' rare appearance at the Press Club. Oakes sat steely-eyed, unmoved. I understand that Gillard's counsel from colleagues that fateful night was that Rudd's personality and his personal crisis at that time rendered him unable to change, thus the advice remained the same: he had to go.

The tumult of the leaks and attacks on Gillard's credibility helped drive Labor's polling numbers down during the campaign, resulting in one of the closest election results in Australian history—seventy-two seats apiece for the two largest parties, with a gaggle of Independents and a Green making up the remainder of the 150 seats in the House of Reps. In the aftermath, the deft political skills Gillard deployed to successfully negotiate a minority government with the Independents after seventeen days of haggling should have turned around perceptions of her abilities and character. She had achieved what Tony Abbott could not, and had delivered government for Labor when many in the commentariat had written her and Labor off. But after a brief media honeymoon, Gillard's successes started to be overlooked as personality politics crept back into media spaces.

Public support for Gillard and her government started crashing in February 2011, after she announced she would introduce a carbon pricing scheme. Her critics claimed she had broken an ironclad promise not to introduce a 'carbon tax'. But on nearly a dozen times during the election campaign she committed a future Gillard government to working towards the introduction of a carbon pricing or emissions trading scheme, which is what she announced: a fixed price moving to a floating price. On election eve *The Australian*, one of her harshest critics, even carried an exclusive interview about Gillard's promise to legislate a carbon price in the next term.

The announcement was followed by a crash in the polls, fed by a growing cacophony of anti-Gillard media voices—mainly based in capital cities outside Canberra—who labelled her an untrustworthy liar and a disgrace. Unsurprisingly, the anonymous malicious gripes of Rudd supporters mushroomed in the wake of Gillard's 'betrayal' and rapidly became the media focus, diminishing the real story of a remarkably stable and productive minority parliament that was in large part due to her abilities as a negotiator and peace-maker.

What was opportunistically never acknowledged by the Opposition, and never by the pro-Rudd and anti-carbon pricing commentariat, was that the art for a prime minister steering a successful minority parliament is to compromise with Coalition partners; in Gillard's case, the rural Independents and lone Green, all of whom had some form of carbon pricing scheme on their wish lists. It was both Labor and Liberal policy, also. Yet Gillard was flayed alive over the announcement and it dogged her days. That she made no headway rebutting attacks on her honesty and credibility says more about the campaign that was waged against her than her communication skills, wanting though they were at the times she needed them most.

The uproar also ignored the reality that promises made by a political party before an election can only become reality in a hung parliament if the governing party can navigate their acceptance through the maze of approvals needed from the disparate Coalition partners. In the May 2010 British parliament the Conservatives, led by David Cameron, formed a coalition with the Liberal Democrats after a hung result. The wholesale redrafting of the Conservatives' agenda as a result didn't prompt relentless bagging of the British prime minister as a liar and blaggard. Our political sophistication is clearly in its infancy.

In June 2011, as the Senate prepared to welcome the Greens as the new ascendant force in a formal alliance with Labor that had also been negotiated with Gillard, the portents for a calm passage through the rest of the parliamentary year didn't look positive. Enemy forces were at work, and they were not just on the Opposition benches.

PART ONE

THE GREAT PRETENDER

PART ONE

THE 'SACKIVERSARY'

15–24 June 2011

It's official. Prime Minister Julia Gillard is a dud. The first female prime minister of Australia is a shocker. Lacking in character, incapable of governing, hopeless, and a liar to boot. We know this because dozens of political journalists in Canberra, plus 'specialist' political commentators who never turn up in parliament, radio shock jocks in capital cities who never grace parliament's doors, and a grab-bag of internet amateur scribes and conspiracy-peddlers who could be anywhere, tell us so in their analysis of Gillard's one-year anniversary as prime minister.

This opportunity to consolidate what's been a relentless bagging of Gillard for months is because it's the 'Sackiversary'. And it's this event—not the economy, stupid; nor asylum seekers; nor running the country—that's consumed the Opposition and the national media for ten days now, leading up to the commemoration of the events of 23 and 24 June 2010. Acres of newsprint and hours of airtime on radio and TV, devoted to dissecting that day and the year since, have been spat out at the public in a stunning overkill analysis of Gillard's weaknesses and flaws.

But what about the good bits? Good heavens, no! She's a disaster leading a disastrous government.

The *Herald-Sun*'s Gillard hater-in-residence, Andrew Bolt, kicks off the media sledge-fest with a column on 15 June declaring her the weakest and most incompetent prime minister since 'at least WWII, with not a single achievement to boast of in a junkyard of failure'. Hers is a 'shameful record of deceits' that 'makes her unelectable' and, just to make sure we get the message, he finishes: 'What's killed Gillard is simply a lack of character. Of gravitas. Of honesty. Dud policy can be fixed. But dud character cannot, and Gillard's tragedy is that hers has been found out.' By whom, he doesn't say.

On the weekend of 18 and 19 June, Fairfax newspapers gratuitously run a poll showing that Rudd is outgunning Gillard as preferred prime minister by two-to-one. Such polls are only designed to create mischief. The person in the prime ministerial hot seat is almost always less favoured than anyone not in it—unless they are still in the honeymoon stratosphere, which Rudd enjoyed when he first became Labor leader. As with Howard vs Costello, or Keating vs Hawke, when you line up the pretender or the deposed against the poor bunny who's having to make the hard decisions, the incumbent is always dudded, particularly if the incumbent is introducing nasties that sections of the public don't like.

When I was political correspondent at the *Sun-Herald* in the mid-2000s, my deputy editor Peter Lynch had the impish idea of conducting a poll of New South Wales voters about their federal Labor leadership preferences and throwing former New South Wales Premier Bob Carr into the mix. Never mind that Carr wasn't in federal parliament and had no intention of coming on down, the huge support for him as federal leader in this poll gave us a spectacular front-page splash, which only served to cast further doubts on the leadership of the incumbent, Kim Beazley. This fanciful story led news bulletins all day, and gathered legs enough to spill into the next day's newspapers and radio news bulletins. It was like a fake bomb that turned atomic, setting off the political world and chattering classes, even though there wasn't a scintilla of reality to it.

The only media outlet at the time to call it for what it was was irreverent political-junkie website, *Crikey*, which accurately described the poll and accompanying yarn, which I wrote, as 'egregious'. Participants in polls will often nominate anyone—a drover's dog, Donald Duck, doesn't matter—as long as it's not the person telling them they're going to get a spanking new tax, have their pensions frozen or their middle-class welfare cauterised. More fool all of us for taking these polls seriously.

For the purposes of the Sackiversary—a brainchild tag dreamt up by the Opposition, and then eagerly adopted by Gillard haters in shock-jock land and quoted respectfully in national newspapers— the Fairfax Nielsen poll works a treat. It is the perfect platform for a feature piece by Peter Hartcher, Rudd's absolute favourite person in the press gallery, who returns the affection and adulation in spades. Asked by his mate for his reflections, Rudd muses: 'At the start, you're a bit too bruised to reflect intelligently. That's being human. But after a period of time you can reflect and learn. For me it's been good to open up discussion of what went right and what went wrong.'

With whom he has held those discussions he doesn't say. But it hasn't been with Gillard or her loyal ministers, and the discussions Rudd's been having with his small mutinous band of caucus backers is about payback, not moving forward. He admits to Hartcher only three mistakes: deferring the emissions trading scheme, failing to be more consultative, and not having more 'greybeards' advising him. But, he says bravely, he's in a 'robust' frame of mind and it has really all been just one big learning experience.

But there are those in cabinet who are anything but happy at this allegedly wised-up and lesson-learned Rudd sitting in the ministerial sanctum as Foreign minister. They see him as still murderous with rage at the woman who took his job as prime minister in June 2010, despite his self-effacing reveries about life after The Lodge.

But then again, he does have God on his side. He was pondering when in Church, he told the *Brisbane Times*, that the main thing was not to sit around and mope. 'The key thing is to get out there and make a difference with the resources that you have at your disposal today.' He wasn't perfect, of course, he was just having a go. 'Whatever your calling and whatever your lot is in life, to take those talents and take those abilities and use them to the utmost—that is what you try and do.' And: 'None of us are perfect and we all fall short of the glory of God.' As the Irish would say: Jaysus! The glory of God does not rest, a holy man should tell the former prime minister, in a vengeful heart.

Rudd has been able to console himself in the last year by busying himself, in the process clocking up a staggering cache of international frequent flyer points as he bustles about breaking diplomatic impasses and brokering peace in our time. But those who know him know he hurts like hell. He watches, he waits, and he plots.

After all, talk of escalating leadership tensions between Gillard and Rudd—or, more accurately, reporting of talk that may or may not be happening—is cranking up nicely. The day before the

Fairfax poll, Simon Benson, Gemma Jones and Steve Lewis wrote a breathless piece in the *Daily Telegraph* about the pair being 'locked' for an hour the preceding day in 'a tense, closed-door meeting'. (Are any high-level ministerial meetings held out in the open?)

When an article starts 'Almost a year to the day since the coup . . .', but it is a good seven days before the actual anniversary, journalistic accuracy clearly isn't a priority. Unfortunately, the *Tele*'s readers weren't told much about the meeting, except for a sniffy suggestion that it was about the temporary banning of live animal exports to Indonesia, a challenging policy issue of the day having catastrophic ramifications for breeders in Australia and abattoirs in Indonesia. This is a real policy issue with real repercussions, but the *Tele* doesn't give us any background.

One would imagine the Prime Minister and her Foreign minister, who are being forced to deal with Indonesian authorities over this unpopular policy, would look grim. But according to the *Tele*—even though it was denied by both Gillard and Rudd's office—the meeting was most definitely about leadership, because their 'body language' showed there was 'renewed tension between the two rivals'. Why? Because the pair walked down a parliamentary corridor into the meeting without talking to each other, the *Tele* informed us.

Here's a thought: maybe holding talks about a grave policy issue is a sombre prospect. The pair aren't exactly BFFs anyway; the parliament has been in a continuous uproar over the issue; and a pesky photographer furiously snapping your photo as you walk into a tense meeting doesn't lend itself to posing and shouting 'Cheese!'. Five photos from *Tele* photographer Gary Ramage's efforts accompany the online article as rock-solid proof of volatile leadership tension between the pair.

The story continued relentlessly: there were 'tremors' evident in Labor ranks, 'renewed rumblings about a Rudd comeback' because of 'shitty' polling, the authors declared. No names, no pack drill, and certainly nothing about the challenging policy dilemma of suspending the livelihoods of 17,000 cattle farmers in the Northern Territory, cutting the meagre livings of thousands of Indonesian workers in affected abattoirs, and crippling a multi-million-dollar export industry.

The authors revealed in the very last sentence why the article's premise was baseless and it should never have been published: 'But claims Mr Rudd could win back the leadership were dismissed, with faction bosses saying his support was the size of a netball team.'

This non-story—and a similar one in the *Australian* about 'rumours' of unspecified 'screaming matches'—sprout legs. Rudd, who on this chill June night has just martyred himself by participating in the annual Vinnies CEO sleep-out, emerges remarkably quickly once the newspapers have hit the newsstands in order to talk to *ABC Breakfast*. He's decked out in a humble blue and white tracksuit and sporting a wee hint of homeless stubble. Reports of a feud with Gillard were a fabrication and those speculating about it should take a Mogadon, he instructs. They'd been talking about the live cattle issue, he says. And no, he's not challenging the Prime Minister. Cue laugh out loud from the prime ministerial suite.

Immigration minister Chris Bowen also urges calm. The photos were being over-analysed, he told the ABC's *AM*. 'I see them working closely together, cooperatively on the matters of national interest of the day. I've seen that first hand, close up,' he says. It doesn't matter what Bowen or anyone says, the media has the bit between its collective teeth, and it ain't letting go.

*

Accompanying the Fairfax poll is a story by Michelle Grattan in the *Age*, reporting that 'rumours' of an unspecified 'row' between Rudd and Gillard are swirling about—no doubt the very same unspecified row which appeared in the *Tele* yesterday. Rumour becomes fact very easily these days; what one media outlet reports in vague, unsubstantiated terms becomes bible when the next journalist runs with it.

Gillard tries to put context around the poll, explaining: 'I certainly anticipated that this would be a hugely difficult period. I'm not surprised about some of the results we're seeing. We are in a phase where we've outlined principles [on carbon pricing] to the Australian people. We've been very, very frank with them about the impacts of carbon pricing on them . . . and we're not at the stage yet where we can fully explain to people the assistance that comes with it.'

Sounds reasonable; logical, even. Australians fear the unknown. We're a conservative lot at heart, and we particularly don't like nasty surprises that come with a price tag. We respond well to fear campaigns, and we love a good bellyache about thieving politicians sneaking their hands into our hip pockets.

Gillard has been hounded and pilloried for stating before last year's election that her government wouldn't introduce a carbon tax. The one and only quote relentlessly trotted out by the anti-Gillardites in the Land of the Lunar Right is: 'There will be no carbon tax under a government I lead.' What is conveniently ignored is that on at least ten occasions during the campaign she committed a future Gillard government to work towards a carbon pricing scheme. In an election eve interview, Gillard even told *The Australian*'s resident political gurus, Dennis Shanahan and Paul Kelly, that she was prepared to legislate such a scheme in the next term.

She would view victory as 'a mandate' to do so, they wrote. To cries from Abbott and media critics that she'd broken a promise, Gillard responded she wouldn't play semantic word games: her proposal was a market-based mechanism to price carbon—a temporary fixed price 'hard-wired' to a cap-and-trade scheme. They could call it what they wanted.

The response then had been fast, furious and inaccurate. One of 2GB's resident Gillard-haters, Alan Jones, branded her 'Juliar'. Acerbic Melbourne *Herald-Sun* economics writer Terry McCrann, who finds it difficult to give a tick to anything Gillard or her government does, described her as 'both dishonest and dumb'. Andrew Bolt, another in the *Herald-Sun* anti-Labor stable of grumpy old men, let fly. She was a liar leading the world on climate change 'by marching off a cliff', he pronounced. The *Daily Telegraph*'s Piers Akerman outdid even his own consistently florid descriptions of Gillard, tossing around phrases like 'mind-numbing duplicity', 'stupendous hypocrisy' and 'pure treachery'.

John Howard performed a triple reverse somersault on his promise to never, ever introduce a GST under a government he led, and was met with no such opprobrium. Unlike Gillard, he consistently lied to the Australian people about his intentions.

In May 1995, in response to reports of comments he had made to a business lunch that he was leaving the door open to revisit the GST as Coalition policy, Howard issued a definitive statement shutting down the talk. The newly re-minted Opposition Leader declared in his press statement: 'Suggestions I have left open the possibility of a GST are completely wrong. A GST or anything resembling it is no longer Coalition policy. Nor will it be policy at any time in the future. It is completely off the political agenda in

Australia.' At a media conference he repeated the lines. 'There's no way a GST will ever be part of our policy.' Reporter: 'Never ever?' Howard: 'Never ever. It's dead. It was killed by voters at the last election.'

Howard won the 1996 election and, after a horror, scandal-plagued first year that saw five of his ministers depart the front-bench, he revisited what had always been one of his tax reform favourites—probably to take the community's collective mind off what a basket case of a government he was leading. In August 1997, he coyly invited the Australian public to go on a 'tax adventure' with him, declining to say whether the adventure would include wandering down the GST path. Six months later, he announced his GST package. As for those pesky previous promises, Howard invented a new caveat. He had always said, he told parliament in April 1998 in the run-up to the October election, that he'd only ever promised not to introduce a GST 'in our first term'. Nonsense. He flat out lied, thrice. Yet the very same commentators who now hold Gillard to ferocious account over what was not a lie, hold Howard up as an example of how to go about things when in government, because he took the GST to the voters at the 1998 election. The double standards are staggering.

In Canberra's Big House on the hill, parliamentary exchanges this week have been dominated by Opposition taunts about the leadership change-over, a year ago, augmented by Liberal Party-sponsored television advertisements claiming Rudd wants his old job back. 'Has the political assassination of a sitting prime minister been worth it?', Abbott demands of Gillard during one question time. Still washing Malcolm Turnbull's blood off his hands from his own coup against his leader eighteen months ago, Abbott is brazen in his attacks on Gillard. All week, it's the same message: she leads 'the most incompetent, the most deceptive, the most dishonest government in modern Australian politics'. Question after question is peppered with accusations and insinuations about Gillard and Rudd. Labor MPs must deeply regret having 'conspired in the political assassination of an elected prime minister' is another taunt, which cutely ignores the fact that Australians don't vote for the prime minister—it's the duty of both party rooms to elect their leader, who then carries his or her party's credentials to the election. If their party wins, their leader assumes the prime ministership unless their party room decides otherwise.

Trying to ram a spear through a slight opening in their opponent's armour is a traditional pastime for any Opposition. Labor's brilliant at it, too. But when Rudd joins in, political game-playing assumes a nastier dimension. Opposition Foreign spokeswoman Julie Bishop rises to her feet and directs a question to Rudd about Australian diplomatic relations with East Timor, PNG and Malaysia in the wake of Labor's latest asylum seeker policy. Wild cheers erupt from the benches behind her: this will be fascinating. Rudd is happy to respond: he leans with lazy nonchalance on the despatch box as he extols the government's policy, while the faces of ministerial colleagues behind him are grim.

When Bishop winks at him and asks a supplementary question, inquiring when he'd be returning to Bougainville, he responds with deadpan delight: it is a 'most sensitive' issue that remains 'contested territory'. It 'must be brought to its proper conclusion', he states, his back straight, eyes wandering to the public and press galleries. 'That is why we should be very sensitive about any external interventions by well-meaning Australian politicians.' The Opposition benches rock with glee at the obvious sub-text. Bishop's question was no polite inquiry about Rudd's travel plans: 'Boganville' is the former prime minister's searing private put-down of The Lodge's current inhabitants.

Rudd is untouchable. Such a malicious parry with an Opposition MP—collaborating in an assault on his own side's Prime Minister—should have earned Rudd malevolent glares from colleagues and a promise by a frontbencher to drag him behind the dunnies after Question Time for a solid talking-to. Instead, some Labor MPs smirk, and ministers stare at imaginary dirty spots on the carpet.

On 24 June, the real anniversary day, the *Daily Telegraph* tosses another bouncer at Gillard's head, announcing the results of an 'exclusive' poll of 600 respondents in four states—a low, unrepresentative sample by usual polling standards—which, unsurprisingly, finds that 'voters in key marginal seats have forgiven Kevin Rudd and are clamouring for him to return to the Labor leadership'. Steve Lewis, Tim Vollner and Neil Keene continue in their best purple political prose: 'One year since Mr Rudd was executed by Labor's faceless men, the electorate has turned on his successor—savaging Julia Gillard's broken carbon tax promise.' Further into the story we find that, rather than a savaging, the carbon tax is supported by 33 per cent of respondents, with 45 per cent opposed. The rest are undecided. It's a reasonable result, given the unrelenting negative coverage given to the carbon pricing scheme since Gillard's announcement.

The *Tele* also pulls the oldest trick in a tabloid editor's well-thumbed handbook, tracking down another person called Julia Gillard, this one a primary school teacher in Mt Eliza. But it seems it's had trouble wringing out of her anything too harshly critical of her more famous namesake. The best it could do was:

'After watching the political assassination of Kevin Rudd, the Mt Eliza woman wouldn't want to end up on the PM's bad side. "I wouldn't want to cross her. She's very quick-witted."' Er, isn't that usually a compliment?

Journalists Nathan Mawby and Chris Gillett have better luck with another Kevin Rudd. He delivers the goods: 'What she did to Rudd, stabbing him in the back, was stupid,' 62 year-old Kevin from Goulburn pronounced. And Julia's a failure, he added. To round out the anti-Gillard coverage, columnist Piers Akerman weighs in, declaring the day 'Assassination Day', tempering his rant against 'liar' Gillard with the observation that Rudd was also a dud, even if he was 'assassinated'. Quality journalism all round from Sydney's biggest-selling newspaper.

The assassination epithet is enthusiastically embraced by Opposition figures in their scripted early morning 'doorstops'. In a remarkable coincidence, Akerman and Tony Abbott are often well-synchronised in message and tone. Surely it's just all that shared blokey activity—they fight fires together as members of a Sydney volunteer bushfire brigade. No way would they ever collude on tactics.

On ABC Radio's *AM*, chief political reporter Sabra Lane spreads the Opposition's message. In an interview with the Prime Minister, she asks: 'The Opposition has labelled today Assassination Day; one of your senior colleagues calls it Liberation Day. Is it a happy anniversary for you?' Her next three questions are about opinion polls, with Lane expressing the view that Rudd's demise was 'in large part' because of bad opinion polling. Gillard responds, as she always does, that she doesn't respond to polls. She also disagrees with the premise of Lane's questioning; but Lane persists, switching her questions to internal ALP research about Gillard's leadership.

At times she hectors the Prime Minister. Questions are accusatory, loaded with judgement: 'He [Kevin Rudd] was tackling the big reforms that you are talking about as well and he had bad polling figures. Isn't he right to feel—what on earth? Why should you be given a reprieve and he wasn't?' In a question about the carbon tax 'broken promise', Lane demands: 'But why can't you just say sorry?'

It is excruciating listening for anyone interested in serious policy questions. This is a week in which the United States has declared a 33,000-strong troop withdrawal from Afghanistan, with Australia's response relatively untested; yet another Aussie soldier has died in that conflict; and Air Chief Marshall Angus Huston has retired as head of the defence forces. As well, Chinese investors have pulled out of a massive port and rail project in Western Australia, and yesterday Optus, Telstra and the National Broadband Network (NBN) signed a significant agreement to decommission the copper network and move Telstra's customer base to the NBN. Rich pickings indeed, with significant public impact.

Interviews that begin by hammering the nuances of opinion polls become a recurring pattern played out for the rest of the day. And on every day parliament sits. And most days when parliament doesn't. As a class, political journalists are obsessed with the minutiae of polls. They are the permanent backdrop to the story of the day; they frame the way journalists think. In news stories reporters editorialise about the context, the meaning, the import and the ramifications for government and opposition of a slight dip here, a slight rise there in published opinion polls. Opportunistic politicians abuse polls in the same way, and frame policies and launch attacks on opponents using polling as a launching pad. Polls are a canker on the body politic.

*

Rudd and wife Therese Rein were going to hold a party dubbed by the media as an Assassination Party, but it's cancelled—in a blaze of publicity, of course. Rein's explanation is a study in disingenuousness. 'Well, I thought it would be nice to honour a promise made last June to have K's former and current staff over to say thank you,' she Twitter-trilled. 'But, given that it seems to be turning into something of a media event, Kevin and I have decided to postpone it. We will hold it a bit later on so we can catch up with our friends and thank these terrific people properly.'

Tosh. One maxim in politics is, if you don't want to rock the boat, don't appear in the media. That's all Rudd has done for the last week—malignantly philosophising on his demise to pet journalists; strewing teasing lines for eager 'mis'interpretation by reporters obsessed with politics, not policy; organising, and then cancelling, a party that could only have been interpreted one way.

As for Gillard, she's spending the anniversary travelling to Perth for a weekend Labor conference. Two of the big issues she said she would immediately address when she assumed office—the mining tax and asylum-seekers—are either legislated or about to be, and the price on carbon is a work in progress. The superfast broadband network is gathering pace; skills, education, and both general and mental health received massive boosts in last month's budget; and parents are receiving school bonuses they didn't have a year ago. It hasn't been an easy or a mind-blasting success of a year but, by any reasonable measure, it hasn't been a dud either.

THE GREEN MACHINE ROLLS IN

July 2011

Federal Parliament is awash with emotion this chilly Canberra morning, Monday 4 July. The new Senate is about to be sworn in, giving nine Greens senators extraordinary power to help shape the nation for the next three years. Hard man of the Liberal Right, Senator Eric Abetz, mutters darkly that the chamber he has sat in for seventeen years will today take on 'a deeper shade of red' when the gaggle of Greens senators assume the balance of power.

Bob Brown, the party's battle-hardened leader, is a veteran of more than twenty years in state and federal parliaments. He and his deputy, Christine Milne, are determined to turn Australia green by shutting down coal mines, converting the wide brown land into a landscape of wind turbines, and roofing its suburbs with photovoltaic cells. News Ltd, and the *Australian* in particular, is determined to hound the Greens into the political wilderness and to shame Gillard for the deal she struck with them on a carbon price so as to create a Labor minority government and a workable Senate. Acerbic News Ltd columnist Piers Akerman warns: 'Brown and his Greens constitute a small and ugly tail wagging a large and dangerously confused dog. At the first chance, voters will ensure this beast is humanely dispatched.'

In a punchy editorial after the 2010 election, the *Australian* made it plain it saw its patriotic duty was to muscle out the traitors. 'Greens leader Bob Brown has accused *The Australian* of trying to wreck the alliance between the Greens and Labor,' it editorialised. 'We wear Senator Brown's criticism with pride. We believe he and his Green colleagues are hypocrites; that they are bad for the nation; and that they should be destroyed at the ballot box.'

Rachel Siewert and Scott Ludlum from Western Australia, and Sarah Hanson-Young from South Australia—Brown and Milne's only other colleagues before the election—are now joined on the pink leather by four newbies who will support or reject government legislation if Labor and the Coalition can't agree. Richard di Natale is a 42-year-old doctor from Victoria with a notable background in public health. Penny Lesley, 50, joining Hanson-Young from South Australia, is a lawyer and teacher. Larissa Waters is a 34-year-old Canadian-born Queenslander, with Honours in Science and Law. Then there's Lee Rhiannon, a veteran of New South Wales Greens politics with a science degree, a Trotskyist family pedigree and a long involvement in women's and union politics.

The party, riding a growing wave of popular support at local and national levels, is now the legitimate third force in Australian politics. The Labor–Greens alliance is a godsend to the conservative side of politics and for those who will use it to renew their attack on Gillard's authority. Jostling for pole position in this exercise are the *Australian* and Gillard's foes within her own party. 'This is,' opines one glum Labor MP, 'the most unpredictable time we're entering since we elected Mark [Latham] as leader.' He thinks again. 'Or Kevin [Rudd].'

Latham is a giant thorn in the rump of his former party. He led Labor for eleven whole months in 2004 and 2005; detonated his chance at the prime ministership by crushing John Howard's hand and nearly head-butting his smaller opponent at a chance encounter during the October 2004 election campaign; suffered a few bouts of pancreatitis and then spectacularly blew up his leadership in a jaw-dropping press conference in a suburban Sydney park on 18 January 2005. Latham recovered from pancreatitis, but continues to spew bile at his former mates. He made a gruesome appearance as a guest TV journalist during the August 2010 federal election campaign, hounding Julia Gillard and fawning over Pauline Hanson; and then, in a dishonourable piece of television on Channel Nine's *60 Minutes*, he recommended to voters they stick their middle finger up at all politicians and vote informal—which a record number did. His barbed prose on the dangers and shortcomings of his former colleagues, particularly Gillard, continue to bite via his column in the *Australian Financial Review* and his regular gigs on Sky News. A world-class hater, Latham dislikes Gillard; but he detests Rudd, which is a perverse, small mercy for the Prime Minister.

Not that it worries the Ruddster. He has more than enough media mates in his corner. Right now, he doesn't want to lose the dynamic created by the Sackiversary condemnations of Gillard and his recent carefully selected appearances in the media. Like manna from heaven, on 1 July a Newspoll bolsters his spirits by revealing that, if an election were held tomorrow, the political death knell would sound for every Labor Queensland MP—except, of course, Kevin from Queensland (who's only here to help). Treasurer Wayne Swan, with a little on his plate in the form of helping frame the carbon pricing scheme and a new mining tax, and run the $3 trillion economy, spends a fruitless ten minutes being inter-viewed by Queensland ABC's Madonna King, who is interested only in the poll and goading Swan into saying that Gillard's a better leader than Rudd. Eventually, he agrees. As he would.

Within hours, the *Australian* has posted an online news story out of the interview. The first sentence begins: 'Wayne Swan has confirmed he believes Julia Gillard is a better leader than Kevin Rudd . . .' Journalists Rob Kidd and Dennis Shanahan continue earnestly that Swan 'initially refused to answer' but, 'challenged that as Deputy Prime Minister he should think Ms Gillard a better leader', he responded: 'I don't need to think it Madonna, I know it.' Scoop of the year! The fact that Swan is her deputy, that he swung in behind the removal of Rudd and that he has been outspoken in his support for Gillard ever since apparently isn't sufficient evidence of his loyalty.

Such heinous pap is par for the course these days. Stories are squeezed out of nothing; headlines created out of nonsense; trivial games are played out on radio and in the national press. Politi-cal journalism is now a game of Gotcha—a hunt for that hint of weakness, the slight intonation or nuancing of words that might indicate something isn't kosher. It's a witch-hunt out of control, where the slightest stumble is magnified to ridiculous proportions, often into stories of national status, when they're in fact based on fluff. Struggling for survival and relevance, we as a profession of political journalists and commentators have collectively debased our craft to the lowest common denominator—writing articles confected out of barrel-scrapings and hectoring. In such stories, the public interest doesn't figure.

The only winner in this game at this point is Rudd, whose remarkably easy manipulation of the media is giving him a saloon passage back, he hopes, to his rightful place in the prime ministerial suite. It seems not to matter to him that his overweening ambition and quietly relentless pursuit of media coverage is a dragging undertow to the government's functioning, and to Gillard's legitimacy. His ardent supporters in the media are prepared to run with him all the way back to The Lodge by giving prominent, one-sided attention to whatever he or his backers want published or aired.

The jostling for prominence amongst political journalists—each wanting to be known as 'the best' or the one who got 'the scoop'— is reaching new heights of silliness. The *Australian*, for instance, is currently running advertisements in its paper showcasing the credentials of Dennis Shanahan. Under side-by-side photos of a teary Rudd after he'd lost the prime ministership and Shanahan posing outside Parliament House with a phone glued to his ear, a headline screams: 'THE DEMISE OF A PM—THE JOURNALIST WHO KNEW FIRST'. The copy underneath reads: 'As political editor of *The Australian*, based in the Canberra press gallery, Dennis Shanahan not only broke the news of the government's planned super profits tax, he exclusively revealed that Labor mutineers were preparing to move against Kevin Rudd. With a career spanning close to 40 years, Dennis knows the goings-on in politics before many politicians do. Read *The Australian* and you can too.'

As is often the case with the *Australian*'s political reporting, don't believe everything you read. Four days before the events of late-evening 23 June last year, Shanahan co-wrote a piece with Patricia Karvelas stating that, if Labor's poll numbers continued south, Rudd would be head-hunted in the worst possible way. He repeated a similar line the following day. But on the morning of the 23rd—the only morning that counts—Shanahan wrote that 'the school of thought that it would be suicide to engineer a leadership change has prevailed'. He continued: '. . . Rudd seems safe to lead Labor through to the election, whether parliament resumes in August or not, and whether the election is in September or October.' The headline on the story left no room for doubt: 'PM's position is secure, party's is not.' No ifs, no buts. There's nothing like accuracy, in reporting or advertising.

No-one, however, holds a candle to the outright malevolence of the cranky old men of Sydney commercial radio. Alan Jones, the spear-carrier for this homely group, has Gillard in his sights; he has done so since she announced in February her intention to introduce a carbon tax. She committed the unpardonable sin of being late for a live interview with him soon after her announcement, whereupon he berated her for her bad manners and promptly anointed her 'Juliar'. He's been distorting, insulting and hounding her since, running a high-profile campaign—along with others at the 2GB stable—to drive her out of The Lodge.

On 6 July, Jones let it all hang out. Gillard, he says, 'is absolutely laughable. The woman's off her tree, and quite frankly they should shove her and Bob Brown in a chaff bag and take them as far out to sea as they can and tell them to swim home.' Classy.

Jones has had some trouble getting his facts right on climate science (and a host of other matters too great to mention), but on Gillard he constantly tells his listeners she's wrong on the carbon pricing scheme, wrong for the country, wrong on the economy. Wrong, wrong, wrong. The car bumper sticker for the discerning Sydney motorist, 'Is it true, or did Alan Jones tell you?', should be letter-boxed around the country. If Jones at breakfast isn't enough bile for a day, listeners can also tune into Ray Hadley in the mornings, and stay tuned for the afternoon show with Chris

Smith. All three have been zealous anti-carbon, anti-Labor propagandists. Hadley is as big a Gillard-hater as Jones.

But Smith is in another realm altogether. He tossed all semblance of objectivity out the window in March when he broadcast live from an anti-carbon tax rally outside federal parliament. He's been fiercely riding the bandwagon ever since, urging his listeners to descend on Canberra next month, as he told his audience on 15 July, to 'rock the Prime Minister's boat one final time'. Some of the listeners this trio allow onto their programs—to deride Gillard as a 'lying bitch', a 'menopausal monster', 'a piece of crap'—defy any radio code of conduct.

2GB is one of Tony Abbott's favourite outlets. He loves his breakfast chats with Alan, and his media staff use Smith and Hadley to air material they couldn't possibly peddle in Canberra.

The Clean Energy Future package is finally announced on 10 July to a media locked up in Parliament House early on a chilly Sunday Canberra morning. It didn't contain many surprises.

Start-up price: $23 a tonne. Start-up date: 1 July 2012. Heavy-polluting companies paying the tax: 500. Compensation package: up to $4.8 billion a year for households, and up to $3.3 billion a year for industry. Cost to the budget (that is, the cost of compensation after the receipt of revenues) over four years: $4.2 billion. Impact on average household cost of living expenses: estimated 0.7 per cent, or just under $9.90 a week. Net impact on the average household after compensation, including tax cuts: $0.20 cents better off. Level of hysteria: ten on the political Richter scale. Level of fear ramped up by Abbott, loudmouth shock jocks and tabloid henchmen: 150%.

Trying to frame an emissions trading scheme to deal with 'the greatest moral challenge of our time', and then walking away from it, was one of many factors in Kevin Rudd's demise. Voters hated him for it; he'd over-egged the omelette in his speeches, committing the mortal political sin of over-promising and under-delivering. On the other side of politics, trying to get an emissions trading scheme through the Liberal party room mowed down two leaders, Brendan Nelson and Malcolm Turnbull, and in 2009 delivered Tony Abbott to the leader's chair. Miraculously, given the normally short shelf life of Opposition leaders, he still sits there. Now Gillard's enemies want it to claim her scalp too—and there's no shortage of little media helpers for that task.

In his usually understated manner, the *Tele*'s Piers Akerman kicked the first ball with this opening line in his 11 July column about the carbon pricing package: 'Not since the notorious Loans Affair contributed to the Whitlam's government's timely downfall has there been a fraud attempted on the scale of Julia Gillard's great carbon tax con,' he bellowed. It didn't get any kinder. He may be yelping at the converted, but Akerman's columns get traction: more than 500 upset souls took to the keyboard to chime in, and Akerman will follow up during his regular appearances on ABC's *Insiders*.

Fellow *Tele* columnist Tim Blair gives the carbon price package his best treatment and, over at News Ltd's Victorian stable-mate the *Herald-Sun*, Andrew Bolt was echoing Akerman in his outrage. 'Julia Gillard's carbon dioxide tax is the most brazen fraud to be perpetrated by an Australian government,' he thunders. Bolt also has a huge following and he uses it ruthlessly, tub-thumping against Gillard on a daily basis on his blog, in his columns, on radio and in TV commentary. The guy spreads his poison wide. The nitty-gritty of the clean energy package remains largely unanalysed in these commentaries, as these ageing gentlemen members of the

Society for the Indignant and Outraged prefer to rely on rhetoric, insults, personal bias and fear-peddling. One wonders if their bile and venom would be directed at a man; the disrespect they show Gillard and the office of prime minister is unprecedented.

Surprisingly, Paul Kelly declares in the *Australian* the package Gillard's 'finest achievement as a political fixer'.

To borrow a Rudd description, Gillard is not a happy Vegemite with the megaphone media criticism of the carbon pricing package, particularly from News Ltd scribes and commentators. Greens Leader Bob Brown is itching for a wide-ranging inquiry into the Australian media—with News Ltd firmly in his sights—and Gillard has it in her 'for consideration' in-tray. Ah, the temptation! For the time being, she contents herself with a stiff warning about her thinking on the media in Australia, and a verdict about the quality of reporting about her government via an address to Canberra's National Press Club on 14 July.

It is a speech brimming with vision for Australia and the place of a carbon pricing scheme in our nation's future. She is candid about herself, the image she projects and the things that move her. 'Australians do want to know more about me and how I'll lead this government in coming years, especially when confronted with new challenges in the future, and that means they do want to know what kind of person I am,' she reflects. 'And look, I'm a decision-maker by nature and I have tended to let the decisions speak for themselves.

'It doesn't come easy to me to expose my feelings as I make these decisions. I was the shy girl who studied and worked hard, and it took time and effort but I got from Unley High to the law and as far as here, where I am today. I've brought a sense of personal reserve to this, the most public of professions. And the rigours of politics have reinforced my innate style of holding a fair bit back in order to hang pretty tough.

'If that means people's image of me is one of steely determination, I understand why. But I don't forget where I come from, why I'm here, or what I've learned along the way.'

Her words are moving and heartfelt. And she has a blunt message for the media: 'Don't write crap,' she says in response to a question from Seven's political editor Mark Riley. 'Can't be that hard. And when you have written complete crap, then I think you should correct it.'

In newspapers the next day the focal point of the coverage is that she was a tearful girl (or an emotional woman holding back tears, take your pick) pleading to be understood; the vision bit about Australia is sidelined. So much for not writing crap.

But forget the Carbon Tax. The really big news breaks on 19 July, when Kev announces to an anxious world that he's going in for heart surgery to replace a leaking aortic valve. It's a funny thing about Kev—he always has big decisions to announce when there's been other big decisions around in which he can't share the limelight.

Rudd marks his end-of-July eight week departure from parliament with a long interview with the *Australian*. Matthew Franklin, a Canberra journalist who met Rudd while both were Brisbane-based, is another of Rudd's media pets. Their chat ends up as a series of 'exclusives' rolled out over a few days.

On 28 July, Franklin 'revealed' that Rudd was urging the Labor Party 'to target the political mainstream to differentiate itself from the Greens, arguing that the movement is at its best when it is a party of the centre'. And here's the dig from the wounded leader-in-exile:

'I will leave it for others to reflect on the position of the Greens on the question of their non-support for [my] carbon pollution reduction scheme as opposed to the current scheme. Others can answer that question; others will provide the analysis.' Others should provide the analysis that Rudd is attaching himself to one of the *causes célèbres* of the political and media conservatives as they line up to attack Gillard over her and her government's alliance with the Greens. But they don't.

The next day, in another of Franklin's rolling 'exclusives', Rudd ranges across his philosophies on life, foreign affairs and his dumping, including the loaded observation that he learned valuable lessons from his aborted prime ministership and the bludgeoning events of thirteen months earlier. Is there an echo in the room? Didn't his mate Peter Hartcher run much the same line in another exclusive interview with Rudd last month in the *Sydney Morning Herald*?

Kev also knows that the key to media success is a consistent presence combined with a dash of theatre. So—aw shucks—what's this? For a Twinings competition, Kev has designed his own blend of tea. As the RSPCA is his charity of choice, if he wins and his tea is produced he's recruited his cat and dog, Jasper and Abby, to flog the hell out of it in a cutesy home-made YouTube video voiced over by the man himself. His voice tinkles and trills and coos as the pets are enticed to partake of the brew. Abby, the golden retriever, laps up what looks suspiciously like milk—a real sleight of hand if ever there was one. Now there's a rich political metaphor.

Bob Katter Jnr, one of the independents in the Lower House and one of the real individualists in parliament, believes Labor will return Rudd to the prime ministership. The 'Man in the Hat' had a long stint in state parliament before galloping into the national capital. Political blood courses through his veins. His dad, Bob Snr, a lion of the Country Party, held the federal Queensland seat of Kennedy now occupied by his son from 1966 to 1990. Bob Jnr started life as a National, but dumped that allegiance in 2001 over policy differences and became an Independent.

Katter talks constantly to Rudd. Their unlikely friendship was forged in the quieter ambience of the Queensland legislature, when Rudd was running the Premier's Department. Their meeting point was Aboriginal politics: Katter's burning aspirations for Aboriginal people, nurtured through decades of living in outback Queensland, has been one of his enduring philosophical touchstones. Rudd, as Secretary of the Premier's Department under Wayne Goss, grappled with modernising the state's attitudes to its Indigenous constituents, which had been less than enlightened under the rule of peanut farmer Sir Joh Bjelke-Petersen. Matters of Indigenous policy made it onto Katter's twenty-point list put to Gillard as a condition of his support for her minority government. Ultimately, he denied her that support when she failed to meet his demands.

Katter refuses to tell me if he's discussed the leadership issue with Rudd but, given the nature of their friendship, it's a sure bet it's been raised over a cuppa and an Iced Vovo. 'I find it very difficult to see how they can't bring Kevin back,' he muses. 'They [voters] want to murder the federal government. She's heading for a slaughtering.' He reckons Rudd could return if Gillard fell on her sword. 'It could be a bit like: "Sorry about that, we made a mistake. We apologise,"' he says of the way Labor would need to sell it to the electorate. 'What's the alternative? It is very much like Whitlam.

The smart people in Labor tell me they are looking down the gun barrel of a Whitlam-style landslide.'

But Labor's smart people are also telling anyone who'll listen that most Labor parliamentarians loathe the bloke who took them to victory in 2007. And the key rural independents who back Gillard—Tony Windsor and Rob Oakeshott, from whom Katter split—are great admirers of the Prime Minister.

Since backing her into the prime ministership, Windsor and Gillard have forged a close bond. The farmer from New England who, like Katter, has state political service on his CV, isn't big on the bluster and bullshit of spin-driven politics; he plays a straight bat. He meets with Gillard weekly when parliament sits, usually late on Tuesday afternoons. It's a mutual admiration society.

Yanking his support away from the Prime Minister is not on Windsor's radar, despite the daily taunts to do so by the Opposition and the fervent desire of Ruddites. Windsor is effusive in his praise of her and the way she's running the minority parliament. 'Rightly or wrongly, it has been determined that this government be given a go for three years,' he declares to me. 'There is far too much pre-occupation with the next parliament. I'm here to work in this parliament, and I'm not going to waste the opportunity in this parliament in order to get re-elected to the next one. This could be a parliament where three or four major reforms occur. I've said to the PM: "Don't be afraid to tackle the hard issues. Let's try and have a go at some of the previously no-go issues." And she is.'

He ticks off the major reforms underway: a realignment of the Murray–Darling rescue package (into which he chaired a parliamentary inquiry), hospital reform, the NBN, carbon pricing. He's played a role in all of them and believes this minority parliament, far from being a wasted opportunity, could be one of the great reforming parliaments. Windsor is contemptuous of the way the media is caught up in personality politics, saying the real story of the government and the revolutionary new workings of a minority parliament are being ignored as the media continues to report as if it's still a two-horse race.

The *Australian* has added Chris Kenny to its stable of right-wing commentators. In another life he was a bad-ass advisor to former Coalition Foreign minister Alexander Downer and played his politics hard. Kenny's disdain for the Labor Party was matched only by his dislike of press gallery hacks, which he generously displayed in fits of rage and ranting if stories weren't to his liking. While he's not resident in the press gallery, he's now in the political commentariat and there's nothing like whipping up a mischievous article on Gillard's deficiencies and Rudd's attributes to satiate the needs of this former zealous Liberal advisor.

Under the blunt headline 'Rudd is Labor's Last Chance', Kenny opines on 25 July that 'now, as the Prime Minister sinks in the public's estimation, a return to Rudd would be perhaps the only leadership change that might be plausible in the public's eye, and therefore save as many Labor MPs as possible'. It would be an act of contrition; it would be a 'reboot of sorts' for Labor. He berates Gillard for her 'condescending tone and language', being out of touch and incompetent. Quite how he gets insights into the psyche of the loathed Labor beast or Gillard is a curiosity, but Kenny is a rising loudmouth in the political commentariat and determined to wreak his own particular brand of havoc on the Labor government.

The raging against Gillard and the constant marking down of her performance is wildly at odds with the reality of the minority government. Despite the government's wafer-thin margin, the parliament is remarkably stable; but it's depicted as though we are living through the last days of Rome. Gillard is implementing reforms and the parliament has passed a record amount of legislation—around 180 bills to date—but the press talks endlessly of a government close to collapse. Australia is economically robust compared to faltering international economies, but you'd be forgiven for thinking the Australian economy is on the point of disintegration. The media's primary focus is on personalities and politics, not policies or the running of the country.

Tony Windsor puts the economic doomsaying down to the Opposition Leader: 'Abbott's behaviour in relation to a lot of this has been absolutely disgraceful.' Hanging neatly in the ante-room of Windsor's Parliament House office is a row of fiercely anti-Abbott cartoons. The pair are not BFFs.

The month ends with the death at 82 of the amazing Rob Chalmers, who spent a record sixty years in the federal parliamentary press gallery. Two weeks before he died, he was still trying to pump out an edition of his *Inside Canberra* newsletter, which has dropped into letterboxes and, in later years, email inboxes every week since 1957. Rob's death is as sad for the loss of a great bloke as it is for the closing of an era in old-style journalism.

Chalmers, although a Labor sympathiser, put all politicians through the ringer. He refused to socialise with them and was disdainful of the trend towards celebrity journalism and the insidious practice of reporters being 'on the drip'—getting stories from politicians and in return giving their sources favourable media coverage. He concentrated on policies and not the entrails of real or imagined personality differences, the prism through which much modern politics is reported. As Gillard said when eulogising him on 28 July: 'Rob reported on the federal parliament for more than half the period since Federation, having covered twelve prime ministers and almost thirty election campaigns. He relished the policy debates that lie at the heart of our democracy and his reputation for insightful and independent political commentary goes unchallenged.'

How many in our current ranks could this be said about?

THE HEART-STARTER
August 2011

On 1 August Rudd's heart operation gets full media attention, even on international wire services, when he goes under the knife at St Andrew's War Memorial Hospital in Brisbane. It's routine surgery, but his family are marshalled at the hospital and wife Therese Rein is at the ready with a media quote. 'We'd like to thank everybody for all their lovely messages of warmth and support and friendship and their prayers over the last couple of weeks,' she chirps before the scheduled 7.30 am operation. Rudd is also broadcasting early, tweeting to his nearly one million followers—twice as many as Gillard, and rising—a hearty thanks 'to all those kind folks wishing me well for surgery. Therese and the kids also want me to thank you all for the support.' This is where Rudd is happiest: at the centre of attention.

The Prime Minister is peppered with questions on ABC Radio Brisbane to see if she might say something that suggests she's not appropriately sympathetic on the occasion of Queensland's beloved son going under the knife. She plays the game, sending him a cheerio and revealing she's spoken to him about the operation and had passed on her best wishes for a speedy recovery.

Few other MPs would thrust their medical lives onto centre stage in such a public manner. Many have and will continue to endure cancers, heart problems, mental illnesses and a range of other medical conditions, and endure their ailments quietly. The three-ring circus that is Rudd Inc. plays to the crowd with such regularity that his limelight-hogging behaviour is normalised. The only thing his colleagues can do is to grit their teeth and watch with fascinated horror.

The media attention on Rudd obscures a seemingly innocuous radio interview conducted at the same time by 2UE's Michael Smith with Labor MP Craig Thomson. The member for Dobell on the New South Wales central coast was the subject of a sensational *Sydney Morning Herald* report in 2009 accusing him, amongst other things, of using his union credit card to pay for prostitutes and to bankroll his 2007 federal election campaign when boss of the Health Services Union (HSU). He sued Fairfax for defamation but quietly dropped the proceedings two months ago, perhaps prompted by further embarrassing revelations unearthed during the legal discovery process.

A handful of Coalition MPs has since been working behind the scenes to probe Thomson's guilt or innocence. With a slim one-seat majority, his scalp would be a glittering prize. Indeed, it is understood the Liberals are so confident of mowing Thomson down that a search is already on for a star candidate for his seat, which Labor holds with a 5 per cent margin. In these unseaworthy days for the Labor mother ship, the Libs believe all they need is a decent candidate and this seat is as good as won.

Smith, a retired copper, along with the 2GB troika—all nakedly political ideological warriors for the Right—underpin the Coalition's media strategy to take the message away from the Canberra press gallery and into hundreds of thousands of suburban lounge rooms. It's a strategy Abbott's minders have pursued since he won the Coalition leadership in 2009. When Gillard had the hide to rob him of the minority government he thought should be his, Abbott concentrated his efforts on causing such chaos that the government would fall within a year. The grumpy old blokes in Sydney and Melbourne radio stations have enthusiastically abetted that aim. Day in, day out they abuse, vilify and insult the Prime Minister. Since her announcement of the carbon tax, they've used their radio programs as vehicles for their hatred, urging their listeners across the country to join a 'Convoy of No Confidence' to Canberra being organised by a bunch of truckers later in the month.

Craig Thomson is now shaping up as a terrific assault weapon against Gillard. Smith asks him whether in April 2005 he signed off on an HSU payment of $2,475 for brothel services, which had appeared on his credit card. 'Yep,' responds Thomson cheerily. 'And you didn't ask questions about it?' Smith pursues. 'Well, on the face of it, I didn't understand what it was.' Well then, who bought the brothel services with your union credit card? 'The union reached a settlement with another gentleman who paid back $15,000 in relation to use of credit cards at an escort agency,' Thomson responds. The view from Rudd's sick bed of the Thomson affair must be a lively diversion for the ex-PM.

Thomson had been grilled by party officials about the accusations when they arose in 2009, but he convinced his colleagues they were baseless. In an act of bravado and to prove his bona fides, he launched the defamation action against the *Sydney Morning*

Herald. Party officials bought his defence; he subsequently won endorsement to run again at the 2010 election, despite the concerns of Labor heavyweights such as former federal minister Graham Richardson—no slouch himself in the controversy stakes—who now earns a crust as one of Gillard's and Labor's loudest media critics.

Gillard isn't asked for, nor does she volunteer, a comment about Thomson's revelations. She has bigger things on her mind: tomorrow night she's entering the lion's den, visiting News Ltd editors in Sydney to talk about the government's agenda and plans for the future. She follows in Rudd's footsteps; he regularly visits newspaper editors in capital cities. When I worked at Fairfax Media, it was a standing joke amongst senior editorial staff how often Rudd just happened to pop in for a cuppa. His courting of media players is relentless. He obsesses about being loved by everyone in the media, be it journalist or editor. And he knows the power of the media. In Opposition and as prime minister, his minders would be constantly on the phone offering news grabs or picture opportunities. 'Would the *Sun-Herald* come and take a picture of Kevin wearing a Sydney Swans scarf?' we were asked late one Saturday afternoon just on deadline. There was no story—Rudd just wanted his mug in the paper at a footy match. We didn't acquiesce.

A few days after the radio interview, the shadow Attorney-General George Brandis demands the New South Wales Director of Public Prosecutions launch a criminal investigation into Thomson. Not for any other reason than ensuring justice is done, of course; the fact that, if an MP is found guilty of a crime that carries a sentence of twelve months or more, they have to leave parliament is surely neither here nor there. This has all the hallmarks of a very slow train crash.

*

Andrew Wilkie, who continues to help deliver a stable minority government to Labor, can't understand how the Gillard he's grown to know and admire can be the same woman the media regularly lambasts. Nor can he understand why her scripted speeches, often delivered in a wooden tone, are at odds with the engaging person he has come to know.

Those who know her confide that she's not a natural public performer, and she mistrusts the media as much as the media now dislike her. Her personality isn't suited to constantly being on guard, defensive and crouching.

Wilkie, who only secured a shade over 21 per cent of the primary vote in his Tasmanian seat of Denison but managed to leapfrog the more fancied candidates to win, is holding Gillard to ransom over poker machine reform. If she fails to deliver by budget night 2012, then it's all bets off. If the Opposition then moves a vote of no confidence in the government, he will no longer feel bound by his agreement with her that he will not support such a motion.

Yet he says he has a warm and friendly relationship with the Prime Minister. They've even dined together alone twice since he helped Labor form government: at the Prime Minister's office in Melbourne's Treasury Place—eating Thai in takeaway plastic containers on a crisp white tablecloth, drinking wine in crystal wine glasses—and at The Lodge in Canberra across the 'big table' in the dining room. These cosy tête-à-têtes were all about 'relation-ship-building', he explains to me.

'She's a nice, decent, intelligent person,' he says. He believes her problem with voters is because she hasn't been forgiven for 'knifing' Rudd. 'The Julia Gillard I've got to know is a decent, smart, nice person,' he repeats, adding that he doesn't doubt the relationship would change if he was 'no longer of any use to her. Although,

I actually think we would still have a friendly relationship. We've learned to respect each other.'

Wilkie meets Gillard every Tuesday afternoon when parliament sits, as do the other Independents, separately. 'Most meetings, she'll go through her folder ticking off my position on the votes coming up that week, what she knows the Opposition has coming up, my views on things, checking that I'm supportive, trying to persuade me to support her on something she thinks I'm not going to support,' he says. 'Our needs overlap. You don't trade a handout for the electorate for a particular piece of legislation, but I do go to her constantly asking for a bit of help with this or that.'

Bob Katter concurs about Gillard's character. Despite his allegiance to Rudd, he says she's a straight shooter and a decent person. And unexpectedly, given how Rudd feels about Gillard's role in his removal, Katter makes a remarkable comment—Rudd, too, has a high opinion of his successor's integrity. 'Kevin Rudd told me that, whatever else I may personally say or think about Julia, she is a very honest broker,' he says. 'I think she is. If she gives her word on something, she'll try to honour it.'

Gillard and her deputy, Treasurer Wayne Swan, lead most of the ongoing regular negotiations with the Independents. Gillard handles most of the interactions with the Greens and their leader, Bob Brown. It's a collegiate system of governing unprecedented in Australia's recent history, and it needs a deft and skilful negotiator heading up the team. All the Independents agree Gillard has those skills and is a methodical, hard worker.

Despite the unique circumstances of the minority parliament, she and her cabinet continue quarantining Australia from the rocky international economic situation. On 6 August, Standard & Poor's downgrades the United States' credit rating to AA+, sparking a wave of financial uncertainty. In Europe, Greece and Ireland are teetering on the brink of ruin and French financial institutions are wobbly. International stock markets are staggering like drunken sailors on dry land and yet Australia, much to the unrecognised credit of the Labor government, remains solid. The Reserve Bank has just kept interest rates on hold; unemployment is steadily low; consumer confidence is stable.

But as far as the electorate and the Opposition are concerned, the Gillard government is the worst since Federation and driving Australia into ruin. The Opposition's negativism has taken hold in the minds of a scared and suspicious electorate, which is unnerved daily by the ferocious anti-Gillard hotheads in radioland and the regular castigations of newspaper reporters.

An effective and humane asylum-seeker policy was one of three policies Gillard declared she would fix on assuming the prime ministership, but it has eluded her government. The latest version, the so-called Malaysia Solution, was announced at the end of July; since then the Prime Minister and her officials have continued their attempts to finesse it. A swap deal with Malaysia, the policy would send one of our asylum seekers back to Malaysia in return for receiving five of their processed refugees plucked from the tens of thousands of poor souls languishing in Malaysian camps.

Gillard is dealt a late night body blow on Sunday 7 August when High Court Justice Kenneth Hayne issues a temporary injunction halting the despatch to Malaysia of an unhappy band of 16 asylum-seekers recently landed for processing at Christmas Island. The Malaysia Solution is further cast into no-man's land the following day when Hayne re-affirms the injunction, pending deliberation by the Full Bench later in the month. Hayne finds the banishing

to Malaysia of any asylum-seekers would breach Australia's international legal obligations. The High Court proceedings have been
launched by lawyer David Manne of the Refugee and Immigration
Legal Centre in Melbourne on behalf of 42 asylum seekers, including six unaccompanied minors.

Hayne's acerbic judgment will undoubtedly become fodder
for Gillard's enemies, within her own party and on the opposite
side of politics. Abbott these days can recite his mantra of 'Stop
The Boats' in his sleep. His attack-dog Immigration spokesman,
Scott Morrison, has morphed from being on the reasonable small-l
liberal side of his party to the hard Right on this issue, following
the same path as Howard's Immigration minister Philip Ruddock,
who began his political life as a 'wet' and ended his ministerial
career with his own daughter denouncing his refugee policies.

The portents are not good for Gillard. While there's been no
criticism of her today, watch this space. Any excuse to savage the
Prime Minister will be avidly seized.

On 10 August, the Prime Minister announces a plan to introduce a
National Disability Insurance Scheme. It's a blockbuster of a Labor
initiative, still in the conceptual stage, but it's the sort of lofty
aspiration that we pay our elected representatives to devise, rather
than indulging in human blood sports. It's swamped, however,
by the growing clamour over Thomson and his escapades at the
Health Services Union. In what looks remarkably like a planned
and co-ordinated state and federal Liberal pincer attack, New
South Wales state Liberal MP Anthony Roberts accuses Thomson
in the Macquarie Street bear pit of 'unacceptable and unlawful'
behaviour. Roberts' particular target is a harmless-sounding
little collective, the Coastal Voice Community Group, which, he

thunders, was registered on 3 May 2006 using union funds and with Mr Thomson as its public officer. 'The group's registration paperwork stated that its principal activity was to operate a volunteer aged-care hotline!' Roberts seethes, alleging it was a front to help Thomson win Dobell at the 2007 election. Thomson bats it back: the same allegations were made in 2009 and investigated by the Australian Electoral Commission, which found nothing to report. The Liberal Party and its federal leader clearly forget, and hope the rest of us do too, that Tony Abbott once famously established a front organisation, Australians for Honest Politics, which raised more than $100,000 to attack Pauline Hanson and her One Nation Party. When in 1998 the Australian Electoral Commission (AEC) asked Abbott to disclose the names of his donors, he refused— twice. Inexplicably, the AEC took it no futher.

The trickle is now a torrent, and the leaks against Thomson from within Labor start. A well-timed leak to the *Daily Telegraph* on the first day of the first fortnight of federal parliamentary sittings, cites a 'senior Labor source' confirming the New South Wales branch of the party bailed out the MP to the tune of $40,000 to clear his legal bills (bankrupts aren't allowed to sit in parliament) and, just for good measure, that Thomson had abused a Salvation Army worker at a poker machine rally.

Steely-faced, Gillard marches into Parliament expecting to be pummelled over the MP in whom she has declared confidence. Thomson sits stony-faced in the backbench bleachers. It takes fourteen questions before veteran New South Wales MP Bronwyn Bishop rises to her feet to ask Gillard if she retains confidence in the member for Dobell, and: 'Has she now conducted an investigation of her own into the allegations surrounding the member for Dobell, and is she satisfied that her confidence in the member for Dobell is warranted?'

Gillard retorts that she has 'complete confidence' in him. He's doing a 'fine job' representing his constituency and she looks forward to him continuing in the job 'for a very long, long, long time to come'.

One of Gillard's faults, say even her supporters, is that she can be blindly loyal. Her first instinct is to protect and defend. In this instance, she appears to have now firmly strapped herself to a bloke who may not be worthy of such loyalty. The Opposition couldn't be happier.

And on and on the leaks and attacks roll. The *Tele* has stories over the next few days detailing Thomson's bail-out by Labor's notorious New South Wales Branch, simply known in political circles as 'Sussex Street'. The total cost of its largesse has now been found to have doubled to $90,000, and there's every indication there are more revelations to come. Channel Seven has its sources too, and reveals that Fair Work Australia is investigating whether Thomson misled it when it investigated the credit card allegations against him in 2010. And the *Sydney Morning Herald* scores a king hit with a story sourced from bills and credit card statements its journalists have in their possession showing Thomson made calls to escort agencies from hotel rooms in Melbourne in April and June 2006.

It's difficult to know who's the keenest to keep the issue burning in the media: forces acting against Gillard within Labor's own ranks or Tony Abbott, who accuses Gillard of treating Thomson like a 'protected species who can do no wrong'.

Tony Windsor, though, is not prepared to judge Thomson or sink the government over it, no matter how bad it now looks or might get. With three others, Windsor held the balance of power in the

New South Wales parliament when, in mid-1992, then-premier Nick Greiner was found by the Independent Commission Against Corruption (ICAC) to have acted corruptly by offering a top public service job to a disgruntled Liberal turned Independent, Terry Metherell. The accusation was that the job was offered as an inducement for Metherell to leave parliament, thus vacating a seat the Liberals would win in a by-election, allowing them to seize back majority control.

'Greiner was being persecuted in the press, persecuted in the parliament—and other independents were part of that persecution at the time—where he'd been nailed by ICAC and then he'd appealed against the ICAC decision,' Windsor reminds me. 'Between the ICAC decision and his appeal, he actually resigned [on 24 June 1992], partly because of the pressure of the media and the pre-judgement that he was guilty. He'd very much been absolutely deserted by the Libs. They reacted to the media and the ICAC stuff and said: "Nick, you have to go. We can't support you."'

Windsor recalls ringing Greiner a few days before his resignation. 'I said: "Nick, just to let you know I won't be supporting a no-confidence motion." The three other independents were going to support it. Greiner needed one vote to survive and that would have been mine. I said to him on the phone: "Nick, you are as entitled as anybody to have your day in court." He said: "I think it's too late. My own people are telling me to go because of the political damage." He said, "You know, it's strange, Tony . . ." because he knew there was a bit of bad feeling between me and the Nats . . . He said: "The Nats are the ones that have stuck to me." His own weak lily-livered people hadn't. Anyway, I think it was a week or a fortnight later that he was exonerated in the courts—not guilty.'

It was actually in August that the Court of Appeal tossed aside the ICAC finding against the former premier. Windsor's point is that politicians shouldn't become judge and jury when there are perfectly good courts to do the job. 'There are certain parallels here,' he adds. 'A hung parliament, a political target, an obvious political strategy. In a majority parliament, they would have all sniggered and just got on with life. Others in the parliament have said to me: "You independents—why don't you drag him before parliament?" I've argued the Greiner defence. There are always these motions from the Opposition to persecute someone. The courts will handle it if he's guilty; if he's not, he's not. It's not my job to be a court; it's not this parliament's job to be a court.'

Notwithstanding that Thomson has not been charged with anything and doggedly asserts his innocence, the Opposition and particular outlets in the media are revving things up to full throttle. This is what it's all about: bugger the policies, bring on the scandal.

And bring on the Convoy of No Confidence, says Alan Jones, who is billed as the star spruiker when it rolls into the ACT. It has been hailed eagerly by media outlets such as News.com as an event that will 'bring Canberra to its knees'. Jones has spent weeks cajoling and demanding his listeners turn up for the momentous day which, he and organisers hope, will force Gillard to her senses by the 'spontaneous' uprising of many hundreds of thousands of ordinary Australians. Tail between her legs, the script goes, Gillard will trot off to Government House and ask the Governor-General for an election. That it isn't constitutionally possible to have a double dissolution election now is apparently neither here nor there.

Come 22 August, the event is a screaming flop. Three hundred people gather on the lawns outside Parliament House, and a ragtag of trucks circle it blowing their horns. Jones, alongside his mate Tony Abbott, addresses the crowd who all holler and howl and demand Gillard's head over the carbon pricing scheme. Perhaps aware of what a dud he's partly responsible for, Jones sensationally accuses the ACT Police of stopping 'thousands' from attending the rally and blocking 'hundreds of trucks' at the ACT border— as he describes it, 'the most disgraceful thing to happen to our democracy'.

Um, no we didn't, say the ACT Police. We actually blocked off roads to help the trucks do what they wanted to do. To round out his stellar performance, Jones insults *Sydney Morning Herald* journalist Jacqueline Maley, who has the temerity to ask him about his role, hissing at her that she's 'a grub' and 'a disgrace'. A great day's work, Alan!

Greens leader Bob Brown is a gentle man, but he is savage where News Ltd is concerned, labelling it 'the hate media'. When the phone-tapping scandal engulfed the Murdoch empire in Britain in July, Brown and his deputy, Christine Milne, reacted with Olympian speed to demand the government hold an inquiry in Australia, to make sure things weren't as grubby in the antipodes. Brown rarely talks to the *Australian* anymore because he fears what will happen to his quotes. 'When you're verballed in headlines and quoted as saying something you didn't, because that paper has a vendetta against me and the Greens, you have to be restricted and careful in every single thing you say,' he says of the newspaper that has vowed to drive the Greens out of power.

'I see prime ministers and ministers and so on going to see Rupert [Murdoch] every time they go to Washington,' he tells me. 'The big problem for them is: who do you see first—the President or Rupert? I'm not in that brigade. I am available; I am here. I am representing a section of the Australian people as a result of their vote. I am not in the game of believing that empire must be paid obeisance—or else.'

I ask him his views on the increasing viciousness in media commentary and on blogs, and the growing shrillness of shock jocks. His reaction is intense. 'I think Rupert Murdoch has done more than anybody else to engender that, and the destruction of personalities to the point of criminal behaviour through *News of the World*. To the public out there, the debate has lost boundaries in sections of that empire. So the licence has gone more and more to people in the electronic media to follow suit. I also think that, as the world becomes much better informed and much better educated, there actually is more compassion and there is a tendency to want to share what we have. But that is against the interests of the powerful rich.'

Brown firmly believes that Murdoch is trying to push Gillard from office, a view shared by cabinet ministers loyal to the Prime Minister. That she's a woman is another push factor, he believes. 'It's a very important component of it—that she's a woman,' he says. 'But she's also in a minority government, in a nation where you'll read every day that majority government is stronger. But [majority government] is less inclusive, less pluralistic, less connected to the wider Australian public. It's winner-take-all, and that's what they [News Ltd] want.

'She [Gillard] doesn't represent that, and therefore she must be brought down.'

The *Australian* has a number of attack dogs in its stable committed to highlighting every real, imagined and invented flaw of Australia's first female prime minister. Amongst those is Glenn Milne, the paper's one-time political correspondent, whose tenure with the Murdoch flagship has been bumpy. Recently re-hired as a columnist, on 29 August Milne produces a scathing rehash of a story that's been floating about for fifteen years: that Gillard, when a lawyer at Slater & Gordon, had a relationship with an Australian Workers' Union official and they shacked up together in a house bought with money allegedly fraudulently obtained through the union.

The story is wrong on many fronts. After a few hours, the *Australian* retracts the column and issues an abject apology online to the Prime Minister.

It isn't the first time Milne's had a crack at this topic. With exquisite timing on 11 November 2007, in the middle of the election campaign in the run-up to the 24 November poll, he produced a front-page splash that received saturation national coverage. The story ran in News Ltd Sunday papers in all states under the headline 'Julia conned by WA lover'. Would a headline writer have used just the christian names of John Howard or Peter Costello, let alone the word 'lover'? Milne's sub-text was that now, a decade and a half on, Gillard's past bad choice of partner made her unfit for office. He managed to insert the totally irrelevant paragraph that: 'Ms Gillard, now dating hair products salesman Tim Mathieson, also dated fellow Labor frontbencher Craig Emerson.' The moralistic tone suggested the lady had a history.

Milne's piece climaxed a ferocious assault on Gillard by the *Australian* during that campaign; its female journalists attacked her for her ear lobes and what she wore. Those efforts were surpassed only by a shabby contribution from acrid reactionary commentator Janet Albrechtsen, who excoriated Gillard for 'showcasing a bare home and an empty kitchen as badges of honour and commitment to her career' and for not knowing how to meet 'the needs of a husband or partner'. Quite how Albrechtsen was privy to the intimate details of Gillard's relationships is a mystery.

Milne took his cue for this latest story from the Right's maven and spear-carrier at News Ltd's *Herald-Sun*, Andrew Bolt, who two days ago blogged mysteriously about 'something that may force Gillard to resign'. 'On Monday, I'm tipping, a witness with a statutory declaration will come forward and implicate Julia Gillard directly in another scandal involving the misuse of union funds . . . I suspect a friend of mine in the media will be authorised to release it first.' Bolt isn't friends with too many media types. He irritates the bejesus out of his colleagues by constantly tut-tutting at them, telling them they're wrong or attacking them on television. But he does share a gig with another of commercial radioland's reactionaries, Steve Price, who can be counted upon to be outraged and offended by Gillard's mere presence.

Later that day, Bolt updates his blog to reveal his mate is none other than that vicious Gillard critic, Michael Smith from Sydney's 2UE, who has read out on air a long and rambling statutory declaration from a former AWU official. And what's it all about? Nothing. Bolt states on his blog: 'There is no suggestion at all that Julia Gillard has done anything illegal or condoned any illegality by anyone.' For the next few days, Smith and Bolt continue apace with their attacks, despite Gillard's constant refrain of innocence and their disingenuous rider that she had done nothing illegal.

Gillard first declared her innocence of any wrongdoing in this matter in October 1995. With *Auld Lang Syne* on repeat, she is again being forced to vehemently maintain she has done nothing wrong. In most cases where journalists have no evidence to support a story and no angles to pursue, the 'story' is dropped. Not in this instance; not for this person. The similarity to a baseless political and misogynistic witch-burning is purely coincidental.

Fire sometimes begets fire and, prompted by Gillard and Swan, cabinet is looking at ways to punish News Ltd. Cabinet ministers are holding preliminary discussions about measures that could include withdrawal of government advertising and acceding to the Greens proposal for a wide-ranging inquiry into the media. This is like using an electric prod on a beast: it will either stir it to wilder antics, or only temporarily cripple its rump.

It is nearly the first day of spring and there's a chance that some bounce will be put back into Gillard's step. But then the Full Bench of the High Court delivers a fatal blow to the Malaysia Solution, permanently staying it. For good measure, the jurists cast doubt over the legality of using Nauru and Manus Island as outpost processing centres, a 'deterrent' to asylum-seekers arriving by boat favoured by the Howard government.

The judgement means the government will have to process boat people onshore, unless it lines up a processing country that provides appropriate access and protections. Malaysia is neither a signatory to the United Nations Convention on Refugees, nor is it a stickler for human rights. This leaves Gillard with a pocketful of problems—and Rudd and his small band of insurgents with a handy whacking stick.

Oh, and Kev, Abby and Jasper won the Twinings Tea competition. More than 85,000 people voted and Rudd's afternoon tea blend—described by Twinings as brisk, lively and invigorating—just nudged out the brew allegedly designed by shock jock Alan Jones, which is smooth, light and distinctive—truthfully, no word of a lie. Australians have a fabulous sense of humour.

ACACIA DRIVE
September 2011

It's Wattle Day and our national flower is a 'unifying symbol for all Australians—there is no other symbol that says so much about us and our land, Australia', enthuses the National Wattle Day Association's website. So what better way to celebrate that unity than to put on an angry face, paint an abusive placard, borrow a coffin, emblazon 'RIP Australia' on a crucifix and head down to inner-west Sydney and the Marrickville office of government Leader in the House Anthony Albanese for a spot of protesting? To really get the party going, you can scream blue bloody murder about Gillard's failings and physically attack Albanese while demanding an apology for his deadly accurate description of last month's Convoy of No Confidence as the 'Convoy of No Consequence'.

To complete the festivities, you can hurl abuse just like the insults those ageing lovelies on Sydney commercial radio use against Gillard. You can yell at Albanese that he's a 'maggot' and 'a liar'. So that's just how 500 Sydneysiders decide to celebrate Wattle Day.

The protest was organised by the Consumers and Taxpayers Association (CATA), another in a conga line of righteously indignant Liberal Party–linked groups, whose principals moan constantly on 2GB about 'Jooliar' and the death of Australia as we know it because of the carbon pricing scheme. Apparently, for people like the members of CATA, freedom of speech extends only to what they say or what they want to hear. Organisations like CATA and the No Carbon Tax movement, or the website Menzies House, aren't interested in hearing any voice other than their own. Nor are the angry tabloid commentators and Sydney's graceless pissed-off old men of radio. It's a connected circle of venom and the arc is wide, and spreading. And that's just for starters: Larry Pickering, KangarooCourtofAustralia.com, ElectionNow. com.au—the internet is alive with groups dedicated to insulting, demonising, abusing, belittling and disembowelling Gillard.

Instead of confronting the angry mob outside, 'Albo', as he's known to colleagues and enemies alike, could have holed up in his office and indulged in some light reading. Maybe the *Daily Telegraph*, the newspaper of choice for most of the punters ranting outside, which today editorialises that the government has 'not so much killed off the Malaysian Solution but euthanised a policy already crippled by its inconsistency, illogicality and hypocrisy'. Or perhaps Albo could have clicked on a *Tele* online news story, rather than the editorial. Ah, here's one by Gemma Jones and Ian McPhedran. But this is odd: is it a news story, or is it an editorial? Cute—it's both! Masquerading as news, it's a mishmash of quotes and strident editorialising, including this objective piece of reporting in a 'news' story: 'When former prime minister Kevin Rudd walked out the door after pulling the knife from his back, he warned the incoming team not to lurch to the Right on asylum seekers. They ignored him. And in a hairy-chested attempt to outdo the Coalition on dealing firmly with illegal arrivals, the government has now paid the price.' Yowsers.

Not up to reading the *Tele*'s version of 'news', Albo? Maybe dial in to the dulcet tones of former Labor senator and Hawke–Keating government minister Graham Richardson. Yes, 'Richo'—the bloke whose political *modus operandi* was showcased in the title of his 1994 book *Whatever it Takes*. The bloke who has figured in many news dispatches over the years, linked to strange and wondrous financial dealings and savage political plots, and who has some friends you wouldn't want to meet in a dark alley. A bloke who is the political equivalent of the 'colourful racing identity'. In the last few years, Richo has attempted to re-invent himself as a columnist and commentator—in News Ltd papers and on Sky News, partly owned by News Ltd. Quite how he passes as a commentator when he's an active political player is an open question.

Today on the Fairfax Media radio network Richo is telling his listeners that he reckons Gillard's goose is cooked. Kaput. 'There's no way she can turn this around. You've got to say it gets worse for her every single day. It never gets better, it just gets worse,' he tuts, declaring it will be curtains for her and the government within the year. The Richo crystal ball is shining bright today. But why would Albo sit inside reading the *Tele*'s version of history or twiddle the radio dial on a lovely day like today? No fun in that, when he can be out and about trying to reason with a bunch of frenzied anti-Jooliars, who daydream of the good old days of lynch mobs and have no intention of listening to his side of the story. Happy Wattle Day!

The rats in the ranks haven't let the grass grow under their feet since the High Court junked the Malaysia Solution. The Rudd forces have decided to seize the opportunity to ramp up the pressure, and have been backgrounding journalists about the alleged dissension in cabinet ranks. Senior Gillard loyalists believe that in the last forty-eight hours Rudd has set his timer on a countdown for a lunge back at his old job. They expect the burn to increase, but they firmly believe it will hit a dead end unless the media give him and his small force more oxygen.

On cue, a hefty blast of hot air pumps up news reporting this second day of spring. Gillard would not be a happy prime minister as she wakens to the fruits of Team Rudd's labours, with a rash of media outlets reporting her time is up. Not really that up, mind you, because all the *Daily Telegraph*, the *Herald-Sun*, the *Australian*, the *Courier-Mail* and the *Sydney Morning Herald* acknowledge—a suitably long distance into the stories—is that no numbers are being counted and she has most of the caucus behind her. Thus, no story at this stage? Wrong! Let's not get distracted by such irritating details; it's the impression that counts, not the facts.

The mass-circulation *Herald-Sun* has continued its modestly understated coverage of Gillard. On its front page, the headline screams: 'Tick, Tick, Tick'. As in: Time's up, Julia! This is the favourite behind-the-scenes mantra of the Rudd forces. The first paragraph of the story by Phillip Hudson asserts boldly: 'Senior Government figures say Julia Gillard has "lost her authority" and have urged her to weigh up whether it's in Labor's best interests for her to stay on as PM.'

They have? Who, exactly? During my inquiries, I've found nobody who's had this fireside chat with Gillard. There's been no tapping on the shoulder, no quiet word in her ear that, since the good of the party is greater than the individual, she should consider vacating the chair. That means Hudson is carrying the message to the PM via his newspaper for others. Who are these mysterious 'senior government figures'? All that a few of Rudd's henchmen need to do is whisper a line or two in a media ear and—hey, presto—a story appears that Gillard is toast, even when there's no chance of a leadership switch now or any time soon. But Team Rudd is in the business of creating a momentum for change.

The pursuit of the 'story' can have unusual dimensions. Rogue journalists will sometimes quote each other as 'sources' or paraphrase other journalists' 'sources'. Before appearing on ABC's *Insiders* one Sunday morning a few years ago, I was chatting with the two other journalists on the panel as our war paint was being applied for the show. One had just taken a phone call from a Labor contact about disquiet within cabinet over a certain policy issue and, dispensing with confidentiality, he breezily chatted to us about it. On air the third journalist, straight-faced and without shame, said he'd been told that morning 'by senior cabinet sources' about ructions over a certain policy issue, pinching and rebadging as his own the other bloke's telephone call. Journalists in the press gallery regularly discuss stories among themselves: who's said what, what it means, the angle of the day. When heads are put together and a collective wisdom arrived at about certain events, it can be tough being the one to break ranks.

It's acknowledged within the government's echelons that its asylum-seeker policy is now a mess. But Gillard has an Immigration minister. She has a Foreign minister—a certain K. Rudd—and a cabinet that collectively decides policy. She isn't the Roman empress, making decrees solo. And Rudd as PM was no slouch when it came to comprehensively stuffing up asylum-seeker policy. Look no further than the *Oceanic Viking* disaster of 2009, when dozens of Sri Lankans bobbed about on an Australian customs boat in waters off an Indonesian port because Rudd decided on a stand-off strategy. He had taken sole control of the operation, and a month tootled by without any resolution. Then there was his Indonesia Solution, akin to the now defunct Malaysia Solution, which burst as soon as it appeared in a thought bubble. Rudd was a serial offender in the asylum-seeker policy stakes, but there's little media memory of these events or reminder of Rudd's complicity in the asylum-seeker disasters now besetting the government.

The *Sydney Morning Herald* has the next best headline on this bright second day of spring—not for what it says, but for its sheer, terrifying size. Has there been an outbreak of war? No, it's 'Labor split over asylum'. The headline shrieks in sixty-point type, reinforced by two emphatic 'bullets' above it: 'Factions in open warfare' and 'Doubts over PM's leadership'.

Framed around the High Court decision, the article's thesis is that: 'The High Court decision was a hammer blow to the struggling government and had MPs and ministers wondering anew about Ms Gillard's tenure as leader . . .' And then it tails off sheepishly: '. . . despite no one suggesting any moves were imminent'. Of all the quotes about Gillard, only one is on the record—from MP Graham Perrett, a Gillard supporter. Alongside the story is a column by Rudd's main man at Fairfax, Peter Hartcher. The Fairfax political editor doesn't believe in erring on the side of balance or keeping his ornate descriptors down to a bellow. 'As Julia Gillard's troops choked back rising panic yesterday, one of her lieutenants compared the government to a "house on fire",' he roars. Warming—sorry!—to his theme, he continues: 'Indeed, there are fires in many rooms. The smouldering problem of the asylum seeker policy has now burst into a full conflagration.' Evacuate the nation! We're all about to immolate!

On ABC Radio's *AM*, chief political correspondent Sabra Lane correctly states that the key players in cabinet and caucus are all sticking firmly to Gillard. 'What we are seeing now, they say, is just a little bit of frustration, that the party is going through a tough time.' New South Wales Right convenor Joel Fitzgibbon backs this up, saying pertinently: 'Well, those headlines are misleading. There is a suggestion that Julia Gillard doesn't have authority. I would suggest to you that if she lacked authority, people who were quoted in that article [in the *Herald-Sun*] would be putting their names to those quotes.' Lane asks Gillard loyalist Graham Perrett about Richardson's sounding of the death knell for Gillard's leadership yesterday, and elicited this knock-out retort: 'Yeah, well. You know, he aspires to be a has-been, doesn't he?'

Such a hearty put-down would never push a resilient bloke like Richo off his rhythm. He is a 'commentator' in much demand; he's already strung Gillard up, and that prediction is the flavour of the moment. His radio comments from yesterday have been picked up and run prominently in Fairfax papers. But he does not disappoint his News Ltd paymasters and has today written a terse column in the *Daily Telegraph* that ticks off any number of reasons why Gillard has failed the leadership test.

News Ltd's columnist and fiercely anti-Gillard ranter Piers Akerman follows the general thrust of Richardson's line, making merry with a thousand choice words registering disgust with the PM. The gist of his inflammatory prose is summed up in the lead paragraph. Under the headline 'Labor's hopes of leadership are lost at sea', Akerman declares: 'This was to be Julia Gillard's year of decision and delivery but the past 12 months have seen an aggregation of disgrace, policy failure and humiliation.' Down in *Herald-Sun* land, Steve Price continues the rants he subjects his radio audience to with a demand for Gillard to step down over the next fortnight. 'She becomes more isolated by the day and the whiff of the prime ministerial killing season wafts around Canberra,' decrees the bloke who never sets foot in Canberra, let alone federal parliament.

There is an earnest push by Team Rudd for the relentless media bludgeoning of Gillard to become a self-fulfilling prophecy. A picture of her losing her grip on power and authority is presented daily to voters and media consumers, despite no evidence being provided to back up that conclusion. The government is suffering policy difficulties, as any government will from time to time, and there is a clutch of MPs who want Rudd returned; but they're a minority desperately trying to entice the media to blow strong wind into their sails. Much media commentary is simply bias and bigotry against Gillard dressed up as 'news', and posturing by media celebrities and wannabes who find Gillard an easy target. It's a vicious circle: the hammering Gillard gets across the country—in newspapers, on radio and on television—leads to her being marked down in the public eye, which then feeds into pitiable polling results in the fortnightly and monthly samples in the *Australian*, News Ltd tabloids and the *Sydney Morning Herald*. In turn, this cycle nourishes and abets Rudd's ambitions.

Yet an under-reported poll which probes respondents' views on real issues, conducted for Essential Media Communications, finds that Labor's handling of headland policies is regarded positively in the community. One of its polls, released in the last week, has found high approval for government decisions and policies including increased funding of health services (89 per cent approve), increasing the age pension (78 per cent) and increasing superannuation to 12 per cent (75 per cent). Astoundingly, given the drubbings the press regularly hand out, approval for Labor's management of the economy and for keeping interest rates low is at a high of 70 per cent, while support for the NBN is at 54 per cent and spending on new school buildings—one of the most ferocious targets of News Ltd—is at 68 per cent. Although rejected by the majority, even the Malaysia Solution received a level of support (39 per cent approve, 45 per cent disapprove); and the carbon tax, which the hysterical commentators and cyber bullies are using as the weapon to bring Gillard down, is supported by 33 per cent.

Yet the same poll finds Labor trailing the Coalition on the two-party preferred vote by 56 per cent to 44 per cent, a perplexing disconnect from how voters should be rating the government if they support so heartily a wide range of its policy initiatives. This is Gillard's hellish challenge: while the big policies are being tackled—185 pieces of legislation to date—the distractions of Team Rudd's activities and the media's obsession with them swamps decent coverage of serious policy issues. The public is ceaselessly assailed with denigrating assessments of Gillard's character and leadership qualities; she is apparently heading a government with little else happening than a great battle of egos. Even when newspapers such as the *Australian* give media exposure to policy issues, they are editorialised as appallingly bad: the National Broadband Network, Building the Education Revolution and the carbon pricing scheme, to name just a few. No wonder the public is confused.

The *Daily Telegraph* is nothing if not determined to stick the course in hunting down leadership mischief. The third day of spring breaks dramatically with a front-page splash by fly-in-fly-out Canberra sessional journalist Simon Benson under the banner 'Let me keep my job', which asserts: 'Under-pressure PM Julia Gillard yesterday made an impassioned plea to keep her job . . .' The story spills onto pages 2 and 3, with claims that 'forces within her own caucus were deep in discussions yesterday about the future of the Prime Minister and the possibility of a return to the man she deposed'. There are other claims that 'phones ran hot' as powerbrokers talked nervous MPs off the ledge.

Two small facts. Gillard did not make an impassioned plea for her job; she did an interview yesterday on Sky News in which she said she wasn't going anywhere as she had too much to do. It wasn't tearful, emotional or passion-fuelled. Second, Rudd has the same support he always had, maybe a quarter or less of caucus give or take an MP who wakes up in a fit of pique on any given day and thinks about knifing his leader—a Labor mindset for many inured to the practice by more than a decade of leadership overthrows. Even Benson admits in his article that factional leaders are united behind Gillard, and that his sources confirm there is no move against the PM. The *Tele* nevertheless sees fit to plaster a cheery three-quarter page photo of Rudd next to the article, all of which sits neatly under a strap banner at the top of the page alerting readers to the 'Leadership Crisis'. It should have put in parentheses thus: *(With our help, tee hee.)*

Saturdays just aren't Saturdays without a dose of Hartcher to sell Kev11 to the *Sydney Morning Herald*'s readers. And he doesn't disappoint this weekend. There's a theme to the message from the Rudd backgrounders: Rudd isn't campaigning for the leadership; he'll wait to be drafted. They believe Rudd will thus be painted as having 'clean hands' if the media does its bit in fertilising a leadership crisis and if the seeds of dissent and discontent being planted were to flourish.

Five weeks into Rudd's eight-week break after heart surgery and it's all going swimmingly. Hartcher quotes one of Rudd's caucus supporters: 'Rudd isn't campaigning, his view of the world is pretty clear—he doesn't have to.' But Hartcher can't help himself; he has to finish with a plea. An impassioned one, even. Dissecting 'the choice' facing caucus—even though there is no choice on offer and no possibility of one being offered any time soon by Gillard—he entreats: 'Are they prepared to forgo their only realistic leadership hope in order to protect the pride and promotions of the faceless men?'

The 'faceless men' was the job-lot tag given by Rudd and Opposition figures to the very visible blokes who rang around on the night of 23 June last year to gauge the mood of caucus—Bill Shorten, Mark Arbib, David Feeney, Don Farrell. They have very recognisable faces in parliament, and their contribution on the eventful night has been acknowledged and their names have been widely reported. Yet this epithet is repeated *ad nauseam*, despite it being misplaced. The label could be said to be more suited to those doing the slow-burn agitating for Rudd behind the scenes, such as Victorian Alan Griffin and Western Australian Mark Bishop. Rudd's campaign relies on anonymity—puppet masters in the shadows. But even describing Rudd's minions in such a way isn't accurate either.

The term 'faceless men' was coined in the days of Robert Menzies' government. On 21 March 1963, press gallery journalist Alan Reid arranged for midnight photographs to be taken of Labor Opposition leader Arthur Calwell and his deputy Gough Whitlam standing under a lamp post outside Canberra's Kingston Hotel as the thirty-six delegates to Labor's federal conference decided the party's official attitude to a proposed United States radio communications facility in Western Australia. Reid's accompanying column accused Calwell and Whitlam of being puppets of '36 virtually unknown men'. The Menzies government adopted the theme with gusto; two weeks later in parliament, back bencher Harry Turner castigated the '36 faceless men' of Labor's federal executive who controlled the parliamentary Labor Party. Thus the term was born, and it has been abused and misused ever since.

Even though Rudd is supposed to be resting after his heart operation—his spokesman has been telling reporters he's not commenting on anything to anyone because he's recuperating— he is clearly so emboldened by the success of the latest tweaking of leadership white noise generated by his team that he manages to struggle off the couch for a few media appearances. There are fabulous photos of a Cheshire-cat-grinning Rudd on the beach at Noosa, his arm slung casually around his son Marcus's shoulders as the sunshine kisses both their cherubic cheeks.

And, look, on this lovely spring Sunday, Rudd is photographed outside his multi-million-dollar Canberra pad with United Nations Secretary-General Ban Ki-moon. Seemingly in Ruddy good health, he chirrups disrespectfully to the UN figurehead: 'Hi, SG!' Imagine if Gillard were to address a visiting dignitary in such a manner—she'd be flayed alive. There's not a question raised nor a peep of condemnation, bar one online report carrying a comment by Labor back bencher Michael Danby that Rudd's greeting was 'unbecoming of a serious foreign minister'. Another newspaper states that the Secretary-General visited Rudd before Gillard— a story without context that could only have been given to the reporter to humiliate Gillard and remind readers of Rudd's stature. Why is Rudd allowed such extraordinary latitude?

Another day, another blow. The *Sydney Morning Herald*'s investigative hound, Kate McClymont, on 9 September splashes an exposé about Craig Thomson's exploits when head of the Health Services Union and allegations against another union official, former ALP president, current vice-president of New South Wales Labor and member of the ALP National Executive Michael Williamson. It's not pretty reading: allegations that the pair received secret commissions from a union supplier in the form of a credit card, and that Williamson 'ran amok' with his union credit card, even paying for his children's private school fees on it.

This is excellent fodder for Gillard's enemies and they have a substantial weapon: Gillard's ill-advised declaration of loyalty to Thomson last month, when she told parliament she had 'full confidence' in the New South Wales MP and looked forward to him staying around 'for a very long, long, long time to come'. It opens up another window of opportunity for Rudd's people to capitalise on a number of issues bedevilling Gillard; beyond this escalating scandal, there's the confusion around asylum-seeker policy and a growing anxiety among Labor MPs about a well-oiled campaign being run by the club industry to protect its multi-billion-dollar pokies business.

In the *Daily Telegraph* the next day, Simon Benson revs up an innovative new Team Rudd pitch: the former PM is a 'changed man' and is ready to 'forgive and forget' if offered back the leadership. Funny, no disclaimers are added that Rudd's practising for his next journey in life as a comedian. But wait—there's more! Rudd is no longer autocratic, has eaten humble pie and has learned from his mistakes, whisperers tell Benson. Despite the tell-tale pointer that this should not be a prominent story—given that these truths are being dispensed by only 'a small group of MPs', and there is no actual evidence presented that Rudd has changed—the reporter does manage a quote from a caucus realist: 'Rudd must think we all have the memories of goldfish.'

The *Tele* has run a preposterous online poll asking readers, who have no knowledge of the Foreign minister other than his theatrical shows, 'Is Kevin Rudd a different man to the one he was as PM?' Notwithstanding the bleeding obvious—that the glaring difference is that he's no longer PM and thus behaves differently—only 31.15 per cent (2714 respondents) reply 'Yes'. But 68.85 per cent, or 5998 respondents, reckon (I'm paraphrasing here): 'Bugger off, what a silly proposition' and respond in the negative. Apparently you can fool some of the people only some of the time.

Gillard and Treasurer Swan are big on the jobs agenda, as have been all governments from Robert Menzies on. Gillard thus announces on Sunday 11 September that a one-day jobs forum will be held on 6 October in conjunction with a tax summit being conducted the same week. The forum will invite eighty representatives and experts from business, unions, government and academia; it will have on the agenda the changing structure of the Australian economy and the drivers of job creation and investment. It will also focus on manufacturing, a devilish problem for Labor. News wire service AAP gives this announcement an underwhelming six paragraphs, which find their way into the back news pages of just two papers.

So September rolls on, an unhappy convergence of scandal featuring pretty boy Thomson and craggy-faced Williamson, and policy challenges over asylum seekers and pokies reform. The thoughts of marginal seat-holders flick constantly to that club down the road from their electorate office, and the one in the next suburb and the suburb after that, and how the powerful consortium of Clubs NSW and the Australian Hotels Association has just threatened to run campaigns against them if Gillard goes ahead with a pokies reform agenda. Clamping mandatory pre-commitment technology on pokies was a prime ministerial commitment to Wilkie to secure his support for the minority Labor government. He's not budging. 'The agreement with Gillard as far as mandatory pre-commitment is concerned is that there'll be mandatory pre-commitment,' he tells me. 'The legislation must be passed by both Houses by the budget. By the time the Treasurer has stood up, it has to be the law of the land. If it isn't the law of the land, the government will know they have lost my support. They have lost certainty of supply and confidence.'

Clubs NSW has powerful friends, a lot of money to splash around and a lot of fear to instil in nervous back benchers. It naturally follows the political habit of the times and conducts polling, which spills mysteriously into newspapers, showing that a mandatory pre-commitment scheme could lose the government up to thirty-three seats in New South Wales and Queensland— a 14 per cent reduction in votes in New South Wales and a 16 per cent reduction in Queensland, wiping out the seats, among others, of Rudd and Swan.

In mid-September Gillard seeks to cut through the illusion of chaos created by her critics to remind Australians she has a reform agenda. In a speech to the Chifley Research Centre she lays out a blueprint for party reform, including the trial of American-style primaries to select some candidates. Attempting to quell the ardour of her enemies within the party, such as Rudd, who have voiced either self-serving or genuine concerns about the influence of the Greens on Labor values, she tells her audience she rejects the Greens as a 'party of protest'. It's a speech to the party faithful, a reminder that she's leading Labor reforms and believes in Labor values.

Her speech receives far less press coverage than a tacky episode of a tacky ABC comedy series called *At Home with Julia*, in which Gillard's character is depicted swathed in the Aussie flag after having sex on the prime ministerial floor with partner Tim Mathieson. Would've loved to have seen a similar scene in *At Home with John and Jeanette*, but such a show would have been so heretical and disrespectful that the storm troopers in the Liberal Party would have shut the ABC down overnight.

Swan is named Euromoney's Finance Minister of the Year, a globally prestigious gong that this year is awarded against a bleak backdrop of serious international economic wobbles from which he has quarantined Australia. Wannabe treasurer, the Opposition's Joe Hockey is scathing. He's also superficial, racist and ignorant about world economies when he tries sneeringly to put Swan in the same category as what he sees as pissy little economies. 'Over the last few years we have had two Slovakian ministers, a Serbian, a Nigerian and a Bulgarian!' he spits in parliament. 'In 2001, there was a Pakistani finance minister. That is quite an extraordinary one, that one!'

Yes, Shaukat Aziz was an extraordinary Pakistani Finance minister—a highly respected Pakistani-born international banker lured back to his native homeland to wrestle that country from its economic woes. When in Islamabad in 2005, John Howard recognised his skills when he enthused that Aziz had endowed Pakistan with 'a well-deserved reputation for being a country that beckons foreign investment and creates a transparent environment for foreign investment'. And Hockey wants to take Swan's job?

Benson in the *Daily Tele* is continuing his run of leadership stories, first about Gillard clipping Rudd's extravagant travel wings (he's spent a staggering $1 million this year and it's rising), and by

22 September he's quoting 'several' senior back benchers claiming that support for Rudd is 'growing significantly'. But several does not a summer make, and Benson concedes in his article that much of the speculation is being driven by 'Liberal Party operatives' (well, they'd know what's going on in Labor, wouldn't they?). Phillip Coorey steals his thunder in the *Sydney Morning Herald* on 23 September with a breathless article asserting that Gillard is on the rocks, because Northern Territory Country Liberal Party senator Nigel Scullion says so. Why? Because Scullion reckons he overheard Kev on the phone to Labor senator Trish Crossin, telling her he was close to snatching back the leadership. 'Rudd nine votes from PM', squawks the headline. Unfortunately for Coorey, not really.

It transpires the supposed phone call took place when the two Northern Territory senators were recently enjoying a bout of cross-party drinking. Scullion had popped by Crossin's office with the odd bottle or two of red, but the details of the night became a little hazy. Who said what, and why, and when? And hey—did it happen at all? Crossin (who, after all, took the phone call from Rudd and, unless she had a political death wish, wouldn't have popped Scullion on to an extension phone) flatly denies Scullion's version. That fact is included in Coorey's story. But if the person who had the conversation flatly denies a mischievous version from a political opponent, is there a story?

Oh, oops—it's on the front page anyway! What's more, Peter Hartcher has leapt into commentary alongside Coorey, opening with the colourful and predictable gambit: 'With the Labor government on the political torture rack over asylum seeker policy, the Liberals yanking in one direction and the Greens the other, it is increasingly wondering whether Kevin Rudd could end the pain.' Hartcher does little to hide his source: 'While he is tempted at the prospect of vindication, Rudd has told colleagues he is not sure he wants the responsibility of trying to rescue a dying government.' (Hahahahaha. Side-splitting!) Hartcher continues, as if the man himself had penned it: 'If he took the job for a second time, he reasons, it would absolve the people who deposed him—Julia Gillard and the faceless men of the Right faction—from their historical responsibility for Labor's dire position.'

Those wretched faceless men again! Rudd is now actively canvassing MPs with chatty phone calls inquiring about life and the universe, but he denies it when asked. He is a denial expert, on many levels.

Don Watson, Paul Keating's former speechwriter, once wrote that politics is a war fought with words. If so, then Rudd is sharpening his weapons—some are totally concealed and some are in their sheaths, but revealing a glint of steel to the enemy. In New York towards the end of the month, when queried about the leadership crisis that he and his small band are fomenting, Rudd resorts to his tried and true instruction—for everyone to have a Bex and a good lie down. But there's a twist: he uses the same line that Gillard formerly used when she was being hounded about her aspirations for Kev's job: 'I support the prime minister.'

The mood is now feverish, perversely in inverse proportion to the threat of a leadership spill any time soon. Rudd does not have anywhere near the numbers now; just as he didn't last week, last month, or six months ago. His supporters know it; two-thirds or more of caucus, who back Gillard, emphatically know it and they background journalists to that effect—almost daily, according to one cabinet minister—but with little impact. If you believe the hyped media coverage, uber scrutiny on Gillard and what is presented as an unstoppable Rudd juggernaut, Gillard's leadership is terminal.

However, sometimes covert operations don't go to plan. Rudd waltzes back into the country from the Big Apple, and when asked on ABC Radio about his leadership ambitions, puts his foot in his mouth. 'I'm a very happy little Vegemite being prime minister . . .' he starts, then quickly corrects himself: '. . . being *Foreign minister* of Australia.' Crikey! Sometimes it's hard being Kev—keeping under control all those conversations and ideas and plots and ambitions that swirl around in one's head.

THE STAGE MANAGER
October 2011

Every Labor MP, even those who say the opposite on the record, knows Team Rudd's destabilisation plan is gathering pace. Rudd and his mates are trying desperately, and with a great deal of success, to turn wishful thinking into positive change. Dennis Shanahan may not have appreciated what he was writing in the *Australian* on the weekend of 1 and 2 October, when he states: 'One Labor MP who is working to have Rudd's leadership resurrected . . . was surprised by the sudden, positive reaction to reports Rudd was gathering numbers.'

Hang on—that's not in the script! Rudd's urgers have been planting the line that the former PM is *not* gathering numbers, that he's *not* running a campaign; that things are looking so bad for the government he just might, just *may be*, willing to be drafted for the good of the party and the nation.

Shanahan's inadvertent slip says much; journalists know Rudd is creeping through the political undergrowth hunting and gathering, but they're not writing it—they're letting Team Rudd ply its trade.

Any 'sudden, positive reaction' is because the subversion plan is working a treat; the stories of a weakened, under-pressure Gillard are now a daily news item, even if she in turn insists daily that she's not weak, she doesn't feel under pressure, she's not going anywhere and she just wants to get on with the job.

But Team Rudd doesn't want things to move too fast. Their plan is to allow Gillard even more time to be seen to be screwing up asylum-seeker policy, stuffing up the mining tax, falling to her knees under the weight of the anti-carbon tax onslaught and being slugged to political death by the powerful pro-pokies clubs lobby. It's the lingering death master plan and Shanahan acknowledges this, quoting an anonymous Rudd numbers man: 'We don't want to go too early, everyone's quietening down now until November at least and probably until next year.'

As with most senior journalists, Michelle Grattan at the *Age* knows the game plan too. Just days after Shanahan's piece, she acknowledges in a column that the Rudd camp doesn't want any 'blowing up' of the leadership too soon. 'The personal strategy of Rudd—who is driven these days by the desire for vindication as much as by rational ambition—is the one he always adopts,' she writes, as if his head is resting on her shoulder as she pounds the keyboard. Further outlining his thinking, she continues: 'He is omnipresent. In current circumstances, this serves several purposes. It keeps him in the public's mind (useful for those surveys of preferred Labor leader); it sucks attention from Gillard; and, when he is received as a rock star in MPs' electorates, it shows caucus members how popular he is, and how useful he could be to helping a lot of them hold their seats.'

Rudd's is a cynical, corrosive ambition that is eating the life out of the government, rocking the wheels off parliament and serving nothing other than the need to fulfil one man's vengeful ambition. Why is this not being written? And why, when Rudd is questioned about the leadership and gives his stock standard answer that he's a 'happy little Vegemite' or other trite and untrue responses, do journalists not hit him with a series of questions about his knowledge of the destabilisers and why he won't call off his dogs?

But what's this? Richo—who is not a journo in the gallery, paid to track and monitor these things—has written a piece in the *Australian* on 7 October under the impressive headline 'Kevin Rudd's treachery will be the biggest obstacle he faces'. Richo starts: 'Not a day goes by where you don't see an article about how a surging Kevin Rudd is going after a doomed Julia Gillard.' He writes that senior journalists tell him that Gillard 'will be gone by Christmas'.

How do they know that? Assumptions and judgements are made based on nothing more than the handkerchief-over-mouth-piece titterings of Rudd's people. The journalists putting a timeframe on Gillard's demise (she's passed deadlines already) couldn't be looking dispassionately at the evidence because even the Rudd camp would concede that Gillard still commands more than 75 per cent of the caucus—roughly the support she always had.

Or do journalists know this, but their 'reporting' is propelled by a need to keep the bosses happy by dishing up sensational stories in a competitive market? The Rudd challenge is a make-believe that wants to be taken seriously, and its main fantasist, One K. Rudd, set his *modus operandi* a long time ago. As Richo points out: 'He has form undermining leaders. He knows how to run long-term campaigns of guerrilla warfare. Mark Latham and Kim Beazley can attest to that.'

Rudd was actually hard at work campaigning long before either of those two Labor leaders; he set his sights on the prize when he entered parliament in 1998. He had a good think about swiping at Simon Crean's leadership at a ballot in June 2003, but didn't follow through because of a lack of caucus support. He had a decent crack when the leadership spilled again in November that year but, after talking up his support and playing the maybe-I-will, maybe-I-won't nominate game for a few days in the media, he pulled out again due to a lack of support and Mark Latham stepped up to beat Kim Beazley. Rudd emerged from the shadows once more in January 2005, after Mark Latham's jaw-dropping resignation in a Sydney suburban park, but he pulled out before the ballot because of insufficient support and Kim Beazley was returned to the leadership.

Then a hungry Rudd got deadly earnest and his prey, the gentlemanly Beazley, was an easy target. For most of 2006 Rudd circled the country, duchessing every factional powerbroker and union heavy in every state; he stitched up the deal when he finally clinched the support of the all-important New South Wales right-wing machine and did a deal with the Victorian Left. He won the leadership from Beazley in a ballot held at 10 am on 4 December, shortly after Beazley's fifty-three-year-old brother David died of a heart attack. It's a day and a year Beazley will never forget.

So, God bless Richo's cotton socks when he writes that it's about time to 'put this phantom challenge into perspective'. The former mover and shaker in the party's Right knows how to count numbers after many decades spent wielding the knife in leadership stoushes. He points out the bleeding obvious: Rudd has no more than about twenty votes, and he knows it. 'Those who are talking up this challenge have had much more success in getting coverage than they deserve,' he understates, fingering Griffin and Bishop as Rudd's main spruikers.

This prompts an instant reaction—but no denial—from a wounded, sombre-faced Rudd when he's quizzed by a pack of journalists about Richo's article. 'There's a thing in politics called relevance deprivation syndrome. Is Mr Richardson suffering from that?' he asks rhetorically. 'Probably,' he answers, then asks and answers another question. 'Is Mr Richardson taking hundreds of thousands of dollars a year in salaries to go out there and bag the Labor Party and the Labor government every day? Probably. In fact, definitely.' Good conversation you're having with a great listener, Kev, but you didn't answer the journalists' questions about Griffin, numbers, campaign and leadership aspirations.

Cripes, here comes another solo Q and A! 'Is Mr Richardson doing as he's always done in the past and acting as some sort of unofficial spokesman for the factional bullies in our party who try to control it from time to time? Undoubtedly.' Great idea to run a press conference for a party of one, Kev, but how about answering a few real questions?

The tax and jobs summits waft by, creating barely a ripple. Meantime, *Daily Telegraph* readers, responding to yet another of the paper's slanted online polls, find Gillard responsible for everything that's wrong with the economy.

Damn, but it's a pain for the stalker when the stalked gets any kind of press coverage at all. No worries—Rudd's mind, and his domestic travel budget, are concentrating on other matters. Here he is today, Saturday 8 October, in campaign mode on the New South Wales Central Coast—popping in for a coffee here, and being mobbed in a shopping centre there. His visit to Deb O'Neill's New

South Wales seat of Robertson is hot on the heels of similar trips in the past week to marginal electorates in Queensland, Victoria and northern New South Wales, where he was greeted with his favourite rock-star treatment.

Of course, he's going to all these politically important electorates only to talk about foreign policy matters, which are right up there on the list of live concerns to financially hurting families in marginal seats. In recent times, he's been known to go missing from important cabinet discussions, but nowadays he's a dead-keen candidate for ribbon cutting, fetes, garden parties, the opening of an envelope—as long as it's held in an at-risk Labor electorate.

Asked about the leadership after receiving, in Ms O'Neill's words, a 'fantastic' reaction to his sweeping campaign-style tour of her electorate, Rudd answers: 'Firstly, let's be very clear about this. I am very happy being the Foreign minister of Australia. I fully support the Prime Minister. I will continue to support the Prime Minister.' It's all too cute: it seems he supports the office of Prime Minister, not the woman occupying it. On the same day in Victoria at the ALP state conference, his numbers man Alan Griffin uses the same words when asked if he was running a campaign to undermine Gillard. 'I support the leader, I support the Labor Party.' What an extraordinary coincidence that neither man can utter the prime minister's name!

As for why he's running around marginal electorates, Rudd tops the pops with this pearler of an explanation: 'What I've been doing for the last week with many of our local members across the country is explaining what we are doing in the aid portfolio, given that many, many Australians are deeply concerned about what's happening in the Horn of Africa.' A Logie for best dramatic performance to that silver-haired bloke with the mop-top hairdo!

The Opposition's Julie Bishop has Rudd's measure. She's been around politics a long time, and she knows a coiled snake when she sees one. She peppers Rudd with questions during Question Time on 11 October, his first official day back in parliament since his cow valve operation. She says afterwards: 'I knew that whatever question I directed to Rudd he would use it as a platform to show off shamelessly, and he didn't disappoint.' Rudd also bursts into print today in the *Daily Telegraph*, opining about feeding the world's poor. Sydney's largest-selling 'battler' newspaper loves One K. Rudd, whether it is pumping up his leadership aspirations in news stories or allowing him to preach in columns—four in the *Daily Tele* in the last month, a few dozen in accommodating News Ltd newspapers in the last year, mostly in the *Australian*.

Former opinion editor of the *Australian Financial Review*, aspiring Liberal politician Tom Switzer, recently told online outlet The Power Index that the first thing Rudd did after his 1998 election to parliament was to hit the phones to opinion editors. 'He called me up at the *Financial Review*, he called up my competitors at the *Age*, the *Sydney Morning Herald* and the *Australian*,' he said. 'He would call every fortnight wanting to get a piece on the opinion page. He became a real relentless pest. If he couldn't get a place [on the opinion page] he would go to my editor-in-chief and ask for him to overrule me. He knew there was a great deal of gravitas and influence on the opinion pages.'

At 9.40 am on 12 October, Gillard notches up a decisive victory with the passage through the Lower House of eighteen pieces of legislation making up the Clean Energy Future Bill which, *inter alia*, establishes the carbon price mechanism and its regulatory body. As the Labor troops erupt in a collective embrace of hugs and hand-shaking, Kevin emerges from the back-bench bleachers where, unusually for a minister, he's been sitting while the votes were counted. As if in slow motion, he walks to his leader and airbrushes a faint kiss on her cheek, his back to the press gallery. With both hands on his shoulders, she responds guilelessly. It's the money shot, and Rudd knows it. Opposition MPs guffaw with laughter; Rudd grins cheekily and gives them the thumbs up.

In a rare burst of insight the *Tele* notes the next day: 'Kevin Rudd yesterday ensured that the final and lasting image as Labor MPs celebrated their political victory was his continuing ambition to reclaim the job that was taken from him last year.' Peter Hartcher does not disappoint one little bit with his bold opening paragraph in the *Sydney Morning Herald*: 'The weakest Australian federal government in 70 years [by what measure, Peter?] has managed to win passage through the lower house for one of the most controversial reforms in decades.'

But surely the passage through parliament of 'one of the most controversial reforms in decades' speaks of Gillard's mettle? She negotiated it with the Independents, she steered it through committees and the party room, she clinched a critical salve for the steel industry in a surprising deal with the Greens, and it will pass the Senate. That's not good enough, though—it's all about The Kiss, and Rudd's ambition. Rudd's managed to shred her momentous victory; just another day on the Kev11 campaign trail.

Then there's another blow. While analysis of the Judas kiss continues twenty-four hours later, titillating the political and chattering classes, Gillard is forced to abandon a vote on an amended Malaysia Solution because Western Australian conservative Independent Tony Crook won't support it. If ever there was a showcase political illustration of how to stand tall and then fall flat in record time, this is it. And much of the blame must fall on Gillard's head.

She knew she might not get the necessary parliamentary support; it was a desperate act in anxious times. Her plan to outrun Tony Abbott—whose obstinate refusal to countenance any of the government's asylum-seeker solutions has been as maliciously driven by pure politics as Gillard's strategy has been compelled by extreme political anxiety to notch up this win—has backfired.

While a catastrophe for the government, it is a godsend for those who wish to bring Gillard down. On 14 October, Richardson bangs the drum again in the *Tele*, noting that 'talk of a challenge will not go away'. And why is that, Richo? 'It is great copy for newspapers, it provides talkback radio with a daily subject, and television news just loves it.' Yes, but what about the reality of it? It 'doesn't mean a challenge will happen', he concludes. Yet he and dozens of other journalists and commentators continue to write it anyway, giving what Richo has dubbed 'the phantom challenge' legitimacy, status and impetus.

Journalists are so clearly driving the Team Rudd train to its destination that it's hard to see what's going to derail it, apart from a blast of responsibility by the nation's media or Rudd deciding to do the right thing and give Gillard some clear air to try and dig her government out of a hole. Hahahaha. (Sorry; I must have been hit by an unusual blast of October Canberra heat.)

So it begins in earnest, as the cabinet starts falling apart. On Saturday 15 October, the *Sydney Morning Herald* runs an article leaked straight out of Thursday's emergency cabinet discussions on the asylum-seeker issue. Comments by Immigration minister Chris Bowen about his attempts to reach a compromise that would appeal to the Independents and Labor's Left are quoted verbatim. The article gives readers a who's who of supporters and opponents in cabinet for Bowen's compromise solution, which would have involved re-opening Nauru as a sop to Abbott in the unlikely hope that in return he would support the Malaysian processing regime. Gillard, states the story, didn't want to give any concession to Abbott and the compromise went up in flames.

It's a serious and deliberate breach of cabinet protocol, designed to dent Gillard. The *Australian* has a more low-key story, quoting sources denigrating Gillard's lack of a 'Plan B' while devoting most of its squadron of journalists to monstering the carbon tax in the wake of its successful passage. When those who have been leaked against start berating the leakers in public, it's obvious that Labor's ship has had holes blown in it and is taking on water. Former leader Simon Crean levels the blowtorch at his colleagues in the Sunday News Ltd papers. The Sunday *Tele*'s version has a glaring front-page story under the banner 'Rats in the Ranks', in which Crean declares: 'The principle of not just cabinet solidarity but cabinet confidentiality is essential to government. It's outrageous that cabinet leaks. People ought to understand the damage this can cause government.'

The media assessment is that the right-wing 'powerbrokers' who installed Gillard in the prime ministership had been 'snubbed' because she refused to back the Bowen rescue plan. What that means is unclear. If, like the mafioso, they expected her automatic endorsement of any proposal they make and feel dishonoured by her refusal to back their option, then it means cabinet can no longer operate as a democratic decision-making body and all decisions must relate to the politics of leadership support groups. Or just maybe this is one of those bullshit lines fed out by the pot-stirrers that ends up in print.

Back on that strange planet where Ruddspeak is the art of saying one thing while thinking or doing another, the aspiring returnee to the prime ministership, out and about at a community barbecue, muses solemnly: 'One of the first principles of cabinet government is that we maintain those discussions among us'. Hilarious! And regarding his drooling leadership aspirations: 'I am not going to go into any such discussion other than to pursue my normal policy of giving you a further example of how Mr Abbott would change the country were he to become the prime minister.' News Ltd journalist Samantha Maiden comments: 'Just how long can Kevin Rudd keep refusing to rule out a leadership tilt? For one long, hot summer, if yesterday is any guide.' And for as long as journalists give Team Rudd carte blanche to gather momentum through an encouraging media.

There's a slight hiccup. A poll today (Monday the 17th) in Fairfax newspapers shows a 3 per cent bounce to the government, even if the obligatory meaningless Rudd vs Gillard question finds—gasp—that Rudd is the people's favourite. The problem for an undeclared challenger who is heavily reliant on transient and superficial polls is that the numbers have to be consistently in your corner. And that annoying little uptight neat freak Stephen Smith keeps getting thrown into the preferred prime minister mix, and garners reasonable support to boot. Plus the right-wing is toying with the idea that he could be a bolter candidate if Gillard is beyond redemption. How irritating for K. Rudd.

No matter. Today Rudd's at home in Canberra with quill and parchment, scribbling a humble piece for tomorrow's *Daily Telegraph* about his ticker operation and reading in the *Sydney Morning Herald* about a massive crash in public support for the government's poker machine reforms after a multi-million-dollar clubs industry advertising blitz. His spirits soar even more when the oracle of News Ltd commentary, Paul Kelly, pronounces on 19 October:

'Gillard has now reached a stage of permanent humiliation.' Quite how a woman of just fifty can have no future other than one of humiliation in perpetuity is one of life's mysteries; but, if Kelly has spoken, then it is surely the truth.

Back in the days when Graham Richardson was running the New South Wales right-wing machine, whether out of Sydney's Sussex Street or out of the Senate, most of what he told journalists was crap. As Bob Hawke wrote in his biography, filtered through now-wife Blanche d'Alpuget's pen, Richardson was an 'archetypal trickster' and a 'gifted liar'. Even Richardson 'fessed up about lies and truth in his memoirs, *Whatever it Takes*: 'In politics you never tell the truth about division in the upper echelons of your own party unless you are declaring public war on your leader.'

Richo spawned a coterie of like-minded cronies in what simply became known as the Sussex Street Machine, and for the past three decades it has made and broken federal and New South Wales Labor leaders. It was, and still is, a trusted maxim that what these right-wing warriors tell journalists is crap, and what they tell their factional foes is crap. One of its current crop of spear-carriers who fits the Richardson mould beautifully is Mark Arbib, former head honcho of the Sussex Street Machine and now a senator. Arbib's a master background briefer whose public utterances are often strangely at odds with his confidential chats. This is the classic MO of the New South Wales bovver boys: give journalists the low-down off the record about a particular strategy, then say the opposite for attribution in the paper. And journalists print their on-the-record quote, often knowing the strategy. It is complicity writ large.

Thus when the *Tele*'s Simon Benson runs a story on 20 October that leads with the opening gambit 'New South Wales Labor Party boss Sam Dastyari is believed to have softened his support for Julia Gillard . . .', readers are in for a rich tapestry of veiled and coded messages. The story states that Dastyari's 'shift' comes as 'support for Ms Gillard from the powerful New South Wales Right faction begins to collapse'. Dastyari confirms he has spoken to MPs, but denies he's no longer supporting Gillard. He'd been ringing around, he protesteth, to try and quell anger in the New South Wales Right over the asylum-seeker issue. 'Rank-and-file members of Labor won't support a change and the culture of the short-term leader needs to come to an end,' pronounces the bloke who is general secretary, and before that was the deputy general secretary, of a branch that for a decade orchestrated a series of state leadership coups.

Julia, you are in even deeper trouble than you know.

While denying it, Rudd tries to share the limelight with Her Majesty the Queen, currently in Oz ahead of a Commonwealth Heads of Government Meeting (CHOGM). Strangely, Aussies love this woman with the jarring title of Queen of Australia, and it's a golden opportunity for some reflected glory. After dashing back to Canberra from the Philippines on 22 October, Rudd prays alongside the royals at St John the Baptist Church in the gracious inner-northern suburb of Reid. When in Canberra, St John's is Rudd's chosen place of worship; when he was prime minister, it was the locale for many a media doorstop, much to the private dismay of most in the congregation. Rudd was raised a Catholic, but he switched to the more upwardly mobile Brisbane Anglican flock back in the 1980s, along the way becoming a firm chum of high-profile socially and politically well-connected Brisbane cleric Peter Hollingworth, who went on to become an outstandingly failed governor-general.

There's a thirty-strong media swarm at St John's, in scenes reminiscent of Rudd's prime ministership. Unusually, there are a few grumpies in the press throng asking testy questions. One reporter quizzes the former PM if it was lucky timing he returned so speedily from Manila so as to be able to make it in time for the church service. How very churlish! 'Try again,' Rudd retorts, lips pursing. The Bishop of Canberra and Goulburn, the Right Reverend Stuart Robinson, and the rector of St John's, the Reverend Paul Black, confirm to journalists that the service is not for dignitaries and VIPs; the Queen had requested only members of the congregation be present so she could experience a 'normal service of worship'. Lucky, then, that Rudd is no dignitary or VIP and is just a member of St John the Baptist Church's congregation.

Rudd may not be able to beat the Queen, but he can be king for a wee bit at meetings before and at CHOGM in Perth. And doesn't he give it his best shot! Over three days of foreign ministers' and leaders' meetings, starting on the 25th, he rushes around lecturing and hectoring on European debt, the Australian economy and climate change, giving twelve different speeches to the point of hoarseness. He compares his resultant throaty rasp to the voice of Hollywood siren Mae West, instantly distressing fans of the ageless sex goddess. Tony Wright drily notes in the *Age* that there is perhaps one small point of similarity, recalling one of West's great saucy lines: 'I believe it's better to be looked over than overlooked.' And overlooked Mae Rudd is determined not to be at this CHOGM, which after all should rightfully be a stage on which he should be strutting as Australian prime minister.

But hell—any stage in a storm, what? Why not crash a rock concert? Remember this date: Friday, 28 October 2011. It's when the Foreign minister of Australia, hoarse of voice, red of face, slightly unsteady of foot, decides he might try and confirm his rock-star status by leaping onto the stage at Perth's Belvoir Amphitheatre, where 4000 young rockers had turned up to a free 'End of Polio' concert. Grabbing the microphone, he starts squawking, as shrieking is out of the question with his voice in mufflers. For what, to a startled audience, seems like an extended period of time, he cajoles and massages with banter and questions, pushing for rounds of applause. 'Are you here to end poverty?' 'Are you here to have fun?' 'Do you want me to sing?' 'I. Sing. Like. A. Cow!!' he drawls, punctuating each word. 'I. Want. Your. Support. To do this. You [pointing the microphone into the crowd]. And you [ditto]. And you [etc.]. And you. And you. Every. One. Of. You.' For weird political performances, this is a medal winner.

On other somewhat sober occasions, when questioned at CHOGM about more banal but important domestic issues like pokie reform, Rudd is all business—or, rather, no business at all. He clams up. Twice. His formerly oft-repeated commitment to poker machine reform has gone missing, reinforced by evaporating public appetite for reform gauged recently by a Fairfax poll. It is such a potent issue in the electorates of Labor marginal seat-holders that any potential leader who will promise to renege on Gillard's deal with Independent Andrew Wilkie to curb the mega poker machine industry could hit the jackpot with nervous back benchers.

And then a festering Qantas dissension breaks loose, a product of months of strikes and skirmishes between the unions and Qantas management and brought to a head at 2 pm on 29 October by the airline's quietly spoken Irish-born boss Alan Joyce. It is a strike-break of gargantuan proportions: Joyce grounds his entire fleet and strands tens of thousands of domestic and international passengers. Within hours, the government has applied for an emergency hearing to Fair Work Australia (FWA) to terminate the unprecedented Qantas action. Forty-eight hours later FWA orders the planes back in the air and instructs the warring parties to enter into three weeks of mediation. Even though Gillard was central to forcing the tribunal action, she has to furiously deny reports in strategically placed newspapers like the *Daily Telegraph* that, on the day he grounded the fleet, she ignored Joyce's telephone calls.

Can things get much grimmer for Gillard?

THE KILLING
SEASON OPENS

November 2011

A funny thing has happened over the last few days as Gillard stepped into the well-known territory of her industrial lawyer past: she took control. Despite a concerted daily effort by the *Tele* to characterise her response to the Qantas action as sloppy and negligent and her public utterances about it as lacking in credibility, she's not brooking bullshit from reporters who trivialise the imbroglio. Asked on 1 November on Adelaide radio 5AA to comment on 'strong' reports she'd ducked Joyce's phone call, she snaps: 'That paper, the *Daily Telegraph* . . . that story ran yesterday and as early as 7.30 yesterday morning Alan Joyce was on the radio saying that story was untrue. So don't be misled by false reports here—that report was wrong.' She urges the hosts, Keith Conlon and John Kenneally, to 'get their facts right' about industrial law and slaps down as 'unfair' another question.

On ABC local radio in Sydney, Gillard lambasts Qantas for being aggressive and extreme and extols her government's actions for getting planes back in the air so swiftly. Within hours, another asylum-seeker boat has tragically sunk off Java en route to Australia, with preliminary reports suggesting more than a dozen deaths. The Gillard government's media inquiry is underway—the temptation to neuter News Ltd's more ferociously biased outlets must agonise cabinet ministers—and within hours the Prime Minister will jet out to the G20 Summit in France to discuss European debt. She's not in the business of getting bogged down in a game of Who Called Whose Bluff in the Qantas dispute when there are more pressing, and real, issues to manage.

In a party room meeting before leaving for Europe, Gillard graciously acknowledges Rudd's hard work at CHOGM. Not so deputy Opposition leader Julie Bishop, who comes up with the line of the day in the Coalition party room meeting. Referring to his star performance at the CHOGM rock concert, she says: 'When Kevin Rudd did his Bon Jovi "Living on a Prayer" impression, 4500 people were instantly reminded why they always thought Rudd was a tosser.' Bishop is a sharp thorn in Rudd's side—she doesn't like the cut of his jib.

Andrew Wilkie talks to a lot of Labor MPs. He's a quixotic political operator who shopped around a few political parties before settling as an Independent. He's a chameleon: a Labor-style economic thinker with a small-l liberal outlook on freedom of the individual and Greens credentials on social policies. MPs and staffers yak to him in the parliamentary corridors, and he reckons the Labor leadership talk is a case of a minority being able to commandeer a lot more attention than their numbers should suggest.

'I have a close relationship with a handful of people in the ALP, and they tell me there's nothing going on,' he says during the first week of the November sittings. 'It's the usual half dozen suspects talking to people and stirring it up. They [Wilkie's contacts] tell me there is absolutely no appetite from the overwhelming majority of people to repeat the mistake of last year.' But that's not what Rudd's thinking, and he's subtly sounding out Wilkie's thoughts on a range of policy matters.

The pair met at Rudd's invitation in the Foreign minister's parliamentary suite on Thursday 3 November. The meeting was about Wilkie's call to Gillard to instigate another inquiry into Australia's decision to join the George Bush invasion of Iraq. It's an issue dear to Wilkie's heart; in 2003, he resigned his post as an intelligence analyst with the Office of National Assessments, citing explosive concerns that the Howard government had misrepresented intelligence material to bolster its case for Australia's blind support for the war.

Wilkie broached the Labor leadership with Rudd. 'I will share with you one observation about the meeting: he was obviously looking for ways to get me on side, to get me on board,' he tells me. 'He wasn't actually asking for my support; if I had to describe Rudd's reason for the meeting, it was more than anything a bridge-building exercise to establish a better relationship with me and to bring me inside his tent. Ultimately, we found ourselves in a situation where I was asking him: "If you were prime minister, what would you do about asylum seekers? What would you do about this, and about that?"' Wilkie says it was clear Rudd wants his old job back: 'And that's perfectly understandable.'

Wilkie left their *tête-à-tête* with an open mind about the Labor leadership, should the question ever arise. He has a warm relationship with the Foreign minister, and says he still feels deeply uncomfortable about the way he was removed.

*

The clubs industry and gambling barons have thrown everything at Wilkie, including threats to sue him, but he's sticking stubbornly to script and repeats that he won't back down. It's a defiantly inflexible position from someone who despises the club industry almost as much as he does poker machines. 'This is an industry that has been ruthless with the government, running this campaign against Labor members in their seats,' he says. 'There is no doubt there is a very loud minority opposing this, but they clearly are a minority. They're just disproportionately in Labor seats.'

And those under-siege Labor MPs are as jittery as hell. Some, such as Mike Kelly from Eden-Monaro and Janelle Saffin from Page—both Rudd supporters—have broken ranks to express their dismay at the Gillard–Wilkie deal. In its highly targeted marginal seats campaign, the clubs industry has bombarded householders with flyers individualised for each seat. A black and white photo of the relevant MP is featured alongside a plea addressed to the unlucky sap: '[Name], why won't you stand up for our community?' It argues that millions of dollars in community support will be jeopardised by the Wilkie demands, that local sporting facilities will close and one-third of jobs in clubs and pubs—a high-intensity hospitality employer—will be lost. It's the gamblers' version of Chicken Little, and nervous nellies in marginal seats are swallowing the clubs' verdict that the sky will fall in if the capacity of gamblers' losses is limited to $120 an hour, instead of up to $1200.

The irony for Gillard—given the protests she faces over issues such as the pokies policy—is that Labor MPs are only parking their backsides on the government side of the parliamentary chambers thanks to the deals she sealed with the Independents, including the poker machine agreement with Wilkie. But now that pact is being used by some MPs to undermine her. Unabashedly pro-clubs, on the same day Rudd and Wilkie chat the *Daily Telegraph* carries an 'exclusive' that the powerful Clubs NSW believes Rudd's gambling policy when prime minister was more 'considered and reasonable' than Gillard's.

Well, duh. Rudd wasn't being stood over by Wilkie to secure a Labor-led minority parliament, as Gillard was. London to a brick, if Rudd had been steering those negotiations he would have shut down poker tables and roulette wheels as well as poker machines just to ensure he secured Wilkie's vote.

Tele journalist Andrew Clennell continues: 'Clubs are understood to privately believe that a Rudd prime ministership is one of the best ways of avoiding mandatory pre-commitment legislation. The clubs believe Mr Rudd could decide, if he became PM, to abandon Ms Gillard's agreement with independent MP Andrew Wilkie on mandatory pre-commitment and that he would be able to reach agreement with another independent, Bob Katter, to stay in office with minority government.'

Wow! I can almost hear Rudd whispering 'If I was PM again' in Clennell's ear. He didn't whisper similar sweet nothings in Wilkie's ear; the pair only talked in 'generalities'. The *Tele* story is powerful, capable of having a high impact on backbenchers who, fearful of losing their seats, may turn to the bloke who can save them from the Wilkie deal. While industry insiders will not name names, it is understood that members of Team Rudd—Alan Griffin is mentioned to me—have been busy bees behind the scenes making it known that their man would toss the Wilkie deal overboard to appease the clubs lobby, which is very appealing to skittish Labor MPs.

What an astonishing coincidence it is then that on the very same day the *Tele* carries a Simon Benson–Steve Lewis special, which starts: 'Kevin Rudd is being urged by key backers within the Labor Party to challenge Julia Gillard for the leadership as early as this month.' It cites a New South Wales right-wing source (who else?) saying the challenge is imminent, even though Rudd doesn't have the numbers; it includes references to the Clubs NSW endorsement of Rudd and the back-bench heebie-jeebies over the pokies policy.

The article states: 'Labor figures behind the push for the former PM to take back the job he was removed from last June have confirmed he was now being advised by his closest confidants not to wait until next year but to launch a challenge as early as the second last week of November. Senior sources within the New South Wales Right claim the leakage of support away from Ms Gillard, who flew out to France last night for the G20 leaders' meeting, was snowballing.

'There are three things that are certain: there is a leadership challenge under way, Rudd doesn't have a majority yet but has enough numbers to be a contender, and they are strategising about how to get it done.'

The report prompts a direct hit from Gillard ally, Communications minister Stephen Conroy, who slams the *Daily Telegraph* for 'clearly campaigning against the Gillard Government . . . they can't even find an MP that they want to pretend is saying something.' Health minister Nicola Roxon similarly tries to reduce the hysteria, telling ABC Radio National's Fran Kelly that the stories are 'ridiculous' and 'ludicrous'. She blames the stories on 'either the media or a few disaffected people' who are 'trying to cause trouble'. For good measure she tells reporters in Canberra that people making comments about coups and spills are 'idiots' who aren't game to put their names to their whispers. 'For all I know it might be the president of the ALP Bennelong branch who's being quoted as a senior source.'

Team Rudd is definitely tiptoeing out from the undergrowth, showing tantalising glimpses of blade, but Team Gillard is on to them. And Rudd is so wanting of media adulation that his game-playing is becoming more high farce than the Shakespearean tragedy he is attempting to craft, in which he will star as the hero who saves the burning building from ruin.

A battery of cameras and microphone-waving journalists attach themselves to Rudd that morning as he saunters through parliamentary corridors batting back questions about the *Tele*'s 'revelations'. 'As I've said a thousand times before, I'm very, very happy being the Foreign minister of Australia!' he clucks, before flouncing off in the infuriating fashion that has become his trademark take-your-leave. 'Guess what, guys, I'm about to zip!' he enthuses, and off he zips, looking for all the world like the cat that's swallowed the cream.

In Question Time, Treasurer Swan tries to provide some perspective for the important issues and what he sees is driving the *Telegraph*'s coverage of leadership speculation. In response to a touch-up question from Manager of Opposition Business Christopher Pyne, he retorts: 'With all of the big issues that are around at the moment—we have a meltdown in the European economy, potentially; we have a very big and important discussion about resource rent taxation; we have huge challenges when it comes to skills; we have, or should have, a big economic debate—all those opposite can concentrate on is muckraking from a newspaper which has its own motives. I do not think anyone on our side of politics would be at all surprised by anything that was written about politics in the *Daily Telegraph*. They are running their own agenda; they have their own motives—and that is entirely a matter for them.' And that agenda, he, Gillard and a bevy of senior ministers believe, is to drive the government out of power, and Gillard as prime minister out of her job. Whichever comes first; it doesn't really matter.

Three questions later Rudd dances around his answer when asked by deputy Opposition leader Julie Bishop if he backs Gillard's poker machine reform policy. Bishop's question was in two parts. She first asked if, in his travels as Foreign minister, Rudd had become aware of any country that has adopted a mandatory pre-commitment regime in relation to gambling, and whether he supported the cabinet's position on this. Rudd answers that he hadn't heard the 'last bit' of the question because of the 'hubbub', and started waffling about gambling not being high on the agenda of international talks. Bishop raised a point of order with the Speaker, emphatically re-stating her question: '. . . this is not a criticism of the Foreign minister; he said he did not hear the end of the question. The question I asked was: does he support the cabinet's position in relation to mandatory pre-commitment? That was the question. So could he be relevant to that part of the question?' The Speaker instructs Rudd to be so, to which Rudd responds: 'I do note the deputy leader of the Opposition required me to be relevant to that part of her question.' He then ignores it.

This is similar to his pirouetting at CHOGM when he was directly asked on two separate occasions to confirm his support for the Wilkie–Gillard reforms. This is the bloke who declared, when he was Opposition leader, that he 'hated' poker machines, that they infected families and corrupted government revenues. Perhaps cautioned by his lieutenants that his refusal to answer the pokies question was not a good look, later in the day Rudd issues a statement saying 'of course' he supports the government's policy, and that he hadn't heard Bishop's question because of the noise in parliament. This is a flat-out lie hiding behind a quarter truth.

Journalists such as Phillip Coorey in the *Sydney Morning Herald* and Phillip Hudson in the *Herald-Sun*, who sit in the press boxes in parliament during Question Time, report Rudd's false defence.

Hudson files Rudd's statement in an online update at 9 pm under the banner: 'Kevin Rudd will support pokies but won't reject talk of PM challenge'. The rest of his article is a lift from the Benson–Lewis story in the *Tele* this morning, without attribution or any evidence that he has sought to confirm the story. A sample: 'Labor figures behind the push for the former PM to take back the job removed from him in June last year have confirmed he is now being advised by his closest confidantes not to wait until next year. Senior sources within the New South Wales right claim that the leaking of support away from Ms Gillard was snowballing. A senior New South Wales right-wing source said: "There are three certainties: There is a leadership challenge under way, Rudd doesn't have a majority yet but has enough numbers to be a contender, and they are strategising about how to get it done."'

This is the way of modern newspapers and online reporting for media conglomerates. A creative sub-editor on the news desk plucks bits of copy out of stories from one or more journalists in their vast stable, maybe adding a dash of AAP copy. Combined with more than a splash of hyperbolic poetic licence, it is then poured into one glorious mishmash, often under one by-line, and transmited to all the News Ltd tabloids. The journalist under whose by-line the story appears may not have a clue about the final story because the news outlets need to feed the twenty-four-hour online story beast makes news gathering, accuracy and fact-checking an anachronism. Despairing politicians who claim they have been misquoted or verballed, or that stories are outrageously wrong or fabricated, are ignored.

Over in France at the G20, Gillard is not having much luck talking about minor issues like the tottering international economy and European debt. It's all about her leadership, which isn't under threat. 'I am very sure about my own characteristics and personality,' she says in response to a clamour of leadership questions. 'So, you know, the newspapers and the media do whatever they do, but it does not worry me all that much.' It makes her scream into her pillow at night and drives most of her cabinet colleagues—with the notable exception of the most frenzied international jetsetter—insane with rage . . . but worry? No point in that; it won't stop anything.

It certainly won't stop the *Daily Telegraph*'s campaign against the carbon pricing scheme. As with the *Australian*, the tabloid's crusade is now months old. If there's a disgruntled Sydneysider who hasn't had a say—the less informed the better—it's not because the sleuths at the *Tele* didn't try their darnedest to find them.

One of the paper's best efforts to date emblazons the front page on 9 November, the day after the carbon scheme passes the Senate. Just minutes after the vote had been taken, the heavens decided to open and an eerie atmosphere momentarily engulfed Canberra. 'Heaven Help Us' screeches the *Tele* headline. 'As the carbon tax Julia Gillard vowed never to impose was passed into law, yesterday marked a dark day for the majority of Australians opposed to it', the paper thunders, adding for dramatic effect that Gillard now stands accused of dividing the nation.

Over at the more level-headed *Sydney Morning Herald*, journalist Lenore Taylor records the government's belief that the new carbon pricing laws will be a political turning point once the 'scare campaign' against it is seen for what it is. Instead of empty bluster, her article contains facts and evidence and even-handed quotes.

Refusing to let go, the next day the *Tele* runs two anti-carbon pricing stories. One is headlined 'Carbon casualties', alleging three million families will bear the cost of Gillard's 'latest levy'. Included is the requisite struggling western Sydney family—or so it seems at first blush. But the hubby of this upwardly mobile Castle Hill family actually earns $150,000 (working 'bloody hard' for it) and he reckons to have to pay any more—well, it's . . . it's . . . it's just 'not fair'!

How much extra will they need to pay, given they earn too much for full compensation from the government? $1.92 a day. Surely the *Tele* could have done better than that. Or just maybe they couldn't find a real struggling family to complain, because those families will actually be better off under the government's compensation package.

Barack Obama and Gillard get on famously. When he touches down in Australia on 16 November it's for a flying visit that of course she, as prime minister, hosts. A few days ago they had both attended an international forum in Hawaii, but this is his first visit to Australia as president and there is much to discuss: stationing American troops in Darwin, the growing international financial crisis, and America's domestic economic woes. A not insignificant agenda is belittled in a sexist and insulting barrage of reporting from News Ltd about the pair's 'relationship'—a theme that then sweeps across the internet and the oceans to land in UK and US publications, and even in the *Huffington Post*.

It is worth reporting slabs of one *Daily Telegraph* article. 'They are a touching pair and touchy pairing,' start Patrick Carlyon and Owen Vaughan under the mocking headline 'The Audacity of Groping': 'Their hands, like disembodied life forms, seek out the other's shoulders, backs and, quite possibly, bottoms. When such targets are out of reach, digits settle on forearms or the nearest available body part. Obama constantly bares his American teeth. His smile alone could power a Third World country. Gillard blushes, like a high school girl who has, finally, after much bedroom plotting, captured the gaze of the football captain. Today her football captain held sway in Parliament. The content of his speech didn't seem to matter; what was important was that he was there and she had invited him.'

Other offensive lines include: 'Gillard glowed, head bowed, as though a new beau was being introduced to the family for the first time', and 'She has added a dash of coquettishness, if not flirting, to US–Australian relations'. Even if we are to believe, generously, that this is a feeble attempt at humour, it is belittling to Gillard the woman and the office she occupies. If it had been written about a male PM—say, John Howard and Margaret Thatcher if they had been prime ministers at the same time—the uproar would have stopped the nation.

And then it all goes quiet. The temperature momentarily drops as MPs zoom back to their electorates before the last critical fortnight of parliament starting on the 21st, which ushers in the long Christmas break. The final fortnight of a year's sittings is the oddest of times in politics; it's when the nasty underbelly of the political beast is exposed at the same time as the best of camaraderie and achievements are celebrated.

Factional foes and allies clink glasses together in remarkably civilised end-of-year drinkies sojourns. Cross-party opponents down weapons and slug back a beer or three together in their suites, animosities temporarily forgotten. Journalists who tear strips off MPs are hosted to drinks by the same backbenchers or ministers they've targeted, and no scribe has yet been poisoned. On the last day, the prime minister and the Opposition leader, whoever they may be, salute parliament, their overworked and long-suffering staff, their own teams and then each other and their respective teams. As this quaint practice is usually preceded by a day of vicious insult-hurling and eye-gouging in the chamber, it must make the average voter wonder about the sanity and stability of our politicians as they transition from cage fighters to gracious toast makers without changing costumes.

Rippling underneath the general air of festivity is the knowledge that everyone in the building has locked in their memory vaults: this also is the killing season. If leaders are going to get knocked off, it happens in a pre-Christmas rush of blood during the November sittings or shortly thereafter. The roll call of leaders who fell on their swords or were knifed in this season is long: Bob Hawke, Simon Crean, Kim Beazley, Malcolm Turnbull. Mark Latham blasted himself out of the leadership in January, technically still in the killing season. MPs striding purposely down the corridor during these last desperate two weeks are either popping into a colleague's office for a tipple, or nipping in for a swig of plotting. This is politics at its best, folks.

Team Rudd's been planning for months for the possibility of a political coup during the pre-Christmas season—planting stories and revving up the appearance of a leadership threat. The fact that their vehicle is just a flashy car with a toy engine is neither here nor there. If only News Ltd can maintain its efforts and be followed by the wider political press, the killing season will live up to its name—they hope.

Then something both unexpected and expected occurs to throw a massive spanner in the flashy car's spokes.

First, the unexpected. On 24 November Harry Jenkins— the genial, often frustrated and highly competent Speaker of the House of Representatives, who before sitting in the chamber's big chair was an active member of the Labor family—resigns his post. He wants to contribute to ALP policy; he's frustrated by the goings-on in parliament, and he's no longer of the mind to spend lonely nights in the House without friend or even foe with whom to break bread.

The expected was the elevation to the chair of Peter Slipper (Slippery Pete even to his mates, the unprintable to his enemies), a done and dusted deal within hours of Jenkins informing Gillard at 7.30 am of his intentions. Political swashbuckler Anthony Albanese, whose dislike of 'Tories' is personal, was pivotal in pulling Slippery Pete away from the clutches of the Coalition and, unshackled by party loyalties, into the Speaker's chair.

The bedlam in parliament from outraged Opposition MPs—who see their capacity to force Gillard from office becoming considerably more difficult with her gaining of one precious extra vote in the House—is a sight to behold. It's high theatre the likes of which even the politically uninterested would pay tickets to see. Such is the outrage of the robbed that, within an hour of assuming the chair, Slippery has tossed out four of his former Coalition colleagues during an uproarious censure motion moved by a furious Tony Abbott. Jenkins has been forced to 'walk the plank' to preserve the government because of Craig Thomson, Abbott sneers, sobbing on the inside.

If Abbott is feeling outmanoeuvred, it's because he has been. Royally. The trouble with Pete has been brewing for months; years, in fact. He's a man with a liking of the high life—good booze, fast cars (as long as they're taxpayer funded, and can take him anywhere he likes) and overseas jaunts (ditto). Stories of late-night drinking, and other activities that allegedly accompany the tippling, have bounced around parliament for a long time. In a case of the political gods having a bloody good belly laugh at us all, he's one of those controversial characters who end up holding all the cards. Think senators Albert Field and Mal Colston—together with Slippery, they make an amazing trio. Of Queenslanders, no less. It's got to make you wonder about the quality of the pool of Sunshine State candidates for high office.

The Queensland Liberal National Party (LNP) had been toying for months with the idea stripping pre-selection from Slipper. In the first days of the minority parliament, he'd already shown that his allegiances were to any benefits he could get from parliament rather than to his party when he'd accepted Labor's offer to be its nominee for deputy Speaker. The convention is that it's the Opposition's prerogative to choose the deputy Speaker, given the new government has dibs on the speakership. So up Slipper went against one of his own, and secured the gig through the combined might of the vote of Labor MPs and the cross benchers—plus one, his own vote.

Labor's tactic on this earlier occasion was clever and cynical. It should have made the sharp heads in the LNP take note that Slipper was more than just an embarrassment with a fondness for plonk and perks—he could be political dynamite. But, instead, the party angered the bloke it had continued to pre-select in the seat of Fisher for nearly two decades by publicly talking up how it was going to chop him off at the knees. The next time the LNP hierarchy was due to consider Slipper's pre-selection was next week. So close, and yet now so far.

One MP who's feeling the pain today is Andrew Wilkie, who's looking like a prime candidate for the Rooster to Feather Duster Award right now. Given his love of media attention and the power he wields over the government, this afternoon he is putting the best possible spin on the torrid events of the day. He does, however, have the good grace to look shaken.

After trying to get hold of Wilkie from 8 am onwards, Gillard finally reached him as he cruised up the hill to parliament in a Commonwealth car at around 8.30. 'It was a brief conversation, just to tell me that Harry Jenkins was going to step down at 9 am, and also to say that as far as she was concerned nothing had changed in our agreement,' he tells me. He's still marvelling at the political creativity of the move. 'I tell you what, the government finishes on a high now. A two-seat majority. From a political point of view, this is a remarkable achievement for the government.'

Will it turn their fortunes around? 'I think it will, because there is now a greater certainty they'll go full term and there's a greater certainty they'll get their legislative agenda and there'll be less need for the argy-bargy and negotiations. It will still happen, but the government will appear stronger, more stable and more legitimate in the eyes of some people.' Yes, it has reduced the Independents' leverage 'a little', he concedes, but: 'They want to keep a two-seat majority, so they will still keep the four of us happy; otherwise, what was the point of this? Suddenly they'll be back to a one-seat majority if one of us is pissed off.'

Wilkie might regret the loss of power and influence, but there's one thing he bluntly admits he won't miss: the thought he could have been the one to hand Abbott the prime ministership. His frankness is disarming. 'I don't have to worry now about being the man to install Tony Abbott. And you know what? That's a huge relief. It was making me sick with worry. That was really, really eating at me—the fact that it was going to be up to me to decide whether or not Tony Abbott was going to be PM.' It's not that he loathes the man; indeed, he admits to rather liking him. He just doesn't want him as prime minister. 'The more time that has gone on, the less confidence I've had in him to be a prime minister. Fifteen months in, we haven't seen a lot of policy out of him. We've seen a lot of wrecking. Nothing adds up any more—the numbers, nothing adds up. That worries me.'

Through all the negotiating and bickering over poker machine policy, he remains a Gillard fan. 'I've developed a lot of respect for Julia Gillard and I want her to succeed. I still think she can win the next election, and that move today has greatly increased her chances of going full term and, in doing so, significantly increased her chance of winning the next election. She just needs time.'

Within hours the payback against Slipper starts, with Coalition staffers and MPs openly gathering in huddles in parliamentary corridors to talk in shocked whispers about the many loaded guns Slipper left for them to fire right back at him and at the government. Maybe it wasn't such a bad move after all, Coalition staffers mutter. Maybe we can kill two birds with one very big stone.

Two days later stories appear in newspapers about an alleged video starring Slipper and a male staffer, as do reports that Labor MPs are 'spooked' that allegations of misuse of travel allowances against Slipper might continue to emerge and be proven. He has already been forced to pay back $20,000 for unauthorised spending. This could get very ugly.

So could Kevin, who is suffering a serious bout of limelight deprivation syndrome. Two days after Slipper's ascension to the chair, he bursts onto the stage and into the media via a book launch, delivering an incendiary blast at Labor's stagnating culture, urging sweeping reforms to prevent Labor becoming a 'marginalised third party'. It's a pre-emptive strike against Gillard's reform agenda, which is due to be presented within a week to Labor's national conference. That conference, he says by the by, should be a 'genuine public contest of ideas'.

Rudd's been at the happy juice again, for sure. It was he who in 2009 presided over the most antiseptic national conference in decades, where not one vote was taken and no debate was allowed. It was Kevin who helped torpedo rank-and-file pre-selections so he could bring supposed star power to candidacies, and it was he who stripped caucus of the right to choose its front bench. It is staggering that he now thinks every person he's worked with and worked over has the memory of a Queensland cane toad.

The killing season is only in its first blush, with the ALP national conference just days away for Gillard to look fondly toward. Politics is a brutal blood sport, no matter how you look at it.

THE LIFE WE'D LIKE TO LIVE
December 2011

As far as stage productions go, Labor's national conference is always a must-see for the sheer bravura of its posturing and politicking. Ah, wait! Sorry, that was a memory from a long distant past. A decade or more ago, the three-day shebang morphed into a study in party harmony for the cameras rather than a genuine forum for debate. Ever since the bruvvers and sistas decided in 1986 to shift the conference to Hobart's Wrest Point Casino (pesky protestors had become increasingly rowdy outside venues on the mainland), Labor's conference soul has been slowly ebbing away.

When the Apple Isle lost its appeal in the early 2000s, struggling families in western Sydney could rest easy that the champions of the workers wouldn't be coming anywhere near them for their biennial conferences; any appearances in the 'burbs of such illuminati are strictly reserved for election campaign speeches, launches and announcements about 'battlers', which are just about the only times these days when ALP leaders can be bothered to visit western Sydney. The upmarket Convention Centre at Sydney's

Darling Harbour—sitting alongside millionaire yachts bobbing on the harbour—became the new venue of choice for the national conference in order to accommodate the swelling ranks of delegates. Well, that was the story, anyway; but it was a somewhat curious explanation, given that the sprawling clubs in western Sydney have auditoriums that can accommodate numbers well into four figures. That Darling Harbour offers great hotels, terrific watering holes for grog swilling and an ambient atmosphere for wining and dining had nothing to do with the decision.

On this day of the conference's opening, 2 December, no-one is more full of the simple joy of being a Laborite than One K. Rudd. His leadership ambitions beam brighter than a Sydney summer day. His striding entrance into the venue is greeted with manic enthusiasm by a pulsing media throng. Journalists stumble over each other and rapid-fire flashlights pop as he slowly makes his way inside. The rock star returns! Where's the stage? But unlike his hyper-vibed performance at the CHOGM concert, this performance must be finely modulated. Rudd needs to duchess his targets, set his media tone to a discreet but audible volume, and ever so slightly flick the Keating switch to vaudeville. As he takes his seat in the conference hall, the former PM's omnipresence shimmers as a sharp note. Eyes glinting, he waits for proceedings to start.

The conference curtain raiser—a hero video of Labor achievements set to some music best reserved for chick flicks—scales new heights of political schmaltz. It's a black and white tear-jerker; Labor loves the genre. These audio-visual treats are trotted out at campaign launches and big functions, the Labor equivalent of the warm-up guy who revs up the crowd. Rudd rates a fractional second mention in the video for his prime ministerial apology to Indigenous people, the reference jammed between lengthier eulogies to

other Labor greats including the very controversial and colourful Father of Multiculturalism, Al Grassby. Towards the front of
the conference room, the temperature rises ever so slightly with
Rudd's contribution to Labor history having been relegated to a
minor footnote.

After restrained applause, on strides Gillard in a carefully casual
ensemble of black slacks, tangerine top, cream coat and neatly
coiffed hair. As she waves to delegates—who stand to cheer her
in a more Liberal-reserved than Labor-wild way—I wonder about
the vacuousness of contemporary politics, in which an effervescent,
smart woman has been forced to undergo public transformation
into a starched and over-scripted political figure. That wonderment
increases as the PM launches into a wooden and off-key opening
speech unlike any I've witnessed at a Labor conference.

My memory of these events dates back to the 1979 Adelaide
conference. It was a raucously drunken, brawling, passionate affair
where delegates ripped each other to shreds, and where Bill Hayden
and Bob Hawke first let loose their poisonous ambitions to beat
the other to a pulp or to the leadership, in no particular order.
And that was just the timid stuff in the bars at night; the real
action on the conference floor made a young girl's eyes pop out of
their sockets.

A boring sermon is livelier than Gillard's address today. I jolt
into the here and now when she starts up a drum roll of Labor
greats: 'The responsibilities of government are the responsibilities
of hard choices. Curtin knew that when he raised conscripts for
military service overseas. Chifley knew that in the industrial winter
of 1949. Whitlam knew it when he ended the bitter debate over
state aid. Hawke and Keating knew it every day they governed.
And we know it now.' I'm sitting in the bleachers, where the

media is always shunted, and swear I can see the back of Rudd's head shake with indignation that Gillard hasn't acknowledged his prime ministership.

As if that isn't enough excitement, the following words fairly crackle with promise: 'Delegates, in these coming days I want us to have a fair dinkum Labor Party conference. We didn't join Labor in our youth because we had no opinions. We didn't come here for a coronation or a campaign launch. We came here for debates, we came here for surprises, we came here to have votes.' Polite applause follows. A few young Laborites behind me titter nervously. Perhaps they don't know what she means. At the last, in July 2009 under Supreme Leader Rudd, there were no debates and no real votes. The prime minister didn't even attend most of the conference.

Is Gillard really proposing that in the next few days there should be a knock 'em down brawl over bedevilling issues such as marriage equality, refugee policy and uranium sales to India? She perhaps wishes, even yearns, for the old days of fiery arguments. But the outcomes are already known before debate has started. There will be a bit of argy-bargy, but it's a foregone conclusion that the platform will be changed to allow for gay marriage; Gillard will tick off a cross-factional deal that will allow federal MPs a conscience vote. A deal's also been done on uranium sales to India, which Gillard champions and the Left opposes. Ditto asylum-seeker policy. Rank-and-file delegates will, for the first time, endorse offshore processing, even though the Labor government has been vigorously trying to ram an offshore processing regime through parliament for months.

And so the irrelevance of Labor's layers of so-called democratic decision-making is made plain—a process where policy-making is supposed to start in the branches, progress up the chain through various committees and then on to state and ultimately national conference for final debate and resolution. Policies that then make it into the ALP platform are supposed to be adhered to by Labor in power, but even Labor idealists know it doesn't work that way. It's a long time since the platform was the unimpeachable blueprint for How Labor Will Behave in Office.

As Gillard reaches a crescendo with the words: 'This is the Labor way. This is the Australian way. We follow it simply because we are us,' I wonder who wrote this fluff. The only plausible explanation is a young Labor scribe penned the words while watching re-runs of *Friends*, swigging a carafe of red and smoking a joint.

The PM finishes with the triumphant line: 'Labor says yes to Australia's future!' Which is silly, too, even if it is just a dab of feel-good rhetoric. It's a line designed to highlight what Tony Abbott would do to Australia if given the chance; but, even so, only a politician with a death wish would say 'no' to Australia's future. Ben Chifley's Light on the Hill speech to Labor's 1949 national conference this is not. It is a long way from Gillard's finest hour, and it will give her detractors and Team Rudd a massive opening.

Within hours the flatness of Gillard's speech and Rudd's omission from the history of Labor luminaries is the febrile buzz of the conference. You can sense the heat rise another notch, hear the whispers of condemnation and the regrouping of Team Rudd. The media is merciless (myself included, on Sky News).

The Foreign minister is an angry little Vegemite, cloaked in the guise of a sarcastic little Vegemite. As dusk settles over the harbour, he's strolling with adviser Philip Green past Darling Harbour's Cyren Bar and responds to a beckoning call from one of a group of senior journalists, including the ABC's Chris Uhlmann, Sky News political editor David Speers and News Ltd's Mark Kenny, who are inside the bar swilling plonk and cogitating the meaning of Labor conferences (a short reflection). They tickle him up about Gillard's speech and he lets forth about being airbrushed from history and mocks her 'Toys'R'Us' speech. As for his successor's 'Labor says yes to the future' line, Rudd, who the journalists think may have cleansed his palate at another bar along the harbour strip, thrusts his middle finger in the air and declares with mock humour: 'Fuck the future!' Hahaha. The Foreign minister has never been a shrinking violet when it comes to letting journalists know what he thinks, but usually it's behind closed doors. The journalists who were present tell me they were startled at how open he was with them, and in front of an adoring crowd. After his outburst, Rudd saunters to the bar where he happily poses for photos with excited revellers. One of the journalists records these thrilling moments on his iPhone.

The expected happens on Saturday. Marriage equality becomes part of the party's platform and Gillard's conscience vote for federal MPs passes, all but ensuring it will fail in parliament when left-wing MP Stephen Jones introduces his private member's bill early in 2012. Party reform proposals to dilute the influence of factional hacks and unions—which were judged by Labor elders such as John Faulkner, Bob Carr, Bob Hawke and Paul Keating as critical to modern Labor's survival—are shunted to a subcommittee of Labor's national executive, which is controlled by the factions.

Before the conference, Hawke had warned the party it was being suffocated by the unions. They represent only 18 per cent of the workforce and yet they constitute 50 per cent of ALP conferences, dominate the selection of Labor candidates and wield a disproportionate influence over policy-making. The postscript to today's flick pass of party reform to a coterie of hand-picked factional insiders is that it damages Gillard, who entered the conference hoping for more radical reform.

Rudd is a latecomer to the reform cause. In his quest to saddle up again for the top job, he is fashioning himself as a voice for a new, grassroots-orientated Labor. It is a self-motivated turnaround. When Rudd was stalking Kim Beazley in the mid-2000s, he criss-crossed the country garnering every factional and union vote he could muster. He owed his leadership in Opposition and his prime ministership to the types he now blackens as Labor's cancerous core. The failure of delegates to embrace radical reform opens up another door for the deposed PM.

Sunday, the last day of conference, dawns to a screaming headline in the *Sunday Telegraph*: 'Humiliated Kevin Rudd plots a leadership coup'. Reporters are only too happy to light a bonfire under the story, which is based, of course, on a smattering of anonymous quotes. A media scrum with One K. Rudd at the centre is the order of the morning. Reporter: 'Are you planning a leadership challenge?' Rudd: 'I'm very happy being the Foreign minister. I've enjoyed the job.' *Enjoyed*? Not *enjoying*? Ah, Kev, get your tenses right, comrade!

Step right up, Simon Crean—party elder and another Labor leader felled a lifetime ago in one of Labor's pitiless leadership putsches. Crean leaps to defend Gillard's omission of the Ruddster from her speech. 'Of course' Rudd was the equal of other leaders mentioned in Gillard's speech, he says indignantly to a press pack yapping for quotes. 'When you look at his leadership . . . getting to [the] prime ministership, his leadership in terms of the G20 recognition and putting us front and centre on the international stage . . . his commitment in terms of the domestic agenda . . . these are all important legacies in a great history of Labor tradition,' he says with a flourish, making you wonder why Gillard bought herself a truckload of strife by not saying this herself. As for people upset about her speech, they're just 'sensitive petals' who need to understand 'the broad sweep of things', Crean asserts. Okey dokey, that's fixed that sensitive petal Kevin Rudd right up.

Gillard's mis-step in omitting her predecessor from her speech, and Rudd's posturing in response, is now trumping every success of this conference, like the announcement of the design of an historic National Disability Insurance Scheme. But it's not just what Rudd sympathisers view as Gillard's deliberate snub in her speech that has delegates gossiping.

A prominent equal marriage rights activist sidles up to me at the ground floor coffee cart to whisper that Rudd attended the celebrations the previous night of the pro-gay marriage group Rainbow Labor, many of whom have spent years agitating for a change to Labor's platform. There was apparently much confusion at Darling Harbour's Cohibar when Rudd appeared, air kissing and enthusiastically congratulating everyone on the success of the marriage equality vote. Attendees did not have amnesia. After Rudd had bounded out, they huddled together and reminded themselves of his refusal when leader to entertain changes to the Marriage Act and his then repeated insistence that marriage is, and will always be, only between a man and a woman.

Rainbow Labor spokesman Neil Pharaoh is very kind about the former leader's attendance at the knees-up: 'It was excellent for him to come and enjoy the celebrations.' But my informant is less impressed: 'He is looking for votes everywhere he can,' he whispers.

'This is exactly what he did when he was hunting Kim Beazley. He promises everything, gives every group support, and then discards you when he's got what he wants. I don't trust him, and I told my friends last night not to trust him.'

Gillard's speech, Rudd's surprise nocturnal bar visits and the pair's frosty avoidance of each other at the conference, as obvious as two repulsing magnets, have become the talk of the 400 delegates, the few hundred business and other observers, and the dozens in the media. The day drags on and, as expected, Gillard wins on overturning a ban on flogging uranium to India. But any after-glow evaporates the moment Rudd takes to the stage to launch the Foreign Affairs platform debate, noticeably relegated to the grave-yard slot in the fading hours of this last day.

It becomes rapidly apparent that this is a campaign speech. Rudd deliberately and provocatively does what his successor failed to do for him just forty-eight hours ago: he praises her, albeit faintly. 'We acted as a Labor team in government,' the Foreign minister says pointedly, lauding his own handling of the global financial crisis and other achievements in his short-lived prime ministerial term. 'A team made up of Julia; of Wayne [Swan, who also failed to acknowledge the former PM in his speech to conference], who is with us here today; of Lindsay Tanner, a former great Austra-lian finance minister; of Chris Bowen, then assistant treasurer . . . acting as a team, acting to make a difference for Australians and keeping Australians in work.'

Rudd's hitting all the right notes, even if his memory is fatally flawed about his own administration. He attacks Tony Abbott as 'Captain Negative', 'Captain Stunt' and 'Field Marshall No'. He quotes from the Opposition leader's 2009 book *Battlelines*, in which Abbott wrote that 'the future lies in the Anglosphere'. 'Pity about the Chinese, the world's second-largest economy; the Japanese, the third biggest; and the quarter of a billion people of Indonesia!' Rudd sneers. The insults roll on. Abbott is a combination of Rudyard Kipling, Biggles and the *Boys' Own Annual*. If the Opposition leader's brave new world 'wasn't so dangerous, it would be hilarious,' he scorns. Gillard's thoughts are surely along similar lines, but not about Abbott.

Gillard in opposition and as deputy prime minister used to talk like Rudd is now—full of political fury, barbed insults and punchy messages. The prime ministership forces the incumbent to turn down the volume. Not so Rudd. With the main prize again in his sights, he's sharpened his political tongue. Gillard is now the hunted, and she's feeling it. Rudd is the hunter, and he's loving it. On cue, Rudd exits stage left and blasts the failure of conference to take 'giant leaps' on party reform. As happened in 1979 and 1982—when the titanic struggle and bitter animosity between Bob Hawke and Bill Hayden swallowed those party conferences—so, too, has this one been marred by a personally spiteful battle. Big, big trouble lies ahead.

Retribution is via a leak of the hitherto 'sealed section' of the 2010 party review by John Faulkner, Steve Bracks and Bob Carr, which bobs up in the Fairfax press the morning after conference ends. If the leak is inspired by Team Gillard to put Rudd in his place, they should be well pleased with their efforts. The *Sydney Morning Herald*'s Phillip Coorey leads with a paragraph that will undoubtedly prompt an infamous Rudd dummy spit: 'A secret Labor Party report has criticised the government led by Kevin Rudd as lacking purpose and being driven by spin, and implies that the former prime minister or his supporters were behind the leaks that almost destroyed Julia Gillard's election campaign.' It speaks volumes about the nature of the increasingly bitter battle being waged between Gillard, her stalker and their supporters that a damning report on the damage that is wreaked on the party by leaks is leaked.

The story gets no better for Rudd. Sprinkled like poisonous fairy dust throughout are quotes from the review about Rudd's spin-driven style and lack of substance, including the killer line that Rudd forged a government 'rich on themes, announcements and talking up a narrative, but short on substance and follow through'. The reviewers castigate the extraordinary number of press releases issued by Rudd, the lack of follow-through on real policies and the absence of a core government philosophy. In echoes of what is happening now, the authors state that every time Gillard was generating momentum in the election campaign, there was 'another damaging round of internal disunity'. The unanimous conclusion of the review committee was that 'these events were designed to cause damage to Labor's election chances, and those involved should be condemned by the party'. They haven't been, and they still walk tall.

Gillard tries desperately to amend for her conference sin of omission. There is a press event the following day at a primary school in the affluent Canberra suburb of Red Hill; it is supposed to be about her London 2012 Olympic and Paralympic Challenge, which is designed to entice youngsters into becoming more active. When she asks the assembled media for questions, the first has nothing to do with children earning gold, silver or bronze awards. Matthew Franklin from the *Australian* asks: 'Prime Minister, do you like Kevin Rudd?' Slightly taken aback, Gillard replies: 'Look, Kevin Rudd and I are working together in the interests of the nation. Kevin has been attending for us the conference in Bonn on our further strategy in Afghanistan and is now pursuing the nation's interests in a number of places overseas.'

Then another similar question: 'Prime Minister, given the weekend's events, are you still able to work—have a functioning relationship with Kevin Rudd—and are you bracing for a challenge from him?' PM: 'The answer is, yes, of course we work together closely in the interests of the government and the nation. Kevin is a very valued part of my team. He's doing a great job as Minister for Foreign Affairs. He's an incredibly active Minister for Foreign Affairs, pursuing our great Australian tradition of middle-power diplomacy, what we like to style as punching above our weight. Kevin Rudd is doing that for our nation, so we'll keep working together, with Kevin pursuing his work as the Minister for Foreign Affairs.'

Of nearly two dozen questions, none relate to children's sport or to the Prime Minister's Challenge. No-one pays the slightest attention to Sports minister Mark Arbib, standing alongside Gillard looking like a dill. The kids must wonder what strange circus has visited their humble schoolyard. Back down the road and up the hill in the Big House, the sound crackles across Canberra of gloves being ripped off by members of Team Rudd.

A tried and true political maxim is: when in strife, divert attention. Big diversions are wars and invasions; little ones are policy launches, reviews and inquiries. A ministerial reshuffle is also the ticket if the collective face of a ministry needs a good scrub and if leakers, destabilisers and turncoats need to be shown the door.

Thus, on 12 December, as the cacophony of leadership chatter intensifies, Julia Gillard announces a reshuffle of her front bench and its slight expansion. It is five days after Communications minister Stephen Conroy announced that a multi-million-dollar tender process for the Australia TV Network (our external broadcaster, focusing on the Asia-Pacific region)—a flawed and messy process unhinged at two critical junctures by political intervention and leaks—has been abandoned and the prize handed permanently to the ABC. The debacle cost the competing tenderer, Sky Australia, hundreds of millions of dollars, which has invoked the fury of the star-studded Sky board and brought down on the government the possibility of a whopping law suit.

The stated reason for the reshuffle is the retirement to the back bench, and after the next election the big wide world, of Small Business minister Nick Sherry. A twenty-one-year veteran of federal politics, Sherry overcame depression and a suicide attempt during his early Senate years to become a productive parliamentary contributor. But none of his achievements matter a whit in the frenzy of analysis that erupts after Gillard's uninterrupted twenty-minute reshuffle announcement. While she emphasises the worthiness of the elevated and lays out her case to assemble the right team to tackle the big challenges of 2012, shoring up Team Gillard frames the media interpretation that instantly floods news sites.

Up the ministerial escalator go Bill Shorten and Mark Arbib, into Industrial Relations and Assistant Treasury respectively. Media coverage howls at the elevation of the 'faceless men', parroting yet again one of the sillier terms of this silly political age. Joining them on the ride up are two able performers, Nicola Roxon (into Attorney-General's) and Tanya Plibersek (Health). Instead of being acknowledged as tough, competent performers who've earned their dues and burst through a very tough glass ceiling, it is pointedly noted in many media dispatches that they're female and they're supporters of the female prime minister. Clearly that makes them less worthy to serve in higher office and makes their support for the PM more questionable, is the insinuation.

Off to the outer ministry goes Victorian left-winger Kim Carr, booted out of his beloved portfolio of Innovation, Industry, Science and Research and handed a pairing of Manufacturing and Defence Materiel. Carr had been nursing resentment about cuts to some of his pet programs as far back as January, and there have long been suspicions in cabinet that Carr is loose-lipped about that confidential body's discussions. Banished too is Attorney-General Robert McClelland, described by colleagues as under-performing ('lazy', is one description) and heading a directionless department; he is given the portfolio of Housing, Homelessness and Emergency Management. Both men are furious.

Before the PM's announcement, the reshuffle has already been the source of forty-eight hours of intense media speculation that would have bored the pants off most readers, listeners and viewers. Surely most Australians don't particularly care who has what ministry, only whether they can do the job? What dominates media coverage, once the new line-up is known, is the old race-call approach: it's about winners and losers, about payback or shoring up support, the media almost unanimously agrees. There is little serious analysis about the flaws and contributions of those who are on the way in or out of the ministerial revolving door.

'Prime Minister Julia Gillard's Revenge in Cabinet Reshuffle', yelps the *Daily Telegraph*, complete with a rogue's gallery of pictures. Under each is emblazoned one of three words, depending on the mug shot: 'Rewarded', 'Spared' or 'Punished'. The ABC's Jeremy Thompson headlines his online story with Bill Shorten's promotion, trotting out the faceless man imagery again. Michelle Grattan in the *Age* says the changes are designed to shore up Gillard's leadership. It is barely scrutinised that the elephant of gargantuan proportions, Kevin Rudd, remains in cabinet.

There are times when politicians use the media to make a loaded political point without trying to be obvious while making a loaded political point. This is such a time. The notoriously media-shy Kim Carr issues a statement saying his demotion does not reflect his performance or achievements, and his change in portfolios was not of his choosing—but, hey, he's honoured to do it anyway. McClelland goes public in similar language, saying he has been moved against his wishes—but, hey, he's looking forward to the new gig anyway.

Kevin Rudd goes one better, tailing an ABC interview on foreign policy matters with the pointed observation that Carr was a very good minister in his old portfolio. 'His period as Industry minister—he was largely responsible during the global financial crisis for ensuring that none of the Australian car companies fell over. Automobile companies around the world were falling over at that time.' Any appearance of a co-ordinated attack against Gillard is purely coincidental. The political point made in these three interviews is that the demotions of Carr and McClelland were about Gillard's maintenance of power and position, thus rein-forcing the thrust of media reporting, and that the decision showed bad judgement and paranoia and has pissed off the wrong people.

Gillard fronts the ABC's *AM* program the next morning to try and spread the message that the team she's assembled is about getting the right faces into her 2012 team. *AM*'s political corre-spondent Sabra Lane is having none of it. Her first salvo sets the tone for the interview: 'In announcing this reshuffle, you said it would give the government the firepower and focus it needed for 2012. Is that an admission that you didn't have focus this year and that you've been firing dummy rounds?' PM: 'Absolutely, you've hit the nail on the head there, Sabra. Incisive question, love. Dummy rounds—love it! I've had a shocker of a year, as you all in the gallery keep telling me. I couldn't pull a trick. I may as well hand the whole kit and caboodle back to Kev, as many of you in the media seem to want. He's bonkers, but at least he'll stop stalking me.'

Sorry, daydreaming again. If only! The sober response Gillard actually gives is: '2011 has been a difficult year, that's obvious. In 2012, I want Australian families to see the benefits of the changes that we've delivered this year and I also want to see us focusing on jobs, the economy and fairness for the future. It's the job of government to deliver change and to publicly make the case for change. So, of course, in considering who should be in cabinet and who should be in the ministry, I have selected people who have got the skills to deliver the changes we need, to keep strengthening our economy, to keep increasing jobs, to have the jobs of the future with fairness as well. But I've also selected people who can publicly make that case for change.'

Lane isn't convinced. She gives free expression to her opinions by way of the questions she then asks: how the cabinet's size has now become unwieldy, how McClelland didn't want to go, how people had threatened to resign. Gillard protests that the commentary around the reshuffle has been silly, particularly about people threatening to resign. 'That is completely untrue,' she says. Twice, for good measure. But Lane shoots back: 'They didn't need to threaten to resign—you know what the numbers are in parliament!'

Incredulously, Gillard retorts: 'Oh, crazy. What's the point of that question?' Lane: 'Well, the point of the question is your numbers are so tight, even you know that, if one threatened to go, that that could possibly lead to your government falling over?' PM: 'So now you're building hypothetical on hypothetical, about something that didn't happen.' Lane finishes with one last commentary before signing off: 'But it's not a good look for Kim Carr—a man who works very hard is demoted!' This is our ABC at work.

Within forty-eight hours the coded call to arms by Carr, McClelland and Rudd has been answered. Journalists bubble with talk about a seismic shift to Rudd, stating but not naming 'up to six ministers'. McClelland and Carr are talking freely about how shitty they are after the reshuffle, but refuse to state if they are in the Rudd camp. Resources minister Martin Ferguson—who has nurtured deep hurt against Gillard since 2006, when she swung the Victorian left-wing behind Rudd without Ferguson's imprimatur—refuses to declare loyalty to her. Insisting it's because he won't indulge in press sports, he says he is 'loyal to the Labor Party'. The old neutral mantra from Team Rudd.

The ABC's Jeremy Thompson leads with this statement: 'Julia Gillard's grip on the prime ministership appears more tenuous than ever, with a group of senior ministers now believed to have swung their support behind leadership aspirant Kevin Rudd.' The 'now believed' is because it was written in both the *Australian* and the *Sydney Morning Herald* this morning. Such is the poisonous nature of undeclared leadership challenges, and the odious reporting in response. It is a cycle of Chinese whispers and pack reporting, with journalists repeating what other journalists have written without elaboration, justifying their copy with words like 'believed to'. By the end of this twenty-four-hour news cycle, the story that's appeared in the morning newspapers, based on nothing more than the words of Rudd spruikers, has been repeated on radio and television and become 'fact'.

McLelland and Carr have been, and still are, firmly with Rudd; even if there were another few ministers who have drifted—either permanently or temporarily, in the wash-up of the reshuffle—those numbers do not a challenge make. Far from it: Rudd has a mountain to climb before he's within coo-ee of his personal Everest. Malcolm Farr, along with the *Courier-Mail*'s Dennis Atkins, rare sane voices in the News Ltd tabloid and online stable, sums it up in one line: 'There is no evidence that any of those promoted in the reshaped ministry were moving to Mr Rudd.'

Rudd is unique in modern politics in that—so far—he's got where he's wanted to go, despite being mistrusted or loathed by most of his colleagues. It is the unswerving, crushing Power of One.

When Rudd's serious pursuit of the leadership started in 2004, he had no support in the caucus. He and a few mates talked up his support constantly; it was a fraught time in opposition Labor politics, with personal enmities and factional hostilities creating a rapid succession of Labor leaders. Rudd had to be in it to win it, and if it took telling fairy tales so be it. I was working in the press gallery then, and one of his colleagues would ring me constantly with breathy exhalations about his man's popularity in caucus. Balderdash.

Even though Kev was forced to withdraw from the ballot in January 2005 due to a dismal level of support, he had no respect for Beazley's mandate and started assiduously courting every key player in every state and territory until, having secured the critical backing of the New South Wales right-wing, he challenged Beazley on 4 December 2006. He won forty-nine votes to thirty-nine.

With stakes as high as grabbing back the prime ministership, Rudd is again single-minded in his pursuit of the leadership prize, despite the overwhelming majority of caucus swearing blind after he lost the job in 2010 that they'd never vote for him again. It's tough to determine what's more scary: Rudd's obsessive personal ambition or the small clique of MPs plotting to return him to office, when the bulk of caucus are still askance at the unsteady hand he had on Australia's tiller when PM. Lucky they're in the minority, no matter what the press coverage insists.

There is a poignancy to Gillard's Christmas Night message. Two paragraphs of the simple ten-paragraph statement stand out: 'At Christmas, for at least one day, we can all live the life we'd most like to live: a life of loving kindness for those we care about most. And this evening, we all know we are not alone, that we all have people to protect and trust, and we all have people who look to us to hope and persevere.'

Pity it's not Christmas every day in the Big House on the Hill in the national capital.

ALL BETS ARE OFF

January 2012

Gillard starts the new year trying to steer the agenda back to the government's achievements. She and her advisers, including the newly recruited head of her political and spin team, Tony Blair's former Director of Political Operations, Scotsman John McTernan, have a communications strategy that will attempt to wrestle the obsessive focus away from Rudd and his shenanigans and back on to the government. It's not a surprising plan: start spruiking Labor's economic credentials, which are affirmed by the way the government has managed to pilot Australia away from the stormy international waters; foster national pride in the strength of the Australian economy; highlight Abbott's weakness in the economic policy area; and demonstrate to the electorate Labor's more solid values and policies.

So on the first day of the new year, Gillard fronts a press conference in western Sydney to announce a quintessential Labor initiative that was foreshadowed at the election: family tax benefits for eligible families. Those with teenagers aged between sixteen and nineteen still living at home will receive from today as much as an extra $4160 a year. The policy has a twin aim: to give an incentive to struggling families to keep their sixteen-plus year olds in school, and to help the burdened purse strings of lower income families. She is flanked by Families and Communities minister Jenny Macklin and two western Sydney MPs, Chris Bowen and Chris Hayes.

After her announcement and a short address by Macklin, the Prime Minister invites questions. It starts promisingly enough—the first couple are about the policy. But before long it's back to everyone's favourite theme. Journalist: 'Will 2012 be a year free of leadership speculation?' Not if journalists keep creating leadership speculation by asking about leadership speculation, Gillard should have replied. But she responds: '2012 is going to be a year in which we are building the economy of the future as well as continuing to deliver fairness.' Journalist: 'Prime Minister, how confident are you that you'll be prime minister by the end of 2012?' It's a tactic designed to elicit any response that can be run as a news grab—a superficial genre of questioning all the rage in some journalistic circles. Responds the PM neutrally: 'I think you'll find I answered those questions in 2011, so have a look at the transcripts.' And with that she thanks the motley media throng and takes her leave, no doubt muttering under her breath that, yet again, she can't get clear air to ventilate policy issues of interest to the community.

And it doesn't get any easier to breathe; One K. Rudd is on the move. Over in Indonesia during the second week of January—on an easily forgotten gig, single-handedly cementing Australia–Indonesia relations—Rudd is asked by Frida Lidwina of Indonesia's Metro TV: 'How do you see Australia nowadays under the current prime minister, Gillard?' Rudd launches into a barely coherent answer about the history of see-sawing relations between the two countries since the 1940s, switching to what a 'very, very friendly' and 'very beautiful' country Indonesia is: 'I go to Bali a lot. I'm here in Jakarta a lot. I've been to Surabaya before. I've been to Sumatra, to Aceh.'

He rounds out this inexplicable response with: 'So when you reflect on the questions of these difficulties from time to time, guess what? In any family from time to time there are a few disagreements. It doesn't stop you, however, from being a family.' It does if you're in the Labor Party, mate, and your name is Kevin Rudd and your sister's Julia Gillard.

To borrow one of Rudd's favourite expressions, a few days later he zips. He's off back to Australia and a spot of campaigning for beleaguered Labor premier Anna Bligh ahead of an upcoming state election, where Bligh is tipped to lead Labor to a rout of impressive proportions. Kev loves nothing better than to don an apron and wield tongs at community barbecues, doing so on 16 January in inner-Brisbane, which the *Australian* dutifully writes up the next day as a leadership yarn. 'Anna Bligh has recruited Kevin Rudd to play a star role in the upcoming Queensland poll, in what is set to be a long and bitterly fought campaign likely to feed into Labor's federal leadership,' writes Rosanne Barrett. Then we get into the heavy commentary robed as news: 'A loss on the scale opinion polls are suggesting could further destabilise Ms Gillard's leadership and pave the way for a comeback for Mr Rudd to the job he lost in June 2010 when Labor knifed him.'

Even in a comment piece this statement would crack laughs. For the best part of the last year Bligh and her government have been intensely disliked. Even her adept handling of the floods, while momentarily lifting her popularity, won't save her skin.

Her opponent, the Liberal National Party's Campbell Newman, is seen as Queensland's saviour. Any possible rout has nothing to do with Gillard. If anything, Rudd is putting his comeback ambitions in a perilous position if his campaigning—which will involve blitzing seats across the state, including in the electorate of Ashgrove being contested by Newman—fails to shift the murderous mood of Sunshine Staters against the long-term Labor government. Then he'd be sharing in the reflected ignominy.

When Gillard and Wilkie chatted about their poker machine deal on the remarkable day Harry Jenkins resigned from the Speaker's chair and Peter Slipper slithered into it, they agreed to meet again after Christmas to progress a policy for implementation in 2013. They had one unremarkable meeting at The Lodge in December, agreeing to meet again in Hobart in January. Thus at 4 pm on Sunday 15 January in a conference room at the arty Henry Jones Hotel, the pair hunkered down again with a clutch of advisers.

According to Wilkie, the PM didn't muck around. 'She said she could not honour the agreement for three reasons: the 2014 deadline wasn't achievable; there were doubts over mandatory pre-commitment; and that she didn't have the numbers,' he tells me. He listens to what she has to offer—a compromise that would involve a trial of mandatory pre-commitment; the attachment of pre-commitment technology to new poker machines manufactured after 2013; limits on the amounts of cash that can be withdrawn from ATMs at poker machine venues; and other measures to help alleviate problem gambling.

Wilkie asks her: 'And if I don't agree?' He says she replied: 'We'll do considerably less.' He interprets this as a threat to 'take it or leave it'. He says he indicated neither support nor opposition, telling her he'd discuss her offer widely with associates. Later that day, Gillard and partner Tim Mathieson saunter over to Wilkie's family home in Hobart's 'burbs for an intimate barbecue, where they wine and dine from 7 pm until nearly 11 pm.

The next day Wilkie trips off to Western Australia to speak to conservative Independent Tony Crook and gauge if Crook will support his tougher approach to poker machine reform. Crook is in unknown waters: pokies aren't a problem in clubs and pubs in the west because Perth's Burswood Casino is the only venue where they're allowed. Crook says he's prepared to look at the legislation. In return, Wilkie says he's prepared to look more closely at Crook's concern that Western Australia doesn't receive its fair share of GST revenue from the Commonwealth.

The other rural Independents—Katter, Windsor and Oakeshott —have previously expressed reservations about mandatory pre-commitment, validating Gillard's concern that any legislation with it as its centrepiece would fail to pass parliament. Crucially, Wilkie now makes public comments that he's 'mindful it takes time' to craft poker machine reforms, 'and we need to do it right'. In media outlets this is reported as indicative that he's about to back down.

Wilkie seeks counsel from his usual sounding boards—anti-pokies Senator Nick Xenophon and gambling crusader the Reverend Tim Costello, plus electorate constituents and others active in the anti-pokies space. On the Wednesday night he speaks by phone with the PM, who is buoyed by his public comments, and he meets with her again at The Lodge on Thursday night. His final meeting to nut out the compromise package is at her suite of offices at Treasury Place, Melbourne, the following night.

'I had this dreadful dilemma all week,' Wilkie says. 'On the one hand, do I be a man of my word and withdraw my support? Or do I focus purely on the welfare of problem gamblers and try and cut the best deal I can?' In one of their conversations, he says, Gillard counselled him: 'Be careful about being a man of your word and withdrawing support, because that's almost selfish. Don't let it stop you helping problem gamblers.'

He tells me that on the night of Friday the 20th—at the same place where they'd once companionably eaten take-away and clinked crystal wine glasses—he informed the PM he couldn't support the compromise package. It was too different to the deal they'd sealed when she sought his support to establish the minority government, and he had no choice other than to stick to his word and withdraw support.

Wilkie says they then discussed how—in an unusually polite and mature political approach—they would sequence their respective announcements the next day. 'She said she'd come out Saturday morning at a press conference to announce the new package, and then I'd stand up in Hobart at my press conference and announce the withdrawal of my support,' he says. I remark sceptically that it sounds odd they made such a chummy deal to sequence their announcements. It wasn't chummy, he responds, just logical; she had to publicly ditch the deal first, then he had to declare he was pulling his support.

Gillard and her team don't remember that final meeting the same way as Wilkie. They believed they had worked through the series of meetings all week and secured his backing for a compromise package he could live with. So confident was the government that the new package had ticked all the boxes that Families and Communities minister Jenny Macklin went on ABC Radio's *AM* the next morning to announce that a trial of mandatory pre-commitment would proceed in the ACT. A few hours later, she and Gillard hold a press conference in Melbourne to announce the government's approach: a trial of mandatory pre-commitment technology on pokies in the ACT; expansion of pre-commitment technology to every poker machine nationally, which could be transformed into mandatory pre-commitment if supported by the trial; a limit of $250 in cash withdrawals from ATMs at gaming venues; and a host of other measures. It is the first-ever comprehensive measure offered by a federal government.

Gillard pays generous tribute to Wilkie, describing him as 'a passionate advocate for change in this area; he has been absolutely tireless in his pursuit of change. He cares deeply about the circumstances of people who have got gambling addiction problems, he knows a number of them personally and his heart has been touched by their story. It is a real tribute to Andrew Wilkie that the nation will move to a full trial of mandatory pre-commitment on the 1st of January next year.'

Asked by a journalist whether she's broken a promise to Wilkie, she says categorically: 'The circumstances in this parliament are clear: I have spoken to every member of the cross bench and it is clear from my discussions with them that there is not the support in the House of Representatives for the Andrew Wilkie plan, for the full mandatory pre-commitment arrangements that Mr Wilkie and I discussed after the last election. [It is] very clear that there's not the parliamentary support. That is also very clear from the public statements made by members of the cross bench.

'So the circumstances in which we find ourselves are as follows: we have to do something about problem gambling; not getting legislation through the parliament is not good enough. It means nothing would change. We have to do something about problem gambling. We also have to recognise that to get legislation through this parliament, we need to get people on the same page, prepared to support change. With the changes that we've outlined today, we will be taking to the parliament for the first time ever a national approach to problem gambling in the laws of our country, and I believe we can secure this through the parliament.'

A few hours later, Wilkie fronts the Hobart media and announces he is withdrawing his support for the Gillard government. He can no longer guarantee it Supply and confidence because the deal isn't good enough. There are two issues at stake, he says: real poker machine reform, and issues of governance and the integrity of politicians. 'While there are many, many Australians who are very concerned about poker machine gambling, there are many more Australians who are concerned that they should be able to trust their politicians; that when a politician makes a promise, that promise is honoured and [that politician] does everything in his or her power to deliver on their promise. We should be able to trust our politicians.'

He won't 'mince his words'—he is very, very disappointed in Gillard, he says, very let down by her. 'The PM made a deal with me. She signed it, and Australians expected her, even if they disagreed with the content of that deal . . . I think Australians had every right to expect the PM to honour it.' In a written statement, he goes further: 'Our democracy is simply too precious to trash with broken promises and backroom compromises. So I will walk, take my chances and so be it.' He is adamant that 'the numbers' are there in parliament for his approach to gain enough support to pass.

Gillard and those senior ministers intimate with the detail of the week's negotiations are gobsmacked. They believe the deal they brokered through the week and sealed the previous night was that Wilkie, after expressing regret that his package couldn't be implemented at this time, would back the reform package without impugning the government or Gillard. The last thing they expected was for him to withdraw his support and attack Gillard personally, besmirching her integrity and accusing her of breaking trust and promises.

Wilkie tells me: 'I think she expected me to say something like: "I'm disappointed that the reforms that have been agreed to haven't been achieved, but the government gave it its best shot, and they will progress meaningful reform anyway." That wasn't possible for me.' And yet he does support the alternative package, saying in a statement: 'In the circumstances, it would be better to achieve at least some reform.'

Not long after Wilkie's comments are aired live on TV and radio, Leader of the House, Anthony Albanese, rings him on his mobile. Clearly agitated, he says to Wilkie: 'I've known Julia since university, and I have never seen her as white-hot angry as she is with you.' Wilkie responds: 'Look, Anthony, we both know we have it in our power to screw each other and that is in neither of our interests. From here what we need to do is get our relationship back on a good working level.'

That is wildly optimistic. Wilkie accepts he's hit Gillard where she can really hurt. 'They were white-hot angry with me for what I said about Gillard and how I focused on it being a broken promise, trust, a question of integrity,' he says. 'I touched a raw nerve. But it was about that! A lot of people care about the character of their politicians, and ultimately it came down to the character of the government.' He then concedes: 'This has done her a lot of harm, but it's not my fault.'

The media slant is relentless: Gillard has broken another promise, this time to save her government's skin in the face of Clubs Australia's marginal seat campaign. Very little is fleshed out about the breadth of the package she has offered, which is the first time a federal government has moved to tackle a monstrous social and economic problem that's been evolving for decades and been highlighted in a string of Productivity Commission reports. Few media outlets paint the compromise package as a significant policy step forward; all accept Wilkie's version of events, casting Gillard as a back flipper and deal breaker.

Even Wilkie can't assure me that it would have passed, and my previous conversations with the rural Independents have indicated they were hesitant about a move to mandatory pre-commitment technology within Wilkie's tight 2014 timeframe. The opening question by ABC Radio National's Fran Kelly to the PM on Monday morning reflects the media trust: 'Prime Minister, you've torn up a written deal with Andrew Wilkie to introduce compulsory pre-commitment limits on poker machines. You welched on a deal?'

The most unlikely backing Gillard gets for her deal is from MP Craig Thomson—he of the credit cards and prostitutes fame—who blasts into print in the *Tele* with an opinion piece applauding the trial of mandatory pre-commitment and branding the compromise package a big political win for Labor. With friends like that, enemies are not required.

Australia Day dawns with the usual promise of community bonding, a spot of imbibing, good humour and the bestowing of honours for home-grown heroes. Gillard is attending a shindig at the upmarket Lobby restaurant opposite Old Parliament House; it has been the setting since the Whitlam days of many political lunches and dinners, where plots have been hatched, illicit relationships nurtured and careers broken. In a rare bipartisan appearance, she and Tony Abbott are there presenting emergency service medals to 100 recipients. It is a relaxed engagement, in a venue affectionately embraced as a Canberra institution.

Earlier that day, Abbott had been asked by a journalist about the Aboriginal Tent Embassy, situated a hundred or so metres along from The Lobby. A crowd is today celebrating the Embassy's birthday—it is forty years since it was established on the lawn in front of Old Parliament House as a place of protest at white Australia's treatment of our Indigenous brothers and sisters. Abbott responded to the journalist's question by saying that much had changed for the better since the establishment of the embassy: 'I think the Indigenous people of Australia can be very proud of the respect in which they are held by every Australian,' he enthused. 'I think a lot's changed since then and I think it probably is time to move on from that.'

As Gillard and Abbott stand together presenting awards, a furious swarm of protestors from the Tent Embassy celebrations converge on The Lobby; it has floor-to-ceiling glass on three sides, and they're banging on it trying to storm the room. They believe Abbott has demanded the Tent Embassy be shut down. Their numbers, while small, are menacing, their chanting loud and angry. The PM's security, worried about the fragility of the glass, decide to remove Gillard; she asks them to also keep Abbott safe.

Within minutes of the protestors arriving, she's tucked under the wing of one of her security detail, dragged out the door and bundled into her Commonwealth car, a shoe flying off in the melee. Abbott follows swiftly after. The pictures of a terrified Gillard running the gauntlet of the angry mob, with the suited arm of one of her bodyguards cradling her, instantly beam around the country and make it onto international news bulletins.

Within days one of Gillard's media staffers, Tony Hodges, is fingered for passing on incorrect information about Abbott's statement through an intermediary to the Tent Embassy protestors; Hodges resigns amid over-excited Opposition accusations that Gillard was behind the information peddling. Meanwhile, back in media-land, the focus is on what a shocker of an office Gillard must have, and the free-for-all means her leadership is again under threat.

As the uproar continues unabated in the media, with the Opposition testing its luck with calls for a formal inquiry into the circumstances of what Abbott calls one of the great security breaches of all time (he must be forgetting the Hilton bombing and two ugly union riots at the Old and New Parliament Houses, among many others), Rudd saunters home from his international jaunts. He's spent January on immensely important missions to Indonesia, New York, Paris, London, Berlin and Switzerland, twice taking a breather from the ardours of international diplomacy to rocket back to Brissie and undertake immensely important campaigning for Anna Bligh.

He hits Brisbane a day or so after Cosima Marriner has written in Fairfax Media on 29 January that Rudd's campaigning is his ticket back to The Lodge. What a lovely welcome home! 'Labor insiders say Mr Rudd's involvement in the campaign for the March 24 election is designed to boost his profile, highlight the disparity in popularity between the former and present prime ministers, remind his caucus colleagues how crucial Queensland is in the next federal election—and inevitably stoke leadership tensions,' Marriner writes. 'This is all about the re-rise of Kevin,' one 'former confidant' of Rudd tells her. 'Kevin is still a strong chance of coming back this year.'

For the love of God, wouldn't it be a good idea to see how Bligh goes at the polls before believing the words of the Ruddster ranters? Marriner talks to Bruce Hawker, who is helping run the Bligh campaign and is a long-term ally of the former PM. Hawker is always handy with tantalising quotes to promote Rudd as a leadership come-back prospect. Rudd is welcome in Queensland 'whatever happens in Canberra in the coming weeks and months', Hawker teases. 'If leadership tension becomes a by-product of his campaigning, you accept there is always going to be residual feeling in the community about the manner of his dismissal in June 2010,' he adds disingenuously.

Marriner's sources—anonymous, naturally—are plumping the line that the ascension will happen after the 24 March Queensland election. Presumably that's after Rudd's miraculously turned a near-certain crushing defeat into an amazing victory. Grateful Labor people in branches across Queensland will rise up in tearful gratitude; federal caucus members will beg for forgiveness and demand his return.

So of course Newspoll and the News Ltd team press the leader-ship resuscitation button on 31 January, courtesy of some ho-hum results. According to political editor Dennis Shanahan, the poll—which has Labor, in his words, 'flat lining' on a 30 per cent primary vote—will 'intensify speculation about a leadership challenge from Kevin Rudd'. In fact, Labor's support, as tracked by Newspoll, has remained static on 30 per cent since the end of last year's parlia-mentary sittings. Gillard has now suffered a three point drop as preferred PM to 40 per cent (within the margin of error), while Abbott rose a point to 37 per cent (well within the margin of error, thus totally insignificant). Nevertheless, this non-news becomes news and is the topic of every journalist's pen today—unlike the Galaxy Poll of yesterday, which found Labor's primary vote had lifted by five percentage points. No fun in that one.

Fran Kelly on ABC Radio National Breakfast kicks it off. She is about to interview Regional Development minister and Gillard loyalist Simon Crean but, before crossing to the minister, she rehashes the Newspoll numbers and states: 'Some MPs now view a Kevin Rudd challenge as inevitable, that's the direct quote, though certainly not before the Queensland election at the end of March.' The Rudd boys are spreading their message wide! Of the sixteen questions Kelly fires at Crean, all but one are about the polls and the possibility of a challenge. Along the way, she quotes two other journalists: Geoff Kitney in the *Australian Financial Review*, and the *Daily Telegraph*'s Simon Benson, who has another article this morning predicting a challenge. Benson is now working on his own law of averages: if you state something often enough, at some stage you might get it right. Gillard keeps outlasting his deadlines, dammit.

A few hours later Crean fronts up to Neil Mitchell on 3AW, who hammers the significance of the Newspoll numbers (you're stuffed, Minister; you're cactus, Gillard). Halfway into what is turning into a torrid beating, the world stands still for a moment and Rudd's people are surely shaking their heads, scratching their ears and wondering if they heard right.

Mitchell: Is this a unified government?

Crean: Yes, it is.

Mitchell: Kevin Rudd?

Crean: I think Kevin is playing . . . Well, he's certainly playing a terrific role in terms of foreign affairs, et cetera. Kevin is a continuing great asset within the government . . .

Mitchell: But he'd cut off his arm to come back as leader, wouldn't he?

Crean: Yeah, but people . . .

Mitchell: Is that a yes?

Crean: People will not elect as leaders those they don't perceive are team players, Neil.

Mitchell: And he is not perceived as a team player?

Crean: I'll leave that judgement to others, but I . . .

Mitchell: Well, do *you* perceive him as a team player?

Crean: I think that part of the reason he lost the leadership was that he wasn't. So, I think that that's a circumstance that has to be dealt with internally by the party whenever they make these assessments. But I tell you what—there's no point having a band of prima donnas unless they operate as a team.

Bingo! Crean has just pulled the cap off the grenade. Out and about in Sydney, a voracious press pack descends on Gillard. Is Rudd a team player? Is he, is he? Are you in strife because of the polls? Can you remain leader? 'Kevin Rudd is doing a great job as Minister for Foreign Affairs,' she bats back, straight-faced. 'It's very important for a nation our size that we do have our voice heard around the world. Kevin Rudd as Foreign Affairs minister is doing a good job in making sure our voice is heard.'

Forget it, PM. Still smarting at having his pokies package changed, Wilkie chucks another bomb into the mix by declaring the Australia Day commotion so 'appalling' he'll support a no-confidence motion against the government in parliament.

Welcome to the new parliamentary year, Prime Minister.

THE CARAVAN ROLLS INTO TOWN

1–18 February 2012

As the 150 members of the House of Representatives, seventy-six senators and their hundreds of staff limber up for another bruising year in parliament, the Prime Minister can feel Rudd's hot breath on her neck. Buffeted for most of January by the cold winds of leadership whisperings, she has been assailed by florid media reports of dwindling numbers, impending challenges and poor opinion polls. Gillard knows the brutal campaign against her prime ministership will continue unabated unless there's a circuit breaker.

The *Australian* revs it up on 1 February, with Dennis Shanahan kicking off the new parliamentary year with the acrid observation that: 'All the signs of a leadership challenge are there now: white-anting, bad polls, bad news, public assurances of allegiance and the impossibility of challenges, as well as warnings that a victory for Rudd would lead to an immediate, and presumably disastrous, election. The destabilisation that began months ago has begun to gather pace.' And plaudits, Team Rudd would say, to the *Australian* for its magnificent job channelling and promoting that destabilisation.

Anna Bligh will feel the thunderous wrath of Queensland voters if the entrenched anger in Queensland is registered in votes at next month's election. But on the election campaign hustings in his home state for his good mate, Rudd continues to present himself as above the federal fray of destabilisation and personal attacks. Simon Crean's comments yesterday? But what a great fella! 'I noted recent comments,' Rudd says, sadness tingeing his voice. 'Can I say this? That I am proud to be a member of a ministry which is hard working and dedicated and in which Mr Crean plays a very strong and supportive role, and in which I play my own part as well and will continue to do so.' Just to be on the safe side, he reaffirms his support for the woman who tossed him out of The Lodge. Bollocks!

Gillard supporters watch Rudd's charade with astonishment. This is the bloke whose temper is short and memory is long. No perceived injustice is forgiven, no dissent brooked. His behaviour when prime minister towards those whom he believed were not servicing his political needs properly was scary and unpredictable and always fuelled by anger and hostility, the causes of which were a mystery. The unpublished recollection of the chaotic Rudd government by one of its high-level advisers provides an instructive insight into the way the former PM treats people around him: 'No adviser, whether official or private office, could fail to be aware of the culture of blame and fear throughout the government,' he wrote. 'The one arose from the other, and they both had their origins in the PM's temperament. It was well known that the PM was very quick to anger, disproportionate in that anger, and wont to take extreme and retributive action against those who had angered him.

'In fact, that retribution was very contingent. It was dealt out only to subordinates—most directly, to staff. Administration staff, flight attendants and the like would cop it for logistics not working out the way the PM wished. But advisers would usually cop it for a more specific reason: giving the boss advice he did not want to hear. This angry treatment of advisers and public servants was very calculated. We all knew of PMO [prime ministerial office] advisers being "put in the freezer" for crossing their boss. It was childish to watch—he would refuse to look at them in meetings and simply ignore anything they said until they gave up and quit, or made amends. In this way he ensured he got obedience, but at the cost, of course, of getting proper advice.

'He sent calculated messages in other ways, too. Public servants could get a dose of the freezer, as plenty of them will attest, but the treatment of Hugh Borrowman—blocked by the PM from becoming ambassador to Germany over some unexplained and possibly quite ancient sin—ensured every public servant knew they displeased the PM at their career peril. And that he had a very long memory.' These traits of Rudd's are well known in the bureaucracy, within Labor ranks, and throughout large sections of the media.

On 2 February, Phillip Coorey in the *Sydney Morning Herald* quotes a 'factional boss' as saying 'there's been quite a shift over summer' and 'she's in trouble'. Coorey adds the newest deadline: Gillard's 'danger zone' is after the Queensland March election, and before the budget. The anonymous factional boss is the only source for the story. Hours later, Fairfax Media online reporters Jessica Wright and Judith Ireland requote the quotes from the anonymous factional boss in Coorey's story, adding a defence of Gillard by Communications minister Stephen Conroy. It's extraordinary how the hot-house of the Canberra political world can fecundate stories, which then grow like weeds. Trace them back to the original source, and they can be as thin as the evidence cited as primary sources.

It's staggering that MPs fuel the fire lit by these articles, which are based on the quotes of figures hiding in the shadows. Climate Change minister Greg Combet, usually a man of careful words, throws caution to the wind as media hysteria hots up. Asked on ABC Radio to react to the factional boss's quotes, which are being repeated authoritatively in most media outlets, he snaps back: 'I lose patience with people who are talking to journalists and there's no name attached to it, and you wonder who on earth it was.' Bingo! Another news grab to escalate the drama.

Many Canberra-based journalists 'covering' the phantom challenge know Rudd doesn't have anywhere near the numbers he needs to take his old job back, yet assertions about crumbling support and fading loyalties fill the lead paragraphs of their stories. The extra spice is a peppering of deadlines for when Gillard's prime ministership will come to a screaming halt, for instance, these snippets from news stories of 3, 4 and 5 February:

Laura Tingle, quoting an MP in the *Australian Financial Review*: 'I don't see how the current situation of Julia's leadership can go beyond Easter.'

Jessica Wright, *Sydney Morning Herald*: 'A senior Labor source told Fairfax Media this week there had been a seismic shift in support away from Ms Gillard over the summer break, with a portion of the backbench now backing former Prime Minister Kevin Rudd in the event of a leadership spill.' The 'seismic shift' over the summer break has grown from the 'quite a shift' quoted by her Fairfax colleague Coorey and already requoted by Wright.

She adds, without any supporting evidence, that: 'It is more likely that any confrontation would occur in May, when Parliament returns for the budget sessions.' Based on the tea leaves, perhaps?

Nick Butterly, *West Australian*: 'Mr Rudd's supporters believe about one-third of caucus is unhappy with Ms Gillard's leadership, but are uncertain how the numbers would fall if there was a vote.' In other words, Gillard has the support of a thumping two-thirds majority of caucus.

James Massola, *Australian*: 'Mr Rudd's backers say the former prime minister can count on at least 25 votes in the Labor caucus, and up to 40 if a leadership spill occurs. While either figure would leave him short of the 52-MP majority he would need in the 103-member caucus, the claims show numbers are being counted and a challenge could come sooner rather than later.' But wouldn't even the mathematically challenged read these numbers as a stunning loss?

The reporting is clearly getting to Treasurer Swan, who says on ABC TV: 'I think the community have had just a gutful of so much of the commentary and speculation that's out there—most of it just a huge beat up.'

Let's pause for thought. If they've been in the press gallery for any length of time, journalists have parliamentarians they trust to tell them the truth; they can at least get a sense of who's telling whoppers and who's telling it as straight as a politician is able. Because they talk to all sides in this particular manufactured political intrigue—the number-crunchers, the liars, the self-promoters, the truth-tellers—journalists know Rudd isn't within a respectable distance of majority support. And yet the stories they are writing are overwhelmingly skewed towards giving the greatest weight to the words of the fibbers, the number-inflators and the wish-fulfillers. What people are saying, rather than what can be backed up with evidence, is the new media reality. But Kevin Rudd does not have, and will not get, the necessary numbers to success-fully challenge Gillard in the foreseeable future, and he will not be returning to the prime ministership any time soon. That's the story—but it isn't one, so it doesn't get a run.

Oh, to be a fly on the wall at the special caucus meeting on Sunday 5 February. Queensland Labor MP Bernie Ripoll has already set the scene for a super fun time, bursting into print this morning in the News Ltd tabloids with a challenge to Rudd supporters to 'bring it on' if they really think they have the numbers to topple the Prime Minister. 'Let's see who commands the numbers in caucus. Let's just do it. They won't, and I will tell you why—they don't have the numbers,' he taunts. Samantha Maiden accurately reports that Rudd has fewer than twenty votes, quoting (yes, anonymously) a 'senior Victorian Labor MP' as saying that yesterday's media reports (yawn) that Gillard had forty-seven votes, Rudd thirty-two and there were twenty-four undecided was 'about as accurate as an East German five-year economic forecast'. Good line, Bill!

Gillard supporters Deb O'Neill and George Georganas don't let the meeting slip by without making a few pointed remarks about the damage of anonymous media briefings and the havoc wreaked by destabilising government. Gillard also talks bluntly about the need for party unity and loyalty; not one MP of the eighty or so who turn up raise concerns. If there are sizeable chunks of caucus unhappy with the PM's performance and want her to change her ways, none has the maturity or bravery to speak their piece.

But, rats! The elephant isn't in the room. The Ruddster's in Germany, on yet another manic burst of international peace-making, which means he is also not at the cosy afternoon barbecue at The Lodge after the caucus meeting. What a shame: Rudd and his lads could have knocked the top off a few stubbies and invited themselves to stay around and bunker down in the familiar surrounds of the prime ministerial telly room to watch veteran journalist Mike Willesee interview Gillard on Channel Seven's new program, inventively titled *Sunday Night*. They could've watched Willesee go straight to the big issue at hand. No mucking about with silly questions about policies, Gillard's vision for 2012 or what it's like steering a minority parliament.

'I appreciate your time,' Willesee starts. 'I guess the most negative thing that you're facing constantly is what we might call "rats in the ranks". You've got people in your team trying to destabilise your leadership. Does that churn your stomach?'

Gillard: 'I wouldn't say churn my stomach, no, and I'm not sure I'd even agree with the characterisation of your question, though, of course, it's a very famous saying. My view about the government is we have faced and continue to face some tough times politically. That is because we've done some big hard things, and, yes, that does mean that politically it's been tough.'

Willesee is having none of it: 'You've got a problem. You've got people in your party moving to oust you from the leadership. I mean, the fact is you've got the Kevin Rudd circus, if you like. It's very debilitating to your leadership and to the government and I really want to ask you: why have you allowed it to go on so long?'

It's a good question, and one that would have soured Team Rudd's beers. Gillard should have been asked this many times before, as Rudd and his band have slow-dripped a flagrant undermining strategy that has seriously tarnished the image of the government. The destabilisation has produced a pattern—one step forward, three back—as Gillard is constantly forced into a defensive position by the spiteful background questioning of her legitimacy by Rudd supporters.

Gillard answers Willesee as she always does: 'I think Kevin's doing a good job as the minister for Foreign Affairs . . .' And: 'I don't get up in the morning thinking about all of this. I get up in the morning thinking about what I need to do leading this nation today to make a difference today and make a difference for tomorrow. So I know it's endlessly fascinating to others, but to me it's kind of dead set boring.'

Willesee: 'It doesn't have to be endlessly fascinating. You could stop it. He's after your job and you could stop it.'

Gillard: 'Look, I'm not agreeing with your questions, Mike, and so no reformulation of them is going to get me to agree with them.'

It's a freak show, for sure: Rudd the ringleader, Gillard the dancing pony. Something's got to give.

The next day a strange thing happens. The Nielsen poll in Fairfax publications shows support for the Prime Minister and her government increasing sharply. The government's stocks have risen by 4 percentage points to 33 per cent since December, and Gillard's rose 6 points as preferred prime minister. The Coalition's primary support fell 4 points to 45 per cent, and its two-party preferred lead dropped by 8 points to 53–47. This should 'give Ms Gillard some reprieve from growing talk of a leadership push by Kevin Rudd', prophesies the *Sydney Morning Herald*'s Coorey, again legitimising the polls as the pre-eminent yardstick for prime ministerial performance.

Coorey's is one view from the Fairfax bunker. Rudd's main media mouthpiece, Peter Hartcher, has a much rosier view, invoking Team Rudd's favourite ticking time bomb analogy: 'The Doomsday clock that ticks towards the end of Julia Gillard's prime ministership has been set in motion, but today's *Herald*/Nielsen poll will slow its tempo,' he proclaims. 'While the poll is a source of relief for Gillard, it is also a source of sustenance for Rudd,' he enthuses. 'It shows him, yet again, to be a vastly more popular Labor leader and the obvious alternative. The poll will slow the countdown on Gillard. If it's the beginning of a serious upward trajectory for her, the Doomsday clock will stop. If it is a one-off, the clock will tick on relentlessly.' All this is based on a poll. Not on policies, not on the Prime Minister's control of government, nor her steerage of the minority parliament. Such a barometer of Gillard's prime ministership speaks loudly about the superficiality of much political reporting.

Now it's over to Our Man in the right-wing New South Wales Bunker—sorry, the *Daily Telegraph*'s political editor Simon Benson, who today reports that Rudd's people are counting numbers (that shouldn't take long). Benson informs us that it's New South Wales 'where the numbers have started to shift the most'. He publishes a list of all caucus members, dividing them into three camps: for Gillard, for Rudd, and undecided. He adds an arse-covering caveat: 'It is a list that many will publicly dispute for fear of revealing their hand.' Or dispute because it's wrong and presumptuous?

Craig Emerson furiously thinks so. Asked on ABC News Radio to explain why he is in the undecided camp, he explodes: 'Where have they been: in Antarctica for the summer? No-one has rung me. And if they'd looked at any of the statements that I've made, including many statements indicating my absolute and total support for Julia Gillard . . . where on earth does the *Daily Telegraph*, or anyone else for that matter, get these lists? They make them up as they go along because they want to create the impression that there's a big leadership issue here, whereas in fact the big issue is that Labor is working for and on behalf of the working people of this country. That involves people in the media drilling down, having a look at the details of some of the policies that we're releasing. But it's far easier to sit down in Antarctica and develop a list of people without ringing them, and then saying that this is their wise counsel as to who is going to support who in some imaginary change of the leadership. It's not going to happen. It's not going to happen. I fully support Julia Gillard. I've now said that for the 473rd time, and I'm happy to say it the 474th and 475th.'

Benson's article finished heroically: 'But as the numbers men say, it's not about the numbers, it is about the momentum. And the momentum appears to be swinging towards Kevin Rudd.' But it *is* about the numbers and, despite the best efforts of Rudd's numbers people to talk up the former PM's level of support, he hasn't got anywhere near enough. Not now; not during the last week, month or year; and not during next week, month or year. The destructive slow death game Team Rudd is playing is killing the government, but it won't return One K. Rudd to the prime ministership.

There is something unnerving about the sight of MPs gathering at St Paul's Cathedral in Manuka, a stone's throw from Parliament House, to bow their heads and worship together before the resumption of mudslinging in parliament and backstabbing within their own parties. Proclaimed atheist Julia Gillard isn't there this sunny

Canberra day, Tuesday 7 February, but a beaming Rudd, who as prime minister staged media stunts and offered pious news grabs after many a Sunday service, was readily available post prayers for a spot of cat and mouse for the cameras.

Reporter: 'Mr Rudd, are you going to challenge?'

Rudd: 'Let me see . . . where's our car. This one?'

Reporter: 'Can you rule it out once and for all?'

Rudd: 'Okay, have a good day, guys, have fun!'

The clip is an instant hit on live news services. God help us, the big tent is up and the circus is in town. And here we are in the fourth estate, taking this man seriously. Here we are, watching and reporting the spectacle of this man trying to bring down his prime minister through guerrilla warfare. Here we are, note-books in hand, reporting his movements and words as if they represent reality.

In the *Sydney Morning Herald* this morning veteran political reporter Lenore Taylor stoutly defends the quality of the press gallery's reporting. 'Is the Labor leadership issue a bizarre beat-up entirely confected by the news media? Certainly not,' she writes. 'Is it an unstable and shifting situation, which may lead to a challenge, and which is notoriously difficult to report? Absolutely. Now is the time of how-are-things-going, what-are-your-concerns, read-between-the-lines conversations.' Sure, but what about the idea that now is the time to check the veracity of what's being whispered; to test it, to discover it's bollocks and to not print it?

In the *Daily Telegraph* Bruce Hawker—Rudd's undeclared campaign manager, who masquerades under the media *nom de plume* of 'Labor Strategist'—says the numbers are swinging behind Rudd and talk of a leadership challenge will inevitably escalate. Hawker shifted into Rudd's office in June 2010 to sandbag the PM against the rising tide of criticism about his confused, centralised government; then, when his bloke was removed from the corner suite, Hawker helped Gillard at that year's election. But he has been sidelined since. Suffice to say many in the ALP don't think fondly of him. That Hawker is the go-to guy for Sky News Australia and other media outlets as a credible 'Labor Strategist' when he is running Rudd's campaign is confounding.

It takes an out-of-town journalist, David Penberthy of News Ltd online's Punch, to write what should be written by courageous press gallery journalists. Under the colourful headline 'Memo Kev: Pee or get off the pot', he writes: 'The speculation about a Kevin Rudd comeback is quite tedious. All that matters is whether he is going to have a crack or not. If he doesn't he almost certainly will not become prime minister again.' Penberthy—who once worked in the press gallery, who maintains good political contacts and has a well-tuned antenna for political bullshit—outlines Team Rudd's obvious strategy: because Rudd doesn't have the numbers in caucus, he is deploying psychological warfare in the hope that caucus and Gillard will eventually despair at the tumult and turn to him. Penberthy's column is the most accurate portrayal of what's happening now in Canberra, and puts into context the distortion of much federal press gallery reporting.

'What Kevin Rudd fails to realise is that there are a significant number of MPs who are so utterly disgusted by his tactics that they are becoming even more resolute in opposing his return,' Penberthy continues. 'MPs I have spoken to since Sunday's little shin-dig at The Lodge said there was a sense of bewilderment and frustration at the way things are currently playing out. Many of these MPs have just spent an uninterrupted month in their electorates and have not been on the telephone to anyone in the press, but have been dismayed by the daily procession of leaks running down their boss. They are not so naive as to ignore the woeful reality of Gillard's start to the year, losing Andrew Wilkie after abandoning mandatory pre-commitment on poker machines, and enduring the acute embarrassment of her dopey former staff member's complicity in the Australia Day fiasco. But despite all this, their anger towards Rudd is more intense than ever. One frontbencher, who like so many others freely describes Rudd in language unfit for a family newspaper, told me that he believed support for Rudd had, if anything, decreased. "What Kevin fails to realise is that this transparent little trick of pissing on Gillard's parade whenever she gets any clear air is galvanising us behind her," he said.'

There are journalists in the press gallery who have been briefed in detail this week about Rudd's battle plans by the man himself. Their names are known by some of their colleagues—two are from the ABC, one from Fairfax, one from News Ltd. These reporters have been entrusted with Rudd's confidences; he is out and about pretending to be Gillard's loyal foot soldier, but at the same time he has spread the battle map across his desk and detailed his strategy to a select group of senior press gallery journalists.

On the ABC's *Insiders* program of 12 February presenter and long-time political journalist Barrie Cassidy raises this matter, quoting from a briefing Rudd provided to the two unnamed ABC journalists. The former PM had told them he intended to challenge for the leadership 'the next time Julia stumbles—and that's probably two weeks, given her form', Cassidy claims Rudd joked. Rudd told the journalists he knew he'd lose the ballot, but he'd go to the back bench and keep agitating until he got his old job back.

The *Insiders* panel discuss the pros and cons of such a strategy—what support Rudd would need in the ballot to keep his chances alive for another crack at Gillard, and various other assumptions in the Rudd battle plan. The extraordinary situation where four journalists have been specifically told how he intends to try and bring down the Prime Minister and yet they haven't blown the whistle on him is not discussed. The three-member panel consists of the ABC's online and TV star, Annabel Crabb; Fairfax's colourful and incisive columnist with a roving brief, David Marr; and News Ltd's online political editor, Malcolm Farr.

The four journalists Rudd briefed know more of the details than anyone else, but others are privy to some of his plans. The general game-play of Team Rudd is well known to most press gallery journalists, even if it hasn't been spelled out in so many words. Everyone except those dubbed the 'B Team', the lower-rung reporters, has been given the word by a Team Rudd whisperer; this is the way Rudd has operated for years now. Those who have been briefed about Rudd's strategy will, presumably, continue to report without qualification his denials that he wants the prime ministership back.

How did knowledge of these briefings seep through to other journalists? Because of the inability of many to hold their own counsel; through the cross-fertilisation of information between gallery journalists; and because some journalists like to boast. I phone Melbourne-based Cassidy; the former Bob Hawke adviser is clearly unimpressed with this turn of events. 'The press gallery knows that Kevin Rudd has personally briefed these journalists,' he says. 'This is very different to a "Rudd supporter" [who usually background briefs journalists].' He remarks: 'What do these journalists intend to do with this information? It means they are encouraging the Kevin Rudd challenge, and they are prepared to play a game. The press gallery wants this challenge, they need it. To my knowledge, nobody in the gallery has asked Rudd himself if he has briefed journalists.'

I email Rudd's two press secretaries, Kate Sieper and Ranya Alkadamani, and ask for a formal response to the following questions:

- As alleged on the *Insiders* program on Sunday 12 February, does Mr Rudd deny briefing specific journalists last week in Canberra about his intention to challenge again for the Labor leadership?
- Does Mr Rudd deny that since November 2011 he has conducted other off-the-record briefings with journalists, including at the ALP national conference?
- Is it a fact that since November 2011 Mr Rudd has visited editors of major newspapers? If so, for what purpose?

By day's end there's no response, maybe because a much-hyped ABC *Four Corners* program on the government will be airing. Perhaps Rudd has been busy positioning the comfy lounge chair in front of the plasma and readying the corn for popping. The show's been the talk of Canberra—it's supposedly an exposé of Rudd and his comeback plans.

The program falls badly short of its hype. Its interview subjects are either out of parliament (former Labor minister Con Sciacca) and irrelevant (the vociferously pro-Rudd Janelle Saffin, who clings precariously to the New South Wales north coast seat of Page); bit players with vested interests (Bruce Hawker and Graham Richardson); or a low-profile former back bencher (Brett Raguse, ALP, Queensland). The only one with any credibility is Troy Bramston, a former Rudd speechwriter resurrecting himself as a columnist in the *Australian*. This ragtag of unrepresentative go-to characters nevertheless manage to elevate the *Four Corners* story into heady news as soon as it airs.

A central claim is that a fortnight before Rudd was removed as prime minister, an anonymous scribe in Gillard's office started preparing a victory speech (the nature of which was unstated and unsupported by any sources). This unverified claim is repeated as fact in stories that instantly flood online news sites, as is another of the program's headline claims—presented as a killer blow to Gillard's credibility—that she had presented internal Labor polling on Rudd's poor electoral standing to colleagues during the fortnight leading up to 23 June 2010. Even though identical research had been published in major newspapers for months before Gillard assumed the prime ministership, the program adopted the editorial line that this, coupled with the alleged drafting of the victory speech, meant Gillard had long planned a strike against the PM.

Gillard appears on *AM* the next morning to try and provide some balance to the media hysteria. Chief political correspondent Sabra Lane hammers the PM about the alleged draft victory speech, even though no evidence has been provided that it ever existed, and no-one has been named as its author. But this doesn't soften the aggressive questioning. Gillard says she did not direct her staff to prepare a speech because she 'wouldn't have seen a need for it. I decided to challenge Kevin Rudd and to ask him for a ballot in the Labor Party on the day I asked him for that ballot.' Gillard had told *Four Corners* that she was not surprised people in her office, and more broadly in the government, were 'casting in their minds where circumstances might get to'.

Journalists with good memories would recall that in the six months before Rudd lost his job, caucus members had become increasingly disturbed by his behaviour. There was mounting back-bench anger that the ship of state was Rudderless; serious concerns within the ministry were expressed about Rudd's mental health; and there was near mutiny within the upper echelons of key departments because the PM would not make decisions and yet wanted more and more briefings, ideas, papers and planning. The show was falling apart. As his deputy and a then-darling of the press gallery, Gillard was the only person in the frame to step up if the balloon went up. A half-decent staffer would have been negligent in their duties if they hadn't doodled a few speech notes just in case she was suddenly forced to take the helm.

Gillard must be given heroine points for stepping up for the *AM* interview, but her attempt to provide some sanity only stirs the gallery into further hostility. Within hours, a story by James Massola appears in the online edition of the *Australian* headlined 'Julia Gillard "shifty" over leadership speech, say Kevin Rudd's supporters'. It quotes the customarily anonymous sources as saying that she 'looked evasive [on *Four Corners*]; she looked shifty in the way she was trying to answer but not answering'. It quotes a disingenuous Bruce Hawker musing that it is 'very unusual' for a staffer to start writing a speech two weeks out from what eventually occurred on 24 June. It quotes 'the Rudd camp' as saying the speech doodling was a 'serious misjudgement by the Prime Minister and her staff'. And, apropos of nothing much at all, it quotes shadow Attorney-General, Senator George Brandis, saying that the Prime Minister had a track record of 'telling lies'.

The only suggestion of balance in Massola's piece is an aside that the Prime Minister 'suggested' she had been misled about the purpose of the *Four Corners* interview. Gillard had, in fact, said quite plainly on *AM* that she had been led to believe the interview was about loftier matters than the leadership. 'I was approached by *Four Corners* for an interview on what was described as the government's progress since 2007,' she said. 'In those circumstances, of course I said yes; my job is to answer questions and explain what the government is doing.'

In fact, an email sent by *Four Corners* executive producer Peter Cronau to the PM's office confirms Gillard's version. It says: 'Our story looks at the progress of Labor in power by focusing on the progress of the government since 2007. It will be examining the handling of the mining tax, the climate change issue and the leadership question.' The 'leadership question' is thrown in at the end to signify its more lowly status in the interview priorities. *Four Corners'* duplicity is evident in other emails sent and approaches made to Labor MPs and ministers. Some offices were told it would be a profile of Rudd; others that it would be on Labor's future. Treasurer Swan was approached and told by *Four Corners'* spruikers that the interview would be about the mining and carbon taxes. The story cupboard was bare until Gillard was lured to appear. I'm told by one senior ABC journalist that the *Four Corners* crew didn't think it had a story and was going to ditch the project until Gillard, accepting in good faith Cronau's description of the program's intention, agreed to the interview. That would be depressing news to her government.

Within two hours of *AM* another online story bobs up, this time on Fairfax websites, penned by the *Sydney Morning Herald's* Phillip Coorey. He's adopted the description used in the Newspoll, of 'shifty' to describe Gillard. The *Age* online has also picked up the same description, now being furiously planted by Rudd urgers. Astonishingly, the *Age* is running not one, but three online opinion polls about Gillard's appearance on *Four Corners*. One gives readers the option of choosing one of four adjectives to describe her performance; the top selection is 'shifty', followed by 'shaky', 'good' and 'incredible'. Influenced by the frenzied reporting, at 4 pm 74 per cent of respondents out of 17,000 votes choose 'shifty'. The other two *Age* polls also ask leading questions. 'Do you believe Julia Gillard's account of the overthrow of Kevin Rudd?' asks one. No prizes for guessing that the overwhelming response is 'no'. The other asks: 'Was Julia Gillard's decision to face questions on *Four Corners* the right one?'

The idea that a professional media outlet that bays for blood if our country's leaders avoid interviews should be framing a question on the wisdom of doing just that is a laugh indeed. But by day's end, every newspaper and online report is running the line that leadership rumblings have been re-ignited by the PM's 'gross' misjudgement in agreeing to appear on the program. Coupled with another poor Newspoll appearing in the *Australian*, the collective judgement of the press gallery is that Gillard has monumentally stuffed up again. Yet this twenty-four-hour news cycle has been built on a hohum television program and the malicious quotes of a clutch of anonymous Rudd urgers.

Meanwhile, a delegation representing 600 workers at Alcoa's Victorian aluminium smelter has been in Canberra for twenty-four hours, pleading with the government for financial assistance to save their jobs. In the same time period, ANZ has announced it will shed a hefty 1000 jobs on top of the recent announcement by Westpac that it will sack 400. Moodys has downgraded the credit rating of six European nations, with the United Kingdom and France possibly to follow, which will have a flow-on effect on the Australian financial sector. But the cream of Australian journalism in Canberra is transfixed by a leadership question that hasn't been put.

*

Special Minister of State Gary Gray believes the genesis of the gallery's feverish leadership obsession is because all except a few ABC journalists were caught offguard by the events of the night of 23 June 2010. Now they are keeping watch—'weekly, daily, hourly'—and jumping 'at every single shadow they see' says Gray, a former ALP national secretary come election campaign director. He's looking subdued as we sit in his parliamentary office the afternoon after *Four Corners* aired. 'Meanwhile, the actual processes of the government continue to work well and, in my view, the cabinet processes and the internal workings of the government are working better than they have worked for over a decade,' he says. 'The press gallery's obsession is with the state of the internal politics of the government and of the party, and the internal politics are not great. It is the fact that in order for a government to get re-elected it actually has to be good at the politics as well as the public administration. I think it's reasonable to say that this government is good at the public administration and poor at the politics.' The former Rudd government, Gray says, was poor at the public administration but good at the politics.

Gray is candid about the problems facing the government in which he serves. 'The government as it currently sits, in the middle of the first quarter 2012, does not have political traction. It does not have the political firepower to ensure electoral success. It is also true that the actual workings of the government—the budget management, the program management, the interplay of public policy and cabinet processes—are actually better than they have been for over a decade. The harsh truth is: if you can't politically position what you do, you get substantially marked down. But we also know that it is the truth that, if you can't manage the business of government, eventually you get found out. And that's what happened to the Rudd government.'

Gray says Gillard's intention and determination is to make cabinet work and to restore cabinet to the central feature of government decision-making, 'and I think she has been remarkably successful', he says. He is adamant that the government's leadership is not about to change, regardless of the press coverage suggesting so. 'For good or for bad, the governing arrangements are very strong, and very, very workable.' Why for good or for bad? 'For good, if you believe in the importance of good administration; for bad, if you are in the category of just wanting the government to change.'

Speak of the devil. When I return from parliament I find in my email inbox a response to my questions to Rudd, attributable to a spokesperson. 'The Foreign Minister categorically denies the allegations aired on the *Insiders* program,' it states. 'The Minister on occasion conducts off-the-record media briefings on policy matters, for instance during the Foreign Ministers' component of the recent Commonwealth Heads of Government meeting in Perth.'

Well, well, well. I email back, requesting an interview with Rudd. The response from Kate Sieper is matter of fact: not much point as he wouldn't venture outside his portfolio. Silly me; of course he wouldn't. What would he say? 'Of course I brief journalists [as both he and I know]; haunt the corridors of major newspapers [ditto]; Oh, and I want my bloody job back.' How refreshingly honest if I received such answers!

The next morning, on Wednesday 15 February, the *Sydney Morning Herald* splashes with another leadership story quoting unnamed Labor MPs saying Gillard had definitely shown them polling about Rudd. 'In the days before challenging Kevin Rudd for the prime ministership, Julia Gillard personally handed to her Labor colleagues copies of secret internal polling designed to undermine his leadership,' writes Rudd man Peter Hartcher, and Phillip Coorey. 'Labor MPs told Fairfax that Ms Gillard used the polling as part of an effort to persuade them to support her for the prime ministership. The revelation casts fresh doubt on Ms Gillard's protestations that she was a reluctant challenger who decided to move against her leader only at the last minute—on the day she openly declared herself.'

The eighth paragraph carries a one-line denial by Gillard through her spokesperson. 'Ms Gillard's office has vehemently denied the allegations this morning,' they write. 'The claims are absolutely false,' her spokesman said.' The denial is clearly not believed; the remaining fourteen paragraphs of the article bolster the premise of the story that Gillard had, as Rudd people have been asserting, given private polling to Labor MPs in the weeks leading up to Rudd's removal as PM.

Buried in eight paragraphs on page two of the same paper is a story about the private health care rebate package passing the House of Representatives. It is a $3 billion quintessential Labor reform—a strike at the over-generous middle class welfare system that John Howard put in place from 2001 to 2006 as he attempted to buy the votes of middle Australia. Labor has been trying to get this measure passed since the last parliament. It will be a hit on upper middle class and wealthy households when it kicks in on 1 July—between $20 and $40 a week. It's a big story with big reader impact, particularly for the *Sydney Morning Herald*'s middle class readership. But it is considered of secondary consequence when lined up against stories about leadership challenges that haven't been launched, sourced from nameless backgrounders.

Labor back-bencher Stephen Jones echoes the frustrations of minister Gray and many other Labor MPs about current media reporting. 'I think there is very little media reporting on the way the government operates,' he tells me. 'Overwhelmingly media reporting is around the leadership and the Prime Minister—the extraordinary circumstances by which the PM claimed office, only surpassed by the extraordinary outcome of the 2010 election.' He is frank about the government's shortcomings, again echoing some thoughts of Gray's. 'In the offices I deal with, we have fantastic policy heads. What we lack in the show is political strategy, and the group of wise old or young grey beards who are able to provide political guidance on how we roll out our policy agenda. If you talk to the caucus, it is recognised. In the 2010 election, the government was put on notice. We were given a second chance.

'When it comes to our reform agenda, I think we've done very, very well. When it comes to key decisions around managing the economy, we've been up there with the best. When it comes to the core function of a political party and members of parliament to explain what it is that we're doing and why that's in the national interest, you'd have to say B plus at the moment, and we need to be scoring AAs.'

What about the Gillard–Rudd sideshow? 'I think it is adding to our problems because we're spending too much time talking about ourselves and not enough time talking about what we're doing and why it's good. At some point in the next twelve months it has to be brought to a head. I think Julia should be given a chance to turn it around. Some may say that's a chance she never gave Kevin. I think we owe that to the leader, we owe that to the party and we owe that to the country. It's going to be tough for her, but it's the right thing to do.'

Without the bolstering efforts of the press gallery, Rudd would be just the Foreign minister; his comeback plans would not have the traction they now have. Journalists in the gallery are keeping mum about Team Rudd's unfolding strategy; as highly respected ABC reporter Heather Ewart says on *7.30*: 'It's no secret in this building that Kevin Rudd and his backers are briefing some journalists about plans to challenge when Julia Gillard makes her next big slip—no matter that they deny this and don't have anywhere near the numbers to succeed or even come close.'

What's being glossed over is that, in the unlikely event that Rudd challenges and wins, he would need to work with the parliament he's inherited: a minority government, where the balance-of-power players in the lower house have agreements with Gillard. He would need to re-stitch an agreement with those Independents—a deal that took Gillard and Swan seventeen torturous days to seal—and the Independents aren't that chuffed about having their deal with their friend Julia ditched. Windsor says his deal was with her, not the government. 'If she stays, the term will probably see itself out,' he tells me. 'If she goes, it's probably fifty/fifty there'll be a parliament. Rudd would have to renegotiate an arrangement, and he wouldn't be particularly brilliant at that.'

In a piece on the ABC's online Drum on Friday 17 February, Barrie Cassidy revisits the question about press gallery journalists and their role in the game-play unfolding against Gillard. It's the second time this month that it's taken a non-Canberra journalist to try and flush out the underbelly of complicity in the attack on Gillard. 'Rudd is campaigning,' he writes. 'Rudd is talking to journalists about the leadership despite his astonishing denial. I know the names of some of those he has spoken to. I know where he said it—in his office on a parliamentary sitting day—and I know what he said. He told them a challenge would happen; he told them he was prepared to lose the first ballot and go to the backbench; and in one conversation, he laughed about the prospect of Gillard stumbling again. Yet the Foreign Minister has categorically denied ever having spoken to any journalist about the leadership.'

There appears to be no follow-up in media outlets the next day to Cassidy's claims, yet the article had prompted an extraordinary 800-plus comments on the ABC website, the majority excoriating the political media. The media caravan rolls on regardless. In an apt coincidence of timing, that Saturday the *Australian*'s weekend edition publishes a list—yes, another one!—of allegedly who is in what leadership camp and who is leaning where, much of it wrong. The accompanying article by James Massola asserts that Gillard has forty-six supporters and Rudd thirty-six, with twenty-one undecided. Among those named as switching to Rudd is Stephen Jones, who has just told me he believes Gillard should be given a chance to save her prime ministership. Defence minister Stephen Smith is forced to go public to say he's been erroneously plonked into the Rudd camp, where he doesn't belong. Secretary to the Treasurer David Bradbury is also mightily pissed off: 'If people are going to write stories where they haven't even bothered to pick up the phone and to ask you a simple question, any journalist—and I defy any journalist in this country that has spoken to me about this issue—that suggests that they had anything other than a definitive answer of my support for the Prime Minister to come forward. There won't be one person that will come forward and say that. Yet these things are printed in our newspapers for whatever purpose.' Former speaker Harry Jenkins is also privately upset at being labelled a Rudd supporter.

Other MPs are publicly mute but privately seethe at the way they have been pegged into the wrong camp, and even angrier they weren't contacted by any News Ltd journalist. Massola also asserts that 'Julia Gillard has sent out her closest ministerial supporters to halt the leakage of backbench support to Kevin Rudd.' No evidence is given to support the claim, except anonymous quotes. In the same paper, Dennis Shanahan and Sid Maher write under a large red 'exclusive' banner: 'Kevin Rudd is prepared to challenge Julia Gillard as prime minister next month, before the Queensland election and the federal budget parliamentary session.' That's a new one; last week it was after the March election and before the budget. But let's not fret about consistency. The article continues: 'The former Labor leader is readying for a strike at regaining the top job in the final March sitting of parliament as Labor MPs fall away from supporting the Prime Minister.'

The third paragraph asserts there are 'claims' the Foreign minister doesn't have the numbers, yet the fourth paragraph asserts boldly that 'the rapid shift in support within the Labor parliamentary caucus in the past two sitting weeks has convinced Mr Rudd's supporters he has 40 of the 52 votes he requires to win a challenge.' Looks like Rudd's fantasy peddlers couldn't synchronise their lines for the *Australian*. Apart from the fact that forty votes is nonsense, surely that's a loss anyway? Ah, but wait—it's all about the momentum! The article continues to deliver the lines straight out of the mouths of Rudd spruikers, who habitually bloat the Foreign minister's support. It's a copybook Rudd play: fake it until you make it.

The publication of lists also harks back to 2006, when Rudd was circling Beazley. Lists were published then, and seeds of doubt sown about Beazley's fitness for office. As federal political reporter for the *Sun-Herald* at the time, I was interviewing

Rudd one day on a foreign policy matter—he was then shadow Foreign minister—and he suddenly, casually, mentioned that he was concerned that Beazley may not be as well as he should be. There was the possibility that a debilitating medical condition Beazley had in 2004, a leaking of fluid to the brain known as Schaltenbrand syndrome, might still linger. I was so astonished I rang Beazley's office; I was promised a medical certificate to prove he was clear of the disease. End of story. It was a sinister, subtle undermining that put me on high alert that Rudd was a sniper in diplomat's garb.

Meanwhile, over at the good ship Fairfax, Hartcher makes the audacious claim in the opening paragraph of his column that 'Kevin Rudd will become the leader' and, amazingly: 'Kevin Rudd is not campaigning for the leadership. He certainly wants it.' Hartcher's long-winded justification for Rudd's behaviour (it's a silent campaign; insubstantial, really) says everything about the devotion of Fairfax's senior political commentator to the cause: 'Kevin Rudd will become the leader, not because he's made a compelling case but because Julia Gillard cannot hold the confidence of her caucus.' Hartcher and others intimately know that Team Rudd has been talking Rudd up for months without having sufficient support in caucus to back up their bravado. Rudd has been personally active in briefing journalists about his plans for at least the last fortnight, and he's been yakking to leading journalists and commentators in Canberra and other cities ever since he lost the prime ministership. His campaign has been consistent, persistent and, to many, as naked as his ambition; it has not been silent or insubstantial. It's just that the people out in the suburbs, towns and cities of Australia, whom Rudd likes to indulgently call the 'good folk', don't have a clue. Because we in the fourth estate don't tell them what he's up to.

RINGSIDE AT THE CIRCUS
19-23 February 2012

It is late afternoon on 18 February when edited video out-takes of a pre-recorded 2009 address by Prime Minister Rudd to a Chinese function anonymously bob up on YouTube. Titled 'Kevin Rudd is a happy little Vegemite', this embarrassing footage of the Prime Minister attempting to speak in Mandarin reveals One K. Rudd in multicolour meltdown—swearing, abusing and screaming at unseen staffers about his script and the flow of the taping. 'Tell them to cancel this meeting at six o'clock, I don't have any fucking patience to do this! . . . The fucking Chinese inter-preter up there—oh, just fucking hopeless,' he spits. 'Just give me simple sentences and I have said this before and tell that bloody interpreter this fucking language he just complicates it so much . . . Just fucking hopeless, I fucked up the last word.' This is the nasty Rudd face so many behind-the-scenes people have seen but few members of the public have, to date, glimpsed. The YouTube post must have sparked a similar hissy fit in the Rudd family household that lazy Saturday.

At 10.30 pm Sky News political editor David Speers, relaxing with friends at a suburban Canberra dinner, receives a call from Bruce Hawker. Rudd's undeclared campaign manager offers the Foreign minister to Speers. Yes, in the studio, Hawker says. Now would be good; any time Speers can get in and record it, Rudd will be ready to roll. Speers heads into the Parliament House studio where, at close to midnight, he conducts an interview that is sure to go off like a firecracker.

Rudd insinuates that the out-takes must have been squirrelled away in the Prime Minister's office or her department and, gee, you have to look at motives, right? 'Well, look, anyone who's got a touch of suspicion about them would say if this was done somewhat embarrassingly a couple of years ago, and it suddenly emerges now, then obviously it's a little bit on the unusual side. But that's for— these are questions for others.' And, heck, I'm not faultless—it's me 'warts and all, and I'm not perfect, I never claim to be. And you would know from my previous statements on these sorts of things that I've never pretended not to swear from time to time; that's been out there for a long, long time. I wish I sweared [sic] less, but that's just the truth of it. And I think we all get frustrated. I get frustrated. I got frustrated then. There was a whole bunch of things I had to do, a very tight timetable, lots on the agenda. When things go wrong you get frustrated.'

This explanation is a whitewash of the demeaning, insulting and abusive treatment Rudd metes out to his staff. One Labor person recalls being horrified when walking past Rudd's office one day to hear him berating a junior administrative staffer: 'Repeat this: "I am a fuckwit." Go on, say it!' And he wasn't joking.

A humble Rudd tells Speers he's learned from his errors. 'I've made mistakes in the past. As to whether, you know, K. Rudd has changed in any fundamental way—that's a judgement for others to make. But I've certainly reflected a lot on the last several years, and you'd be a mug if you didn't learn something from the past.' Like the art of revenge, perhaps? On he continues . . . about learning, about wisdom, about how he'd do things differently, like delegating more. It's a line or two he's been practising for months now; with Hartcher, Franklin, Benson. Keep saying it and maybe someone will listen. Or he'll get it right. One or the other. 'The bottom line is I think you do learn,' he says. 'And what I've tried to learn is: do less in a given working day rather than trying to do everything. I also think it's important to delegate more and be sort of happy and content about that. On top of that, most importantly, consult more broadly as well.'

In the wee small hours of Sunday 19 February, One K. Rudd has just declared to Gillard: 'Game on, sister.'

It is an active day, this particular Sabbath. Yesterday Darren Cheeseman, a Victorian MP whose hitherto claim to fame was for being one of the rotated marginal-seat-holding 'nodding heads' placed strategically for the cameras behind PM Rudd during Question Time, told journalists that Gillard should step down for the good of the party. News Ltd's scribe Samantha Maiden quotes Cheeseman, and ramps up the tempo by writing that Gillard was being 'publicly urged to resign now' by some unnamed 'senior ministers and marginal seat MPs' as the government 'descended into open warfare . . . the shock tactics significantly heighten the leadership crisis, and are designed to blast the Prime Minister out of office in favour of Kevin Rudd.' This has long been Team Rudd's game plan: they also want Gillard to pull on the challenge—just not now.

Independent Andrew Wilkie stokes the fire by leaping onto Sky News and declaring he's convinced Rudd will challenge Gillard.

All through 2011 he'd thought this unlikely, until he talked to Rudd late that year. 'I must confess, for a while I thought it was just media mischief, right up until I had a ninety-minute meeting with Kevin Rudd—Kevin clearly wants the job back,' he says. 'That is entirely understandable . . . There will be a challenge and I suspect he may well be successful, and if he is successful then I will aim to work with him to get the sort of policy outcomes I want to see.'

Meanwhile, in the Twitterverse, Victorian Labor MP Steve Gibbons gives Rudd a free character assessment: 'Only a psychopath with a giant ego would line up again after being comprehensively rejected by the overwhelming majority of colleagues,' he offers, to silent cheers from the majority of caucus. He later issues a statement stating that the ALP is 'certainly bigger than Kevin Rudd'; that Rudd had lost his former job and the support of his colleagues because of a 'chaotic and deeply offensive style of leadership'; and he urges his comrades to stick with the incumbent. 'Federal Labor cannot afford to adopt the strategies of the New South Wales branch of the party in regularly changing leaders just because the going gets a bit rough . . . being in government, especially under the current circumstances, is extremely difficult and no place for prima donnas who have had their chance.'

The following day, Monday 20 February, all the major newspapers are full of Team Rudd–inspired stories about Gillard being urged to stand down or to bring on a ballot. In the *Daily Telegraph*, Simon Benson states boldly that 'almost half the cabinet has switched allegiance to Foreign Minister Kevin Rudd, his backers claimed last night'. No evidence is given to support this contention. Support among key cabinet members for Ms Gillard is collapsing, writes Matthew Franklin in the *Australian*. Again, so evidence is offered to substantiate this claim.

Over at Fairfax, Rudd's man on the spot opens his column with the inexplicable observation that: 'The anonymous person who tried to claw at Kevin Rudd by leaking video footage of him swearing in exasperation has, inadvertently, done him a tremendous favour. It is a three-part gift to the man who wants to be prime minister again.' Apparently, thinks Peter Hartcher, the gift is that: (1) it makes a challenge inevitable; (2) it gives Rudd an opening to make a 'job application' to caucus members; and (3), incredibly, the sight of a seething, angry Rudd swearing at his off-camera underlings actually humanises him. Hartcher's loyalty knows no bounds. He finishes with the intrepid observation: 'As he returns, in all likelihood, to the prime ministership in the weeks ahead . . .' Phil Coorey, more grounded about Rudd and more informed about politics than Hartcher, comments: 'Rudd does not want to be seen as the aggressor but, if Gillard does not bring on a ballot, a Rudd loyalist will.'

Gillard stalwart Simon Crean is the advance man for her forces today. He appears on Sky News and tells reporter Kieran Gilbert: 'I think the Prime Minister's got to have the conversation with the Foreign minister and make a judgement based on it. Kieran, this nonsense has to end. This is strangling the Labor Party of any oxygen in terms of what is a very positive message, I think, that we've got to tell.' He adds the salient fact that Rudd has 'never mounted a challenge before unless he's been certain of the challenge, and he's only done it once even though he's talked it up many times before'. Next up Crean's on ABC Melbourne radio telling Jon Faine that Rudd doesn't have the numbers to challenge and that the undermining is wrecking the government and pulling its vote down. For good measure, he has a kick at the *Australian*: 'He's well short of anywhere near a majority, and even the *Australian*'s analysis keeps changing by the day, and it's still wrong.'

Next up Crean is off to the Fairfax radio network; on 3AW he is even blunter about Rudd's duplicitous ways and his lack of support in caucus. 'The Foreign minister is disloyal and he's been undermining Gillard for months,' he says. 'Now Kevin hasn't got the numbers, we know that,' he tells interviewer Neil Mitchell. 'His problem, and he knows it, is he can't convince his caucus colleagues. That's why he has to go on some sort of public campaign. But the public campaign drags the ship down. And that's what has to be stopped.' As for the *Australian*, Crean wonders whether Rudd tried to 'sell them the Sydney Harbour Bridge as well' when he was shopping his inflated numbers. In all three interviews, Crean pushes the line that Gillard has the option before her of sacking her Foreign minister for disloyalty.

At a press conference, allegedly to discuss his real work at the G20 Foreign Ministers' meeting in Mexico, Rudd purses his lips with distaste when asked about Crean's comments. 'I am disappointed by his remarks, because they are based on an untruth,' Rudd solemnly asserts. Licking his lips is more likely; the plan is going swimmingly—all except the teensy little inconvenience that he doesn't have anywhere near the numbers to successfully challenge Gillard and now is not the optimum time. Not to worry; it's all about the momentum, and Team Rudd is in over-drive.

It's true that leadership challenges are about creating momentum, but the leadership challenges of the 1980s and 1990s—John Howard vs Andrew Peacock, Bob Hawke vs Paul Keating—were based on realistic chances of success. Nothing equates to the stealth campaign of sabotage that's been conducted against Gillard since she took the job just twenty months ago. Forget good governance, or keeping

Australia on track internationally, or parliamentary stability; the only aim has been to force sooner or later what now appears inevitable—a leadership ballot.

And so it comes to pass on the other side of the globe. In the wee small hours of 22 February—1.20 am Washington time, 5.20 pm Canberra time—Kevin Rudd resigns from his portfolio, declaring he has lost the support of the Prime Minister and citing attacks by colleagues. Labelling the leadership speculation he has been instrumental in promoting as a 'soap opera' he wants nothing to do with, he refrains from laughing out loud when he denies he's been plotting a comeback. 'I can promise you this: there is no way, no way I would ever be party to a stealth attack on a sitting prime minister elected by the people,' he hilariously asserts, to the thud of incredulous Labor MPs fainting across the country. 'We all know that what happened then was wrong, and it must never happen again.' Journalists back in Australia who've been privy to his long-term strategy immediately and without comment start pounding out stories reporting his claims of loyalty. He doesn't declare a challenge, saying he will consult widely with family, friends and colleagues before making up his mind.

But of course he *has* made up his mind, because he then launches into a mini campaign speech: 'There is one over-riding question for my caucus colleagues and that is: who is best placed to defeat Tony Abbott at the next election? Mr Abbott, I believe, does not have the temperament or the experience to ever be elected and hold the office, the high office of Prime Minister of Australia.' All but blaming Gillard, whose credibility Team Rudd has been whittling away through its campaign of undermining, he concludes: 'But at present, and for a long time now, he's been on track just to do that.'

At 6 pm in Canberra, just after Rudd's Washington press conference, Channel Seven's national political reporter Mark Riley goes to air with a story highly damaging to Rudd: that Clubs Australia officials had been told by Rudd's chief number counter, Alan Griffin, that Rudd was mobilising to take back the prime ministership and he would then tear up the Wilkie–Gillard agreement on mandatory pre-commitment technology limiting betting on poker machines. 'Clubs Australia did meet with an MP close to Kevin Rudd in late November,' Clubs spokesman Jeremy Bath says in a statement to Seven. 'It was made clear at that meeting that Kevin Rudd was sympathetic to the concerns of clubs and that as prime minister he would kill mandatory pre-commitment.' Clubs Australia was 'encouraged' to continue its campaign against the Wilkie–Gillard approach 'and was advised that we should target a select number of MPs. Clubs Australia then sought confirmation of Kevin Rudd's support through a known Rudd ally, which we duly received several days later,' Bath continues. Griffin admits to the meeting; however, he denies he even mentioned Rudd's name. Channel Seven states that Rudd denies the story outright, but I was also told in November that Rudd's lieutenants had been visiting Clubs Australia with clear messages about Rudd's revised position on pokies.

Gillard supporters believe it is this story—which Riley has been working on for some days and which Rudd had attempted to muzzle with the threat of legal action—and not Crean's remarks that has spurred Rudd into action. They believe his decision to resign from the ministry and spark what in all likelihood will be a leadership ballot is because his new position on poker machine reform was about to be unmasked. There is also rising anger among his caucus colleagues at his increasingly outrageous posturing, suggesting his support could drop even more than its current dismal numbers.

On the ABC's *7.30*, Bruce Hawker jumps into the interviewee's chair to champion the Rudd case. He peddles the line that Rudd has been much maligned to the media all day by government people trying to 'make life difficult for Kevin'. No word of a lie; he actually says this.

Next up on *7.30* is an interview with veteran back-bencher Mark Danby that should set the hares running. He is interviewed by Melbourne-based Heather Ewart. After running a lengthy clip of Rudd's Washington press conference and cutting to left-wing factional powerbroker and pro-Rudd agitator Senator Doug Cameron (who says with straight face: 'I must say I'm extremely disappointed. This came out of the blue!'), Ewart saves the best to last. Speaking to presenter Chris Uhlmann, Ewart says Danby has given her the names of three of the four journalists briefed by Rudd on his strategy: two from the ABC, and one from News Ltd. She then runs a pre-taped interview, which I understand journalists in the Canberra ABC bureau—from where Ewart was reporting—did not want aired.

Ewart: Is Kevin Rudd actively undermining the Prime Minister, and how?

Danby: Heather, I know Kevin well; he's a very subtle operator. I can't believe the claim that he met four journalists on three separate occasions to outline a program to undermine in two stages the Prime Minister. I appeal to him to say that this isn't so. If it isn't so, then we can go on; but, you know, if it is, it's a smoking gun and this'll have to be over Monday—Sunday or Monday. The public and Australia can't put up with it any more. Again, I appeal to Kevin Rudd: please say it ain't so that you met with these four journalists to discuss this two-stage program. If it is, there's only one choice for you.

Ewart: And what is that?

Danby: Resign.

Gillard and Swan, and their teams, now have a strategy. They've seen Rudd in the last few hours; they know how he operates, and they know his script. They've had enough. Over recent days they've decided that if it comes to a head, it will be time to call Rudd for who he is, and his strategy for what it is. They will drop the charade about the former PM's lost-way government. They plan to answer Rudd's call to arms with as many bullets as they can put in a chamber, with as many senior ministers brave enough to fire a few rounds and tell the real story about Rudd's time as PM, and the destabilisation campaign he's been orchestrating all year.

The tactic has been devised at the highest levels of government, with key political government advisers—John McTernan, Ben Hubbard and Sean Kelly from the PM's office, and Jim Chalmers from the Treasurer's office—joining with their bosses to craft a message to the Australian people. Other senior ministers will also be involved.

Straight after the explosive Danby accusations air, Environment minister Tony Burke appears on *7.30*. He was scheduled to talk about the Murray–Darling, but that discussion was promptly sidelined. He gets straight to the point: 'Everybody has had enough of the stealth and undermining campaign that has been going on through the caucus and through the media for a very long time. And, you know, the fact that Kevin's been openly campaigning for the leadership has been the worst kept secret in Canberra.' Ah, yes, but the best kept secret by the media cognoscenti. And as for the courting of reporters in Rudd's year-long campaign, Burke states: 'People have talked up through the media and got away with some pretty significant lies to journalists, claiming high levels of dissent within the government.'

At the same time Burke is telling it as it is, Treasurer Swan issues a media statement with a devastating critique of his former boss.

For the sake of the Labor movement, the government and the Australians which it represents, we have refrained from criticism to date. However, for too long Kevin Rudd has been putting his own self-interest ahead of the interests of the broader Labor movement and the country as a whole, and that needs to stop.

The party has given Kevin Rudd all the opportunities in the world, and he wasted them with his dysfunctional decision-making and his deeply demeaning attitude towards other people—including our caucus colleagues. He sought to tear down the 2010 campaign, deliberately risking an Abbott prime ministership, and now he undermines the government at every turn.

He was the party's biggest beneficiary, then its biggest critic; but never a loyal or selfless example of its values and objectives. For the interests of the Labor movement and of working people, there is too much at stake in our economy and in the political debate for the interests of the Labor movement and working people to be damaged by somebody who does not hold any Labor values.

Julia has the overwhelming support of our colleagues. She is tough, determined, forward-looking, and has a good Labor heart. She has a consultative, respectful relationship with caucus, while Kevin Rudd demeaned them. She's cleaned up a lot of the mess he left her and has established a good Labor agenda. She's delivering major reforms, and getting things done that her predecessor could not. Colleagues are sick of Kevin Rudd driving the vote down by sabotaging policy announcements and undermining our substantial economic successes. The Labor Party is not about a person, it's about a purpose. That's something Prime Minister Gillard has always known in her heart, but something Kevin Rudd has never understood.

Swan's strong words and Burke's performance are designed to fire up Gillard's supporters and show Rudd and his lieutenants that the real man will now be exposed. Too much is at stake to protect him any more; for the sake of the government and the country, Rudd has to be unmasked. How different things might have been if, on 24 June 2010 Gillard, Swan and others who had worked with Rudd had spoken out frankly about his unsuitability for office. Instead, he was able to martyr himself and use their protection of him as a cover for his toxic comeback ambitions. What a price to pay.

In case nobody noticed him resign the first time around, on 23 February at approximately 9 am Canberra time, Rudd holds a second press conference at his Washington hotel. He is 'shocked and disappointed' at the accusations made against him, he sniffs; he is a victim of a vicious personal campaign. It's a question about 'the future of the leadership of our party and our country—not about personality. It's about trust and it's also about policy and vision.' He launches into another mini campaign speech, about restoring business confidence and revitalising manufacturing, which is surely a sop to one of his ministerial supporters, Kim Carr.

The man who blew Kim Beazley out of his job through systematic undermining and factional backroom dealings says: 'When this comes to a head it really does need to be recognised that the future government of Australia is not about the power of factions, it's about people's power, and the people of Australia have a view on the future leadership of their country.' It is difficult to watch without cackling uproariously. And with that, Rudd deploys his trademark 'Gotta zip!' and off he motors to catch a plane home.

Sky News and other TV channels have carried the press conference and are at Washington airport when Rudd arrives, gladdening the heart of the former PM; he gives an extra dimension to the old gag that, if you value your safety, don't stand between a politician and a television camera. Watching footage of Rudd grinning from ear to ear, sweeping through the airport greeting well-wishers with a cheesy grin then turning a sombre face to reporters, is like watching an actor playing multiple characters. Which Kevin will appear next?

Danby's call for Rudd to explain himself makes it into a column by Deborah Snow in the *Sydney Morning Herald*, but it does not form the basis for any news story in any other mainstream media outlet. It appears that no gallery journalist has put Danby's questions to Rudd. In the *Sydney Morning Herald*, Hartcher opens his column with two rhetorical questions that have only one answer: return my boy to The Lodge! He writes: 'Kevin Rudd will now present the Labor Party with a shocking prospect—would it like to be electable? Or would it rather continue indulging its personal distaste for Rudd all the way to electoral defeat?' Hartcher carries a potent message that Rudd and his camp have been polishing for months: that if Rudd loses, he will 'repair to the backbench' and prepare for a second strike.

It is close to an acknowledgement by Rudd himself that he doesn't have the support to win a ballot any time soon, and again underlines his destructive intent and that of his lieutenants: that even if Gillard thumps Rudd by a resounding majority in a ballot that is certain to be called by the PM, Rudd will again not accept caucus' decision and will continue to wreak havoc on Gillard's leadership and the government.

Michelle Grattan in the *Age* carries the same message from Team Rudd. 'If she [Gillard] wins convincingly, Rudd will be seriously set back. But if the bad Labor polls continue, as likely, that will not be the end of the matter. From the backbench, Rudd would be able to make trouble. If the vote is closer than expected, Gillard could expect a second challenge later.'

Swan follows up last night's devastating statement with an appearance on ABC Radio's *AM*. He does not intend to miss his target; this is make-or-break stuff for the Treasurer, a normally cautious politician not given to angry outbursts or hysteria. 'The fact is that for some period of time now, with increasing frequency, Mr Rudd has been undermining the government,' he says. 'And of course I watched his press conference from Washington, where he said he would never be part of any stealth attack on a Prime Minister. Well, it's pretty clear now, particularly given events in recent days, that Mr Rudd has been directly involved in that sort of attack on the government and the Prime Minister.' There was 'no doubt' Rudd sought to tear down the 2010 election campaign, he says. He had lied about not briefing journalists on this plan to take back his old job, and 'at every step where we've been putting in place important reforms, Mr Rudd has been in the background undermining government decision-making'. There has been no more lethally accurate character assessment of the failings of a prime minister in modern Australian political history.

Simon Crean has also tucked into some serious super foods for breakfast; his aim just keeps getting better. He tells 3AW:

'What I find is insidious is those that seek to run their campaign covertly. Now Kevin talks about stealth; I mean, this has been a covert operation, and he's up there operating the drone twenty-four hours a day, because he never sleeps. He's always manipulating something. This is a campaign that has been relentless. It's had an impact. It needs to be called for what it is. It's a pity it has taken so long for it to be called.' As for the former Foreign minister's Washington performance, Crean congratulates him for resigning but says Rudd should have acknowledged what everyone knows he will do: run for the leadership. But Rudd has more to do yet, people to ring, limelight to bathe in—and his foot soldiers need to test his numbers while he's in the air, returning to Australia. This hasn't quite gone to plan, now; they wanted another month or so.

The saturation of anonymous and unverified stories that have been drip fed all year from the Rudd machine has so troubled Michael Gawenda, a respected former editor of Melbourne's *Age*, that he pens a provocative column for ABC online's The Drum. Under the headline 'It's time to let the facts get in the way of the story', Gawenda takes aim at Canberra journalists. His thesis is that those 'playing the game of protecting anonymous sources and promoting their falsehoods are lying, and retailing the lies of Rudd and his mob'.

Gawenda asserts: 'At his two bizarre press announcements in Washington, Kevin Rudd spoke as if he was a total innocent, as pure as the driven snow, morally virginal, having never ever been involved in the grubby politics of undermining, white-anting, wounding and ultimately destroying an opponent. And reporters, some of whom knew that none of this was true, reported it all without comment, without letting us know that they knew, personally, that it was untrue. This is "he said, she said, they said" journalism. It is meant to be "straight" but what it is in reality is timid and ultimately dishonest.' Gawenda's conclusion is direct, unequivocal and accurate; the rules of engagement in Canberra no longer serve the public interest: 'They encourage and support dishonesty from politicians and, yes, dishonesty from reporters and commentators.'

Gawenda predicts that millions of words will be written and broadcast by Canberra journalists about the Gillard–Rudd fight over the next few days, but: 'I can't help wondering how many of them, because of the rules of engagement in Canberra, will be unable to tell us what is really going on. On the evidence so far, there are reporters and commentators—as well as editors and broadcasting bigwigs—who have allowed things to be said and reported that they know not to be true.' This is the third column in as many weeks from a respected non-Canberra based media professional aghast at the distorted politico–media information loop in federal politics.

But will his potent comments change anything?

WHO'S THE RINGMASTER NOW?

23–26 February 2012

At a little after 10 am on 23 February a steely faced Gillard calls for a ballot to be held on Monday the 27th, and promises that if Rudd wins she will move to the backbench and renounce further claims to the leadership. She calls on her predecessor and wannabe successor to pledge a similar troth. 'It is now evident to me, and I think it is evident to the Australian people, that there has been a long-running destabilisation campaign here to get to this point where Kevin Rudd is clearly going to announce that he wants to seek the Labor leadership.'

Gillard's in South Australia, where she grew up happy and confident in a close family; she feels in control here. In measured tones, she takes aim at Rudd for 'sabotaging' the 2010 election campaign and for crippling the government. 'The government that Kevin Rudd had led had entered a period of paralysis.' In a masterful understatement, she says: 'Kevin Rudd as prime minister always had very difficult and very chaotic work patterns.'

Within half an hour Rudd's wife Therese Rein holds her own press conference, further developing the 'people power' theme test-run by Rudd in Washington. The campaign strategy is clearly emerging: to bypass caucus and harness the love of the masses to push Rudd into office. It's a novel approach for someone who's been banging on for months about the need to revitalise the power of the caucus and the party.

An hour or so after Rein concludes, Industry minister Kim Carr outs himself as a Rudd supporter, the first minister to do so. No surprises there; his former cabinet colleagues recognised a while back that, for as long as he actively supported Rudd, he should not remain in a Gillard cabinet—hence his demotion in December. Trotting out a familar theme, Carr describes Rudd as a changed man who has a 'breadth of vision for the nation'.

The senior Rudd government policy and political adviser disagrees. His recollections of the events of 23 June 2010, written after the 'period of madness' was over, were a private way of making sense of it all: 'However impossible it was to process at the time, working for the Rudd government was an experience of historic dimensions, in the way that any cautionary tale is historic,' he wrote. His conclusions about the singular destructive power of Rudd and his damaging effect on the government are chilling: 'Is it the case that systems of government are so large, complex and robust and involve so many actors that even the most wilful political leader cannot control them; or can a leader's extreme personality and style make good government practically impossible? I used to be a believer in systems, conventions and good government sailing serenely on over the chaos of even the most extreme personality. I'm not any more.'

The adviser grouped the flaws in Rudd's governing style into six categories: (1) the radical centralisation of decision-making to

Rudd himself, even though he wouldn't or couldn't make decisions; (2) Rudd's chairing of a terrible cabinet process that ignored or wasted the skills of his ministers and officials; (3) Rudd trying to do too many things; and (4) trying to do them too quickly; (5) his neglect of policy in favour of an overweening focus on political and media considerations; and (6) a culture of blame and retribution he personally nurtured that stifled honest advice and undermined decision-making.

The former adviser recalled torturous cabinet meetings that went for hours, with Rudd using them as his personal briefing sessions. He didn't pre-read cabinet papers and had no truck with pre-cabinet briefing sessions, so he would waste hours in cabinet, even when the agenda was short, and then he'd put off making decisions. Unresolved issues piled up and decisions were often deferred until the last minute, by which time the best and most considered options had fallen by the wayside. 'It became standard practice for most ministers to arrive with minutes to sign or papers to read for the long unproductive hours in cabinet . . . [because] ministers were afraid of making mistakes and incurring Rudd's wrath, the PM having let it be known that 'the consequences of a ministerial mistake might be severe'. The cabinet agenda was full of 'minor regulatory decisions a minister would normally make on his or her own . . . To say that it is not a good use of a PM's time to be checking each line of a routine document is an extreme understatement. The battle within government for a PM's attention is intense, and every minute has an opportunity cost. Time spent checking the paperwork for a government board appointment is time spent not reading intelligence material from the front line in Afghanistan.'

And on it went. Rudd had a 'reflexive fear' of even momentary unpopularity; was chronically indecisive; constantly invented and re-invented agendas, but could never nail a big decision and had no leadership capacity to 'go into a defensive crouch and absorb a few days of punches to hold a position that would serve him well in the longer term'. The more he delayed decisions, the more he would make grander plans and demand big agenda items from his ministers. The staffer's hypothesis was that frenetic activity 'was a way of forestalling the need for decisions he simply found too difficult to make. In the same way as a procrastinating student at exam time will tidy his room, cut his toenails and even write an email to his mother rather than pick up a textbook, the PM needed all these ancillary policy debates to avoid making difficult decisions about the big things everyone knew needed to be sorted: tax, CRPRS [the carbon pollution reduction scheme] and asylum seekers. It's no accident that these were the three issues Julia Gillard had to triage when she became PM.'

Rudd had come to office with a reputation as a policy wonk, the adviser wrote, but it was 'something we never, ever saw behind closed doors. His instinct was invariably for the politics of a policy problem—how it would play with stakeholders, how he would explain it in the media, what the timing should be around announcements, and in what form.' Rudd's favourite put-down line to departmental officials and his own policy staff was: 'That's a fine idea, but how do I explain it on *Today Tonight*?'

Rudd could not switch from the 'sound bite' mindset of Opposition leader—sprinkling superficial morsels for the media from pre-breakfast to after dinner—and, according to this adviser, the media didn't want him to: 'Having trained so much of the media to snack on small announceables all day long, he wouldn't have been able to change their diet back to three square meals a day, and the fact is he didn't want to. The freneticism of 2007 [the campaign] was not a strategic choice, it was a pure expression of the incoming PM's preferred working style. Whatever the reason, it was no way to run a government.' Rudd's obsession with the media meant the government's modus operandi revolved around turning him into the 24/7 news cycle. 'It meant every substantial policy deliberation became not a matter of solving a public policy question, but a cluster of potential attack points or announceables. Nothing had a coherent whole beyond a succession of nights or mornings won or lost in the evening news bulletins or newspaper front pages.'

Rudd refused to listen to bureaucrats because '. . . he simply didn't like the way officials thought: of practicalities, long-term consequences, consistency with other policies. These all became an unnecessary burden in his management of the politics and the media cycle. Nearing the end, he seemed to take each piece of considered policy advice as a personal affront/thinly veiled invitation for him to commit political suicide.'

This is the chaos that some in the media and in the caucus want the highest political office in the land to return to—no matter the damage such regression would ultimately inflict on the government and the country.

To round out the day, Robert McClelland, the disgruntled dumped Attorney-General, declares himself as a Rudd supporter on the ABC. No surprises there, either.

Dozens of reporters and cameras have crowded into Brisbane airport waiting for Rudd's plane, due to touch down a little after 6 am on 24 February. They're keening for the undeclared contender to front and dispense his version of the crisis he's manufactured. What's his Bruce Hawker-inspired line of the day? The extended live coverage is akin to that afforded a visit by the Pope or the President of the United States; it is starkly disproportionate to the level of interest in voter land. If the letters to the editor and torrents of posts on news websites are a guide, people just want a capable government and for the sniping to stop.

When Rudd does saunter off the plane and shortly afterwards addresses the media throng, he's not yet done with the striptease. Without providing any evidence, he insinuates Gillard and her supporters are threatening the careers and pre-selections of his supporters. He babbles on about trust and confidence and declares as 'fundamentally untrue' what his cabinet colleagues and his former staffers know: that he ran a chaotic and dysfunctional government. He trots out the line that the leadership question is 'ultimately about people power' (how would they all fit in the caucus room?). Then, after his third press conference in twenty-four hours, off he waltzes. Ostensibly, he is again going to consult with family and colleagues before 'deciding' what everyone knows he will do: take Gillard on in the ballot.

What is this unnerving charade about? He tweeted from the plane before he flew out of Washington: 'Spent time today outlining 5 big policy priorities for the future. Have a read, tell me what you think.' The priorities are: restoration of business confidence; revitalisation of manufacturing; health reform; education; and the reform of the Labor Party. He'd run the agenda at one of his Washington press conferences, also. Give us a break—tell us this isn't a prime ministerial pitch. He did the same thing before the 2007 election: he loves to group his campaign priorities into fives. Why won't he just declare his candidacy?

This pantomime is deeply disquieting. His Labor colleagues, the federal Opposition, his family and friends, journalists . . . everyone knows Rudd's deep, abiding and obsessive need to return to the prime ministership. His job application interview on Sky News after the YouTube video was posted was transparent, as were his comments in the United States. He and his supporters have been plotting revenge for more than a year, yet no-one in the press corps is calling this spectacle for what it is: an acutely disturbing piece of self-indulgent theatre.

Reinforcing how dangerously capricious Rudd could be, Attorney-General Nicola Roxon tells ABC radio that Rudd told her in 2010, when she was Health minister, that he wanted to take over the entire health system, which he rather fancied putting to a referendum—possibly within months, at that year's election. Planning for a referendum can take at least a parliamentary term—negotiating with the States and the Opposition to secure bipartisan support, and educating the public. But fantasist Rudd wanted it held, like, *now*. Roxon was summonsed to The Lodge to discuss it with him; there were no briefing notes, nothing prepared, but the meeting still lasted a harrowing seven hours.

It can often take a non-politician to speak a truth that, at a time like this, is likely to be more believed. And so it is when John Mendoza, Rudd's former chairman of the National Advisory Council on Mental Health, reveals he quit his job in June 2010—a week before Rudd was removed as prime minister—because of the former PM's dysfunctional leadership. Mr Rudd's style was erratic, unpredictable and chaotic, the distinguished professor says. 'The Australian public is now starting to understand that he wasn't knifed in the back. In fact he was removed for his own well-being, and for the government of the country to function,' Mendoza tells ABC radio. 'This man is not fit [to be] prime minister.' He praises Rudd's cabinet colleagues, 'especially all the senior ministers', for being 'extraordinarily loyal to Kevin Rudd not to disclose his shortcomings up until this point'.

The big moment finally arrives later that day. At his fourth press conference in twenty-four hours, held at Waterfront Place, Brisbane, Rudd finally declares his hand. Surprise! He's running against Gillard, and running on the question of trust—a relationship he says Gillard has lost with the Australian people. 'In politics, trust is everything,' he opines, po-faced. A second campaign theme, already road tested by Rudd in Washington and by Bruce Hawker on *7.30*, also emerges: the attacks on Rudd are being orchestrated by 'the spin machines of faceless men'. It's a disingenuous, easily disprovable claim made more astonishing because it comes from the bloke whose own destructive coterie of truly faceless men has been white-anting the Prime Minister and wreaking havoc on the government for a year.

The real strategy—to harness his popularity with the public so as to bypass caucus—is now the most dominant theme. He wants the very people who know him best, his caucus colleagues, to be bullied into transporting him back into The Lodge by some sort of weird people power movement. He and Hawker are off their rockers.

Rudd presents himself as the one who has been wronged, as someone who has been loyal, responsible and totally above indulging in sniping at the boss from behind the bushes. He is asked by a reporter to categorically deny that in the last sitting week of parliament he briefed senior press gallery reporters that he was planning to launch a challenge against Ms Gillard and, if he lost, he would go to the back bench and make a second challenge. Without a glisten of sweat on his upper lip, Rudd replies: 'My discussions with journalists remain confidential, but can I say my position with all those journalists has been one that I have supported the leadership of the current prime minister.' This is a monstrous fib, as many reporters in the room know. Rudd starts to get testy; this isn't the way this is supposed to go. They need to show me deference, to ask me easy questions!

Earlier in the day Gillard offered to release journalists from their off-the-record confidentiality restrictions about past conversations they may have had with her—she urged any journalist who had evidence that she had ever undermined or plotted against Rudd to come forward. Now, when asked to match that offer, Rudd bristles. 'Journalists should adhere to their own code of conduct, which you as a profession repeatedly say to me you are fundamentally about upholding, rather than being in it and out of it at your selective convenience,' the contender sniffs. In a word—no, he won't match Gillard's offer. He can't. Some members of the press corps breathe a sigh of relief.

Rudd dismisses out of hand Professor Mendoza's serious and sobering assessment of his mental health. There are none so blind as those who will not see.

An hour later, Gillard responds in yet another press conference. The leadership contest is about character, strength and temperament, she says. The best line is one Rudd won't like: 'I worked damn hard in days of chaos and paralysis to keep his government running.'

Readers of the country's major newspapers wake on 25 February to a string of stories again pumping up the 'second challenge' option, thus ensuring the media will continue to slowly roast Gillard well beyond the ballot, even if she wins handsomely. The *Sydney Morning Herald*'s Phillip Coorey reports: 'The Rudd camp believes it needs more than 30 votes to keep alive the prospect of a second challenge after Monday's ballot.' Nobody is quoted; the story isn't sourced.

It is an incredible thesis. Thirty votes in a voting caucus of 103 does not constitute a reasonable platform from which to launch another leadership assault. When Paul Keating challenged Bob Hawke for the first time in June 1991, he managed a respectable forty-four votes to Hawke's sixty-six—40 per cent—making a second crack, which happened five months later, a foregone conclusion. The conspirators' claims that thirty votes (about 29 per cent of caucus) represent a decent platform to continue a destabilisation campaign is stretching credibility.

If, as is likely, Gillard beats Rudd with two-thirds or more of the caucus backing her, it would represent the biggest whacking of a Labor challenger in recent political memory. The most significant defeat in thirty years was Simon Crean's over Kim Beazley by twenty-four votes in June 2003. If Gillard survives as prime minister after rising above the contentious removal of her predecessor, the daily savaging meted out by the media and the best efforts of Team Rudd, it will be a remarkable achievement and should, in the real world, forever bury Rudd's ambitions.

The *Sydney Morning Herald* also carries another specially commissioned poll revealing Rudd as the popular choice of voters by 58 per cent to 34 per cent. Yawn. Over at the News Ltd stable, the *Australian* reminds readers of the magnetic power of One K. Rudd, exemplified in its special poll, also conducted over the weekend, showing Rudd as preferred PM by 53 per cent to 30 per cent. The News stable has gone all out, with its tabloid mastheads carrying a special (they are all special; very, very special) Galaxy poll. It shows similar bolstering results for Rudd, with his hometown paper, the *Courier-Mail*, enthusing: 'Kevin Rudd is twice as popular as Julia Gillard among voters and could deliver a significant boost to Labor's support base if he returns to the top job.' The Nielsen, Newspoll and Galaxy polls run mercilessly in media outlets all day.

Former speechwriter James Button lets fly in Fairfax outlets with similar complaints to those of the senior policy adviser quoted in this chapter. Rudd was vindictive, rude, contemptuous; he held grudges for years and made crushing demands on staff who, if he felt they opposed him in any way, would be put in the 'deep freeze'. In meetings he emanated 'a kind of icy rage that was as mysterious as it was disturbing', Button comments. It is a measured piece, carrying a heavy message that Rudd was and is unfit to govern, that he has serious personal failings and should not be entrusted with high office.

As for the constant unsubstantiated accusations about Gillard's loyalty, Button writes: 'I have no idea of the precise moment at which she decided to challenge Rudd, but I am certain that she had been as loyal a deputy as he was likely to get. Through the hard months of early 2010, she had long talks with him to keep him on track. Of all the whisperings I heard against Rudd until the time I left Canberra in April 2010, none involved her.'

Over at News Ltd, David Penberthy of *The Punch* has another crack at Canberra-based political journalists. He reminds readers that in the past off the record was used for only one of two reasons: to protect whistleblowers, *à la* the Watergate scandal, or to add texture to a story. 'The type of stories we have seen about the Labor leadership could be described as dump-and-deny . . . we in the media should reflect on our complicity in this type of journalism,' he writes. 'It's my view that we have not only damaged ourselves, but more gravely we have let down the public by feeding them stories which look thin, tendentious, convey deliberately misleading sentences to blur the origin of the information.'

Penberthy cites Rudd's risible press conference, when he denied backgrounding against Gillard. 'If he had in fact ever criticised Gillard on background, what does it say about political journalism that we would rather knowingly play along with the bullshit and keep the truth from the public, out of respect for a clubby and highly questionable journalistic convention?' Just like the earlier articles by Michael Gawenda and Barrie Cassidy questioning journalistic integrity, and Penberthy's previous attempt to strike up a debate within our profession about accountability, I don't see it going anywhere.

Mid-morning, Bruce Hawker arrives at Rudd's Brisbane home, running the gauntlet of popping camera flashes and pesky reporters. He utters what will surely go down as one of the sillier lines in political history: 'I think the PM should actually think about whether she stands on Monday.' It defies comment.

Despite Gillard's poor polling, the guerrilla war waged against her for months and the promotion of Rudd's cause in the media, two-thirds of Gillard's ministers have now declared they will stand strong beside her. A roll call of senior Labor MPs has spoken in the most strident terms about the former PM's failings. Wayne Swan, Simon Crean, Nicola Roxon, Stephen Conroy, Tony Burke, Tanya Plibersek, Kate Ellis and Peter Garrett have all attested to the dysfunctional, myopic, dangerously self-serving Rudd prime ministership.

Pitted against them are ministerial colleagues Martin Ferguson, Kim Carr, Chris Bowen and Robert McClelland, all with axes to grind over either being dumped in the December reshuffle, rolled in cabinet on some pet project or just embittered by previous factional or personal issues with Gillard. And then the popular 'Albo' joins them. In an emotion-charged press conference in Sydney, Albanese declares he will vote for Rudd—not because of a lack of belief in Gillard's leadership, but to right what he considered was the wrongful removal of a prime minister. Gillard is immediately gracious in response. Albanese had offered his resignation before he went public with his support for Rudd, which she refused. He's a 'great Labor man with a great Labor heart'. Senior Channel Ten reporter Paul Bongiorno, a well-known Labor fan, tweets to 'Albo': 'I'm so proud to have a name ending in a vowel after your gutsy performance today!' Awww, a bromance to brighten our day!

It's Sunday 26 February and the Fairfax papers carry a dose of realism: Labor's most marginal seat-holders would rather risk an electoral wipe-out than back Kevin Rudd as leader, a poll finds. The *Sunday Age* surveyed twenty members of parliament with the slimmest margins and found just five intend to support Rudd in tomorrow's caucus ballot, with some predicting his popularity would evaporate were he to return to office.

Gillard supporters appear to have been busy over at News Ltd. Its tabloids run with a lurid story penned by Samantha Maiden about Rudd viciously running down Gillard a year ago at Adelaide's Stag Hotel as 'a childless, atheist, ex-communist' and vowing revenge. Along with other witnesses, Labor front-bencher Kate Ellis and an Adelaide lawyer attest to his vengeful behaviour that night, in what surely must be becoming apparent to the public and his blinkered caucus followers as a clear pattern of disturbing public and private behaviour. The lawyer describes Rudd as being on a 'rampage . . . out of control'. His behaviour was erratic: 'We are talking using foul language. It was a combination—he was cuddling up to these people taking iPhone pictures of him, and liberally spouting off . . . it was kind of funny because it was shocking. But to be talking that way to strangers was extraordinary.' Another witness says: 'He was telling anyone who would listen: this was "Kevin07, the comeback year".' In a familiar response, Rudd's spokeswoman says the story is a lie.

At 11 pm, Rudd hops off a plane in Canberra to a frenetic shoulder charge of cameras and microphones. He looks strained, and not because he's always too wired to sleep properly. It must be finally dawning on him, now that his lieutenants have started testing support, that there's such a thing as one too many challenges. Of all the politicians over the years who have striven to be numero uno, Rudd has turned his efforts into serial offending on a grand scale. As Mark Latham—formerly a trenchant critic of both Gillard and Rudd, but now just an obsessive Rudd critic—noted tartly in a column in the *Australian Financial Review* last week: 'The first thing is—Gillard can count, and he can't.'

IT'S SHOW TIME!
27–28 February 2012

A carnival atmosphere envelopes parliament when a leadership bout occurs; visitors, families and hangers-on roll up to drink in the atmosphere. Electorate staff and interstate journalists descend; national TV shows set up camp and cameras in makeshift studios on the front lawns. Parliamentary guards sharpen their eyes and ears, particularly in corridors where pesky journalists loiter; political staff flatten their noses to the ground to detect any last minute movements. All that's needed are a few hot dog stands, dancing girls and popcorn.

Neatly pressed and scrubbed, MPs wearing serious looks scurry in to parliament early on 27 February—ensuring they get their persuasive last hurrah quotes on camera at the 'doors'. To explain to the uninitiated, 'doors' are supposed to be impromptu media stops outside the entrances to Parliament House used mainly by backbenchers. There are two of them: one at the Senate and one at the House of Representatives. (Ministers get to avoid the doors, as the entrance to the ministerial wing is blocked to the nuisance media.) Once upon a time this was a chance for journalists to get an unscripted, even honest, answer from our federal representatives. But now backbenchers are rotated by party strategists to deliver a message about the issues of the day devised by political spinners in dawn telephone hook-ups. The hapless backbenchers are given their marching orders, and then pushed in front of the cameras. Other backbenchers are pedalled around the morning breakfast programs, mouthing similarly devised one-liners or sprouting the key message for the day.

But not today. This is the stuff of gladiatorial survival, and in this battle we are being given unvarnished character assessments of the candidates.

Ministers hit the airwaves before backbenchers arrive for doors, pumping up their candidate and responding to the stories in this morning's newspapers. Warren Snowdon (Veterans' Affairs—Gillard), Stephen Smith (Defence—Gillard), Penny Wong (Finance—Gillard), Robert McClelland (Emergency Management—Rudd), Chris Bowen (Rudd)—they've all been out there, spruiking their candidate and responding to yet another Newspoll in the *Australian*. Of course, it shows Gillard in the popularity doldrums, with 53 per cent preferring her opponent compared to her 28 per cent. Peculiarly, however, the poll shows that Labor has reached the dreamy heights of a primary vote of 35 per cent—a twelve-month high that only shows yet again why fortnightly polls should be taken with a grain of salt.

Backbenchers begin to arrive. Laurie Ferguson, a blunt-talking western Sydney MP, gives reporters a dose of reality and a touch-up to Rudd and the media in equal measure: 'We've had sniping, undermining, backbiting, for the last year or two by a fairly major force in the party. With that out of the way, I don't think journalists are even going to listen to him.' All Gillard can do is hope and pray he's right, because if the Rudd camp has its way Gillard will barely get a minute to savour her expected victory.

Nearly every major newspaper carries the Team Rudd attack line for the day. Ben Packham in the *Australian* has clearly been briefed by the usual propagandists, and can't dig deep and find a positive angle about the likely Gillard win: 'Kevin Rudd has left the door open to being drafted as Labor leader at a later date as he heads for defeat and the backbench in today's caucus ballot,' he writes, ignoring the fact that Rudd's already on the backbench after resigning his ministry a few days ago. 'A key Rudd backer said if Julia Gillard won today's ballot, the party could be looking for another leader within months unless her standing with voters improved.'

In the *Sydney Morning Herald* Rudd's spruiker, Peter Hartcher, gives it his best possible last shot. 'Gillard is destined to win the ballot but that will not break this impasse,' he thunders. 'As the next election day approaches and Labor's unelectability is confirmed, rising panic in the caucus ranks could fuel a second Rudd strike in the year ahead.' This is Team Rudd's final, caustic swipe at Gillard: you can win, but you can't run from us; we will get you, eventually. The statements are designed to cause such despair among wavering MPs—with their promise of more instability and ugliness to continue, regardless of the size of Gillard's win—that they will fold and vote for Rudd.

Aimed at the waverers, left-winger Doug Cameron is running the same spoiling line on the ABC: 'If Julia Gillard wins today and we end up in the same position as we are now, in terms of the polls, in several months' time, then my view is the same people who installed Julia Gillard will be looking for a candidate to replace Julia Gillard.'

Rudd is over on Channel Seven's *Sunrise* program, today being hosted out of Canberra, chatting chummily with old pals Mel and Kochie. 'Brekky Central' is his former home, the media vehicle he deftly used for years to build his profile. Warming to his campaign theme—that the factions he played like a Stradivarius to topple Beazley are really a canker in the Labor Party—Rudd reflects, with a touch of the evangelical: 'I'm resting very calm in my skin. It's very tough when you're up against the combined factions of the Australian Labor Party.' He pauses for effect, continuing sombrely: 'Sometimes you've got to take a stand, even if you think it's going to be really tough. It's the right thing to do. People out in the community have told me: "We need a change, put your hand up. Have a go."' Kochie and Mel nod furiously. Ah, but will he accept the verdict of the collective umpire today if it goes against him? 'I would not initiate a further challenge against Julia,' he says carefully. In other words, not bloody likely.

So the showdown begins:

10 am: Rudd and a band of supporters start the walk down the corridor to the caucus room. Rudd is smiling, but looks tired and slightly grey. It's a band of a dozen merry men and women who are flanking him, including ministers Martin Ferguson and Robert McClelland. It's a classic Rudd illusionist trick: if you don't have the numbers, make it look like you do.

10.05 am: A determined-looking Gillard arrives. She only has eight supporters flanking her but they're heavy hitters, including her deputy and Treasurer Wayne Swan, and ministers Craig Emerson, Nicola Roxon and Tanya Plibersek.

10.54 am: Phillip Coorey of the *Sydney Morning Herald* tweets that Gillard has won 73–29. There's fierce competition among gallery journalists to be the first to break the news, so everyone has their contacts in the caucus room. Within minutes, Lyndal Curtis repeats Coorey's numbers on ABC 24. Right now I am commentating on Sky News with David Speers and Kieran Gilbert in the Parliament House studio. Speers is wary of reporting the figure, but does so with the caveat that it's come from other journalists.

11.10 am: Speers receives a text from inside the caucus room, and announces the Coorey tweet is wrong. They're still counting, he says. Oops for Coorey and Curtis.

11.13 am: Speers announces there's a recount underway. Things are getting tangled in the rush to name the victor. It's only minutes away anyway. I must have missed the news that there's a fat reward for the first journalist to announce the winner.

11.18 am: Speers gets another text and announces Gillard has won 71–31.

11.20 am: Caucus returning officer Chris Hayes addresses the media pack and declares: 'Julia Gillard has won the ballot seventy-one votes to thirty-one. I have just declared Julia Gillard re-elected to the parliamentary party.' Oh, and there was no recount, he says. Oops again for the fourth estate.

11.30 am: The victor and the vanquished, together with their side-kicks, leave the caucus room. Gillard has a spring in her step, her head up, looking determined to get on with the job. Rudd has a strange beatific smile plastered on his face. Gillard's is an emphatic victory, her winning margin one of the biggest in Labor leadership ballots and Rudd's vote one of the worst. It also represents about the level of support Gillard had in caucus after Rudd was removed from office in June 2010. Rudd had his core band of supporters then, as he does now; apart from the straying of a few ministers, nothing has changed. Acres of newsprint have been consumed, thousands of words broadcast and many months wasted on useless treachery while the government has had a country to run. As *Daily Telegraph* political humourist Joe Hildebrand tweets: 'Given today's decisive result I'd like to put personal politics aside and offer sincere congratulations to Tony Abbott.'

At 12.45 pm Rudd strides into the caucus room to give his press conference. Shortly after conceding he has lost (reality at least!) and congratulating Gillard (hmmm), he starts on a rambling roam across the past and present. It's like an election night concession speech, except this time the defeated candidate seems to be on a spooky high. With his family hovering, Rudd covers his work in the foreign ministry, his achievements, his staff, his life, the universe. He accepts 'without qualification and without rancour' the verdict of caucus. He will bear no grudges, he promises; he wants to be part of the healing process and wants to continue as the member for Griffith. 'Our purpose is to serve the nation, not ourselves. Our purpose is to serve the people of Australia, not ourselves.' Good line; seeing is believing.

Rudd says he will dedicate himself 'fully' to the re-election of Gillard and her government. 'My task as a member of this parliament and a thirty-year long member of the Australian Labor Party, as its former leader, as its former Foreign minister and as its former prime minister, is to now throw my every effort in securing Julia Gillard's re-election as Labor prime minister at the next election.'

How different things would have been if he'd honoured a similar noble commitment he made in June 2010. And how much smoother the Gillard government will now perform if this time he honours the pledge he's just given. It's doubtful: the bouquets have only just been presented to Gillard and she's yet to give her victory press conference, but the brick bats are already being hurled. News.com, in one of its instant updates, reports: 'Labor MPs warn she might have only six to eight months to improve the Government's stocks, saying if she does not deliver she may face a "tap on the shoulder" from her own supporters.' This is a reheat of a line carried in the *Herald-Sun* this morning by Phillip Hudson, potently run again by News Ltd after the ballot. The media conglomerate has no intention of giving her the slightest break.

Gillard probably wouldn't be bothered about her 'friends' at News Ltd; it's not as if she should expect anything different. At 1.10 pm, having now been endorsed as Labor leader three times in the last eighteen months—on 24 June 2010, after the 21 August 2010 election, and today—Gillard strides into a press conference disporting a straight back and a firm manner.

She is as magnanimous in victory as Rudd appears to present in defeat. She appeals to the community to get behind the government, pledging to get on with the job of governing the country. The leadership question is resolved, it's determined and the Australian people 'rightly expect government to focus on you, for you to be at the centre of everything that government does . . . this political drama is over'.

Gillard admits she should have explained to the electorate much earlier why Rudd was removed as prime minister. It was a mistake not to honour Rudd's achievements at the ALP National conference in December, but she does so now. And she sympathises with him at what she says must be a 'difficult and disappointing' time—a 'tough' day for the former prime minister, minister and now backbencher. Given how she's suffered from the slings and arrows of Rudd and his team over the last eighteen months, she is being gracious indeed.

And what of us in the fourth estate, those with the duty and responsibility to bring balanced news and commentary to the Australian public? Gillard responds with disdain to a question from the *Financial Review*'s Laura Tingle: 'I've seen estimates in newspapers that Kevin Rudd was very likely to win, Kevin Rudd was going to be supported by half the cabinet, Kevin Rudd was going to get forty-five votes and so on and so on and so on. Estimates here, estimates there; lists here, lists there. What we now know is the truth. Obviously my caucus colleagues have overwhelmingly endorsed me to continue to be Labor leader and Prime Minister. I asked them to give me that endorsement because of my strength and capacity and ability to do this job ... It's not easy for my caucus colleagues to give that endorsement in circumstances where everybody who likes to read the tea leaves of opinion polls is telling them to do something else. They've done that because of their sense of passion about the Labor purpose I have outlined for the future.'

Despite the media's blindness to Rudd's unrealistic and destructive need for redemption during the last eighteen months, there are now some for whom his generous concession speech and pledge of loyalty don't ring true.

Question: 'Mr Rudd hasn't renounced, as you asked him to, all future leadership ambitions—he's only said that he won't challenge you a second time. Doesn't that mean that his presence as the member for Griffith into the future is still sitting on the back bench as a reminder he may come forth again?'

PM: 'I don't think it's fair for to you to re-interpret Kevin Rudd's words. What he has just said is that I will have his strong support to take our party forward, take this government into an election in 2013 and to fight that election and win. That is what Kevin Rudd has said today.'

But what Kevin says and what he does are different things. Despite her decisive victory, Gillard should still beware of his hot breath on her neck. As long as Rudd is in parliament, there will be no rest for her and no stability for her government.

Tony Abbott needs little encouragement to reiterate his primary attack on Gillard: that she lacks the trust of the Australian people and they deserve another election. Now (pretty, pretty please)! It's an exhortation he's been repeating endlessly since he dealt himself out of minority government in August and September 2010, when his negotiating skills with the Independents were found wanting. In Question Time he springs to his feet to ask the Prime Minister the first, and obvious, question: 'Given that one-third of her parliamentary colleagues and a quarter of her cabinet colleagues have today expressed their lack of confidence in her, how can she claim to have a mandate to continue as prime minister?'

It's not a difficult question for someone who's just emerged from months of a blowtorch to the belly from her enemy within, even if Abbott has liberally enhanced the actual percentages of the caucus and ministry who supported Rudd (it was a shade over 28 per cent, not 33.3 per cent). A spirited Gillard reminds Abbott he only beat Malcolm Turnbull by one vote in the most recent of many Liberal leadership showdowns. Touché.

Abbott's pettiness is an irrelevance. All eyes in the press and public galleries are trained on One K. Rudd, just as he likes it. He's sitting on the backbench next to Labor's Anthony Byrne. He's grinning and joking, acting for all the world like God's in his heaven and all's well with the world. It's either the brave charade of a graceful loser, or else his love of the limelight has over-ridden his humiliation. Occasionally he glances down and a pensive look shadows his face, but just as quickly it's gone and the cheesy-grinned Rudd is back.

Leadership challenges can be anti-climactic: all that build-up, all that tension, a prolonged session of game-playing, then it's over in a flash. But with Rudd, it's never over. He's mesmerising to watch, but equally as mesmerising is trying to predict which Rudd persona will now prevail: the graceful loser who will pummel anyone who doesn't stand up for Julia, or the avenging angel who cannot forgive or move on. If the latter is still lurking beneath the cheery surface, a poll running for the last few hours in the *Brisbane Times* online—they're his people, in his state—should give him food for thought: two-thirds of respondents don't give a whit about the leadership battle—Labor will get walloped anyway.

Question Time ends at about 3.20 pm, and normality resumes—except for a brief interlude from Bruce Hawker, who blames the factions for railroading his man (wrong: the factions split), and who grudgingly tells journalists that he 'suspects' the only right thing to do is for the parliamentary party to pull behind Gillard because 'she is going so badly in public opinion polls, that if we don't do that we're heading for a disastrous defeat in the coming weeks, months or years'. It's a classic backhander from a sore loser.

But what about a gracious winner? Reality is suspended again when Sky News reports that Senator Mark Arbib is about to resign. Huh? The public face of the 'faceless men'—and after his girl won the leadership contest? Yep! The man who's allegedly been stacking two Sydney electorates so he can move to the House of Representatives and go to the top—Treasury was in his sights—and who only two months ago in the reshuffle pushed for and got higher duties as Assistant Treasurer, wants out for the sake of his family and to help the Labor Party heal and rebuild. That's his explanation, anyway. Clearly someone's spiked the water coolers in Parliament House.

It's 28 February and a line has been temporarily drawn in the sand. It's the reshuffle that's now motivating us reptiles of the political press—whether the ministers who strayed to Rudd will be punished, and who will get the plum job of the Foreign portfolio; the usual piffle that doesn't entrance the public.

When Fairfax's Phil Coorey breaks a hard-to-believe story on the *Sydney Morning Herald* website late morning, the twitching in the press gallery becomes convulsive. Another dose of show time! Someone—very, very short odds on a New South Wales Right operative—has planted a story that Bob Carr has been approached to take Arbib's Senate slot, and that he won't consider it unless he's given the coveted Foreign portfolio. With all the ambitious up-and-comers sloshing about inside the Labor Party, it defies belief that this sixty-four-year-old former premier of New South Wales—whose government, critics claim, nearly bankrupted the state while he was heading it for a decade from 1995 and had hidden within its ranks many a colourful character—could saunter into the Senate and one of the best federal portfolios on offer.

At a press conference about the roll-out of the national broadband network, Gillard is asked if it's true. She responds that Carr has indicated 'for a long period of time' that he's not interested. Sussex Street's head honcho, Sam Dastyari, tweets that, although New South Wales Labor would love to see Carr in the Senate, he has 'unfortunately' said no.

Hah! It must be true, then. Julia, what have you been led into—and after such a definitive victory?

PART TWO

THE FAILED
AVENGER

PART TWO

THE SECOND SACKIVERSARY

1–25 June 2012

It's official. Prime Minister Julia Gillard will be rolled by Kevin Rudd. We know this because we've been told so for three months by political journalists in Canberra, by 'specialist' political commentators who never turn up in parliament, by radio shock jocks in capital cities who never grace parliament's doors, and by a grab-bag of internet amateur scribes and conspiracy-peddlers who could be anywhere and who tell us so in their analysis of Gillard's second anniversary as prime minister.

If the chorus sounds drearily familiar, it's because time has marched on by a year, but the script has barely changed—only a few adjustments are necessary. As the Second Sackiversary draws near, Gillard is still a woman hunted and haunted by Rudd and his gang. The media is so fascinated by the former PM that he continues to dominate the media space, even though he has no ministry and no prospects of returning to his old job, despite his continuing aspirations. It seems immaterial to many in the commentariat that unemployment, inflation and official interest rates are now all under

5 per cent—a phenomenon not seen in Australia for forty years—or that Gillard and Treasurer Swan have achieved this despite the persistent headline distractions about Gillard's allegedly terminal leadership and Rudd's imminent resurrection.

Phillip Coorey at the *Sydney Morning Herald* gets in very early on the Sackiversary Mark Two celebrations by publishing his views about where things stand Labor leadership-wise almost two weeks beforehand, on 11 June. Again, the sense of *déjà vu* is mind-bending. He predicts the week beginning 24 June will be a critical and fraught one for Gillard—she will return from a heavy international trip of important meetings, where Australia's economic and environmental credentials will be feted, to what? Drum roll: '. . . reminders of her second anniversary in the papers, all bound to stir leadership talk. Rather than bask in the adulation for Australia she would have witnessed abroad, one of her main tasks will be to ensure she is leader when the week ends.' Back to the real business of governing, then.

The new deadline for her prime ministership? Well, for Coorey it's a case of pick-a-date. He reckons that if she's not gone by the end of the week, 'there could be a move in late August, when Parliament resumes, or the more traditional December. Yet no one in the Rudd camp will guarantee that nothing will happen in that last week of June.' Apparently the bovver boys at New South Wales head office are restless. It stands to reason, I guess: with Labor out of government in New South Wales there aren't any of their own premiers to organise coups against, so the feds will just have to do.

But wait, there's more! The Rudd camp is relying on an old favourite. 'Natural momentum will continue to grow,' one Ruddster confides to Coorey—or perhaps he's just played the ol' broken record down the phone. 'These things are hard to control,' the record scratches out.

Ah, sweet memories of the Momentum Waltz! And didn't it work a treat for Rudd last year? One of Coorey's final observations is this: 'The Rudd camp hopes Gillard will get the message and walk because no one wants another challenge.' He should have added: 'Least of all Rudd, whose supporters would fit inside a telephone booth.'

It doesn't matter where Gillard turns, Rudd and his team are there: watching, planning, whispering. Behind the scenes, Gillard continues to lead the ongoing negotiations with the Independents over most legislation her government intends to introduce, resulting in a remarkably stable minority parliament with an impressive legislative output. The sheer force of the wall of criticism meted out to her in daily media digests must addle her ability to stay on track, but surely nothing in the media compares to treachery within your own ranks. When Robert McClelland rises to his feet in parliament on 21 June and resurrects the seventeen-year-old Australian Workers' Union (AWU) affair that News Ltd publications have tried previously to use against the Prime Minister, the term 'rats in the ranks' doesn't do his actions justice.

Under cover of parliament and ostensibly speaking to the Fair Work Bill, McClelland makes a thinly veiled reference to an issue involving Gillard and her former boyfriend Bruce Wilson, at that time an official of the AWU who was suspected of embezzlement and fraud. Gillard, then a lawyer at Slater & Gordon, had been providing legal advice to Wilson and the AWU from time to time.

Former Attorney-General McClelland starts by making a plea for the Bill to be strengthened—to increase penalties and give union members a way of triggering investigations if they suspect corruption.

'Officers have sought to obtain personal benefit or benefit on behalf of others at the expense of members of their union,' he tells the House of Representatives. 'Reported instances include not only misapplying funds and resources of the union, but also using the privileges of their office to attract and obtain services and benefits from third parties. Aside from issues of profiteering, secret commissions and tax avoidance, these undeclared benefits can compromise officials. Rather than diligently representing the interests of their members without fear or favour, they effectively "run dead" as a result of these side deals. This is no less than graft and corruption in its most reprehensible form, and it occurs at the expense of vulnerable members whose interests they have been charged with representing.'

McClelland then winds Gillard into his narrative: 'To borrow the words of Prime Minister Gillard, she said on ABC Radio on 9 May of this year: "Let me say I never want to see a dollar that a worker gives a union used for any purpose other than the proper purposes of representing that union member's best interests." Indeed, I know the Prime Minister is quite familiar with this area of the law; as lawyers in the mid 1990s we were involved in a matter representing opposing clients. Indeed, my involvement in that matter has coloured much of my thinking in this area and resulted in me moving amendments on 17 September 2002 to actually strengthen the powers of the Federal Court of Australia.'

McClelland makes another oblique reference to the Wilson dispute: 'As I mentioned, these issues also arose in those matters that I was involved with in the mid 1990s, which were filed in both the then Industrial Court of Australia and the Federal Court of Australia. There are a number of matters, generally under the name of Ludwig and Harrison and others, but probably most relevantly matter number 1032 of 1996.'

A few vague references is all it takes. A remarkably well-briefed Andrew Bolt of the *Herald-Sun*, one of the loudest of the anti-Gillard media mouths, immediately airs the yarn on the newspaper's website. The following day, the *Australian Financial Review* has the story; and in the Senate, the Coalition's George Brandis, also extremely well briefed, and Barnaby Joyce, again extraordinarily well informed about the goings-on at a union nearly two decades ago, use the Senate to all but accuse the Prime Minster of complicity in her old flame's corrupt activities.

Brandis also raises a curious question, with an obvious answer: What is McClelland up to? 'One can but wonder why it is that Mr McClelland, as a backbench member of the government, chose to draw attention to those matters from the 1990s—matters concerning which, as a solicitor, he had direct and thorough knowledge. One can but wonder why, in particular, Mr McClelland chose, in a very pointed way, to throw a spotlight on the Prime Minister's knowledge of those matters,' he muses to the Senate. One can indeed wonder why. That McClelland is a seriously disgruntled dumped minister with both feet now firmly in the Rudd camp surely has nothing to do with his contribution to this debate. Is it just another of those strange coincidences that keep tripping up the Prime Minister? No: one of Gillard's stalkers has become more visible.

News Ltd's Samantha Maiden tells us on the actual Second Sackiversary, 24 June, that Rudd has been spotted pumping iron in the parliamentary gym, which has been interpreted by some parliamentarians as a sure-fire indication he's limbering up for another go at the leadership. They must be some serious oddballs—maybe they think Rudd means to knock Gillard out, which is the only way he'll ever get his old job back.

But back to the main yarn, where Rudd's dogged and desperate gang of troublemakers has told Maiden that Kev's comeback is on track because the PM's just lost another fifteen supporters. In a feedback echo from many similar stories published in other media outlets over the last year, enthralled readers are informed that Victorian and New South Wales right-wingers have split and half of them have gone over to the former prime minister. Now an August strike against Gillard is the new deadline. But, gosh, poor Kev would be a 'reluctant' challenger, Team Rudd murmurs to Maiden. You have to feel sorry for the guy: all he's ever really, really wanted to do is rescue the government and return it to those days of calm, steady, functioning administration he steered so luminously during his time as leader.

Dressed neatly in a blue and white tracksuit, Kev was inspecting housing for the homeless in his home town of Brissie two days ago when Maiden, with a photographer in tow, was dead lucky enough to catch up with him. He'd just spent another selfless night sleeping rough with the country's most influential, politically valuable chief executive officers so he could raise money for St Vincent de Paul. (Odd that—I thought he'd dumped the Catholics for the more socially useful Anglicans. But I guess the C of E doesn't have anything to match this super-networking gig.) 'Slept with 150 CEOs last night' he Twitter-boasts, 'exhausting . . . but raised a lot of money for Vinnies!' Stop it, Kev—you're making us weep! He refused to respond to Maiden's leadership questions, she reports, but her 24 June story is all about leadership, anonymously sourced from people clearly close to Kev and rounded out with juicy information from deep inside the Rudd bunker.

Let's rewind and recall an episode leading up to Gillard's first anniversary as PM. On her First Sackiversary, I noted: 'Rudd, who on this chill June night has just martyred himself by participating in the annual St Vinnies CEO sleep-out, emerges remarkably quickly once the newspapers have hit the newsstands in order to talk to ABC *Breakfast*. He's decked out in a humble blue and white tracksuit and sporting a wee hint of homeless stubble. Reports of a feud with Gillard were a fabrication and those speculating about it should take a Mogadon, he instructs . . . And, no, he's not challenging the Prime Minister. Cue laugh out loud from the prime ministerial suite.' The more things change the more they stay remarkably the same, for some people.

Over at the *Sunday Age*, Misha Schubert pumps up the line that sixteen Gillardites may have drifted (clearly briefed by the same Ruddsters as Maiden), but qualifies it with the observation that '. . . convincing a demoralised caucus to take another leap of faith (especially after how the last one turned out) takes some doing'. Schubert's assessment of the leadership situation is measured: 'Several Gillard backers conceded the caucus mood was grim but insisted only a handful of MPs would actually be prepared to cast a different vote right now. "There's a bit of despair about our position, but the bulk of the people who supported Julia last time haven't moved," said one. "Without a major defection or two, they just can't make it happen." Many of those eager for a Rudd reprise also conceded the momentum for change was not evident this week.' Bad luck for Julia; her longevity is now being assessed on a week-by-week basis. But a thought: with business as usual, with nothing changing, with nobody drifting, with no real or confected leadership tension in the air—why is this a story?

An anniversary wouldn't be any kind of celebration without a Newspoll and the ponderings of Dennis Shanahan, which the *Australian* bowls up on Monday 25 June under the gleeful headline:

'ALP still down, two years after Rudd hit'. The government's support continues to 'wallow' below the levels recorded before the 'coup that removed the first-time prime minister', Shanahan tuts. It grinds on for twenty-three wretched paragraphs about how dismal Labor's vote is, what a wreck the party is, how nothing Labor does is going to shift the vote, and: 'As parliament prepares for the final week of sitting before the winter break—the period Mr Rudd was rolled in 2010—speculation continues within Labor ranks that Ms Gillard will be removed before the end of the year, and that Mr Rudd is the logical replacement because of his public popularity.' Before the end of the year! That's a lot of caucus meetings between now and then to talk up.

Strip away the massaging of the message, however, and there's one fundamental in the Newspoll: Labor's primary vote is about the same in this poll as it has been in the last few polls. So no story on the two-party-preferred front. But there is something new—another time limit on her leadership. 'Before the end of the year' is a bit generous, though, but it does give Shanahan plenty of wiggle room to adjust the deadline if need be.

How did the media get stuck on repeat? A mere four months ago, on 27 February, Gillard won a record-smashing victory over Rudd in a party room ballot. The margin of seventy-one to thirty-one was the biggest victory in four decades of Labor leadership stoushes, but Gillard's legitimacy was questioned immediately. A fair swag of senior journalists either weren't willing to believe she'd been voted by her caucus as a prime minister worth keeping, or were unhappy at the outcome of the ballot. And in their eyes, she committed sins.

The first one was on Friday 2 March, when she strode into the parliamentary prime ministerial press conference room with former

New South Wales premier Bob Carr at her side and announced he would be the Senate replacement for Mark Arbib—and the next Foreign minister, to boot.

This was an idea floated with Gillard by the boss of the Sussex Street machine, Sam Dastyari, after Arbib sensationally quit on the same day as February's leadership ballot. It seemed such an unlikely and audacious move, because of Carr's chequered reputation, because of the questions it raised about the motives of New South Wales head office, and because it would mean the much-prized Foreign portfolio would be flicked to an outsider when Gillard had many capable people eager to fill the slot.

So when Dastyari denied the initial media reports about the move, revealed by Phillip Coorey in the *Sydney Morning Herald* the day after Arbib resigned, he was believed. Journalists at the time should have realised the opposite was indeed true, because in New South Wales ALP-speak denial usually turns out to be confirmation. Gillard had also denied the report; at the time, she was speaking the truth. There'd been instant internal push back against the idea from senior colleagues when it was raised by Gillard on the day Arbib quit; as a result, she had temporarily shelved the plan. But after the idea of the 'elder statesman' bolstering her firepower with his polished media persona and long-standing interest in and knowledge of foreign affairs continued to be an attractive option, Gillard stared down the disgruntled in her ministry, notably Simon Crean and to a lesser extent Stephen Smith, both of whom didn't want the plum ministry going to an 'outsider'. After over-ruling them, she charmed Carr only the day before their joint press conference into joining her Senate team and ministry.

It was messy, but it was an outcome Gillard wanted and she exerted her authority to achieve it. But in that period between the initial media reports and the Gillard–Carr press conference, press gallery journalists rushed to condemn the PM's lack of judgement and authority, even though she was still in the planning stages of her reshuffle and Arbib's replacement was still being decided.

The *Australian*'s Dennis Shanahan slammed Gillard on 29 February: 'The authority conferred on Julia Gillard through her crushing victory over Kevin Rudd as Labor leader has lasted less than 24 hours. The Prime Minister is too weakened to act as leader and can't stop potentially disastrous decisions and campaigns of retribution by factional leaders and ambitious ministers.' Coorey joined in on 1 March: 'A bungled attempt to woo Bob Carr to Canberra to serve as foreign minister has raised fresh concerns about Julia Gillard's authority, just days after her resounding victory in the leadership ballot.'

And on the morning of the joint press conference, gallery heavy-hitters were searing about Gillard's total lack of authority and political nous. Lectured Michelle Grattan in the *Age*: 'The aborted attempt to get Bob Carr into Parliament turned an opportunity into an own goal.' Thundered Simon Benson in the *Daily Telegraph*: 'The events of past days have exposed the Prime Minister as lacking any authority or political judgment. How she could botch this beggars belief. Carr could have been the injection of intellectual capital, statesmanship and political commonsense that the Gillard government needed to turn around its political misfortunes.' Shanahan rounded out the condemnation: 'Julia Gillard's ability to turn good news—a brilliant political strategy, a poignant moment, or an opportunity to become strong, credible and assertive—into bad news and dumb politics appears to be boundless.'

The day after Carr's appointment was announced the *mea culpa*s were grudging. Grattan led with a backhanded acknowledgement:

'Julia Gillard has pulled out a sensational reshuffle trump card, recruiting former New South Wales premier Bob Carr to add lustre to her government as Australia's new foreign minister. Ms Gillard *belatedly* [emphasis added] decided to ignore the claims of Defence Minister Stephen Smith . . .'

Coorey was magnanimous, but attempted to cover the gallery's collective arse for rushing to judgement: 'Bob Carr is headed to Canberra as the next minister for foreign affairs after Julia Gillard reasserted her leadership and overrode internal objections to recruiting the former NSW premier. In a coup that shocked all but her closest colleagues . . .'

And Shanahan was still lecturing: 'Julia Gillard arrived at the right decision to appoint Bob Carr as foreign minister after going about it the wrong way for the wrong reasons. How it will all turn out is still unclear but the Prime Minister has undoubtedly regained lost ground and authority in the past 48 hours.' But Shanahan is not inclined to let Gillard off the hook; he continued: 'The brutal reality is that Gillard has put her leadership on the line by appointing Carr, but the brutal corollary was her leadership was finished if she hadn't.' This is such a jaw-dropping conclusion it defies analysis.

It was left to gallery guru Laurie Oakes in the News Ltd tabloids to give Gillard points for political acuity and authority. 'That's one for the books. Julia Gillard unbotches something. Turns failure into success instead of the other way around . . . For days the PM had been lambasted in Parliament and the media for weakness because she had allegedly allowed a few senior ministers—particularly Defence Minister Stephen Smith—to veto the recruitment of Carr. But suddenly on Thursday she discovered a spine—and a bit of political nous—and decided to revive Plan

A despite the opposition from her colleagues. It was a show of strength.'

Gillard got a few other noses out of joint with her reshuffle. Supporter Joel Fitzgibbon, who some colleagues suspected had briefly flirted with the Rudd experiment in February before sticking with Gillard, was not a happy Vegemite at all when he was offered and rejected what he considered a junior portfolio too lowly for his talents. Somebody should have reminded Gillard that it's perilous to let a New South Wales right-winger walk away shitty from negotiations about jobs and perks, but that's what happened with Fitzgibbon, an MP who has no fear of the media and a sound knowledge of the way messages can be planted and spread, even if he often leaves his paw prints on his work. Then there was former minister and Rudd supporter Robert McClelland, who was left without a ministry to bless himself with. In the space of three months he'd gone from the dizzy heights of being attorney-general; through a demotion in the December reshuffle to the stitched-together portfolio of Emergency Management, Housing and Homelessness; finally landing with a thud and sweet FA in March. He was perhaps the unhappiest of all the unhappy little Vegemites who'd set up at the Team Rudd campsite.

For any other prime minister, making choices about ministers is seen as routine business. For Gillard, the media and political temperature was still ratcheted so high that all her decisions and actions were viewed through the prism of the perceived quality of her leadership, which for more than a year detractors in her own ranks and the media had mercilessly found wanting. As News Ltd's Malcolm Farr tartly noted: 'The Gillard prime ministership is like a badly scalded arm. The mildest touch can cause pain way out of proportion to the force behind the blow. Even when she does nothing unusual, remarkable or even particularly clumsy, the Government ends up screaming in agony.'

And scream in agony it did on 24 March, when Anna Bligh and her state Labor government were swept away on a tidal wave of hostility from Queensland voters at the state election. Campbell Newman's Liberal National Party snagged a staggering seventy-five seats, leaving Labor with just seven, which didn't even give it official party status.

Rudd had campaigned vigorously for his 'good friend' Anna; he had been the most visible federal parliamentarian on the hustings, blitzing seats and kicking up a media storm. He'd tried to use his campaigning for Bligh as a de facto campaign for his own return to the leadership, ahead of a ballot he'd wanted after the March state election but ended up with in February. He'd been endlessly photographed as he was mobbed up hill and down dale. Oh, look—that apron does look fetching, so photogenic!—as he was furiously snapped at community barbecues. What about a street walk? By all means! And look how many voters and microphones are trailing me!

After all that mighty effort, not one dividend was reaped. Rudd had been routed in the February contest; Bligh had been super routed in the March competition. Life can most definitely be unfair sometimes, bugger it.

It was Gillard, of course, who endured the savaging after the Queensland debacle, notwithstanding that she'd only stepped across the border once during the campaign and that the voters there had let it be known for at least a year they intended to pick Bligh and her ratty team up by the scruff of their necks and hurl them into oblivion. However, inconvenient truths do not sell papers down south—flagellating Gillard does. 'If Julia Gillard were a coal miner, her canaries would not just be dead—they would be dead, buried and cremated,' pronounced Coorey in the *Sydney Morning Herald*. 'Julia Gillard's party is just about over as Labor routed in Queensland' screamed the *Daily Tele* headline over a florid piece by Gemma Jones.

The bottom line from Graham Richardson in the *Australian* was that, like Bligh, Gillard was a liar and would go the way of her female state counterpart. And, of course, they both have Trouble with Blokes, he asserted. 'One other factor for the PM to consider is that both she and Bligh have a problem with men. More specifically, men have a problem with them.' So if men have a problem with strong female leaders that's the woman's problem, right, Richo? You gotta love the Aussie male logic; it is so enlightened.

And Kev? Despite being the most popular politician in the Sunshine State, despite lending his considerable weight to Bligh's campaign, despite campaigning his active little arse off for a few months for his gal pal, he got off scot free. Indeed, Team Rudd was whispering in the ears of federal reporters that the five seats that fell within Rudd's boundaries had recorded less of a dramatic swing than across the rest of the state.

But a rout is a rout by any other name, and no amount of message massaging could make it anything other than one of the greatest collective middle-finger thrusts from voters in Australian political history, even surpassing the thumping the toxic New South Wales Labor government received at the hands of angry voters the previous year.

And then there was April. Capital A for Awful. The month can be summed up with two dynamite names: Craig Thomson, Peter Slipper. On 3 April, Fair Work Australia concluded its drawn-out three-year inquiry into Thomson's use of a union credit card when he was boss of the Health Services Union before entering parliament in 2007. It found 181 alleged misuses of union rules and workplace laws but it didn't release the report, and it wouldn't say who was responsible for the significant number of transgressions. Regardless, the pressure increased on Thomson—and on Gillard, who had heroically misplaced her loyalties in standing by Thomson since the furore around his spending habits erupted last year.

Then there was Peter—ah, the Trouble with Pete! When Labor vaulted him into the Speaker's chair in November, in a risky political move intended to subtract a precious vote from the Coalition's count, Slipper's enemies within his party—of which there were and remain many—privately vowed he and the government would pay for their treachery. Happily (and surely purely coincidentally) Slipper was blindsided on 21 April by allegations of sexual harassment and fraudulent use of commonwealth car entitlements.

On the afternoon of 20 April former Slipper staffer James Ashby filed a statement of claim in the Federal Court alleging the misconduct by the Speaker. The following day in the *Daily Telegraph*, in another surprisingly handy coincidence, Canberra-based journalist Steve Lewis had a string of exclusives on all the implications of the court action. He provided the background to the case, chockersfull of spicy details that could only have been gathered days, even weeks, before publication.

Lewis' comment piece kicked off with the understated observation that: 'Julia Gillard is facing a grave crisis that threatens to derail her government's already slender grip on national power. In the history of Australian political crises, the allegations filed in court against Peter Slipper are among the most serious ever raised—and they rank as potentially deadly.' Slipper had no intimation of the court documents before they were published in the *Tele*; he was overseas on a delegation, and was thoroughly and comprehensively ambushed by both Ashby and the newspaper.

Within two days Slipper stood aside as Speaker to defend himself. At the same time Thomson was feeling the media and political blowtorch over his alleged union credit-card spending habits. Despite no charges being levelled against him, on 29 April Gillard insisted that he quit the Labor Party and sit on the cross benches. Her disbelieved explanation was that a 'line in the sand' had been crossed. Down goes another vote for the government; up goes another black mark for Gillard; out goes another call from Team Rudd to impugn the PM's integrity.

The combination of the Craig and Peter troubles prompted a torrent of fury from Canberra's media elite. Given that Gillard had been overwhelmingly endorsed as PM a bare eight weeks before and the option of revisiting that decision any time soon was beyond silly, the press gallery, urged on by ever-avenging Ruddster angels, was now demanding her head. And what a similar chorus they sang after thorough briefings by Team Rudd.

No prizes for guessing which publication led the charge, with a colossal overkill penned by its best and brightest. And of course Rudd's man in the Fairfax foxhole did his bit for the cause too, together with a not-so-recent convert to the vitriolic anti-Gillard camp, the queen bee of the press gallery, Michelle Grattan, who turned positively feral.

Here are snippets from the verdicts of the gallery. In a crowd surge attack, all were published on 30 April:

Troy Bramston, *Australian*: 'Concerns about Julia Gillard's handling of the Peter Slipper and Craig Thomson scandals have refreshed leadership speculation as Labor MPs fear a massive loss of seats at the next election . . . Although a leadership putsch is not under way, Rudd's backers are assessing his support for a new leadership tilt.'

Peter van Onselen, *Australian*: 'Kevin Rudd is firming for another shot at the prime ministership. It has happened because Gillard backers can no longer see how she will rise in the polls. Saving seats is the mantra. Some of the Prime Minister's closest supporters are withdrawing their veto of a return by Rudd, prepared to tolerate its inevitability even if they won't withdraw support for Gillard. That's how Gillard's demise is being described, as "inevitable".'

Dennis Shanahan, *Australian*: 'Australia is facing a crisis of confidence that is affecting the economy, and the actions of Julia Gillard have made this crisis worse. While the Gillard government still hangs by a tangled thread, the nation's broader political and economic life is ebbing away.'

Chris Kenny, *Australian*: 'Julia Gillard's terminal government will go down in history as an ill-conceived, shambolic and dysfunctional administration. All that remains to be known is when it draws its last breath and whether Gillard, or another martyr, will be at the helm.'

Phillip Hudson, *Herald-Sun*: 'The dark clouds Julia Gillard sees over the Parliament are the clouds over her Government, her leadership and her integrity.'

Peter Hartcher, *Sydney Morning Herald*: 'It's because of this transparent insincerity that the electorate gives her no credit even when she does do the right thing. Gillard's government is in dire condition because the Prime Minister fundamentally lacks the trust of the Australian people. This act of political "tricksmanship" will help her with short-term political management but do absolutely nothing to build trust. Quite the contrary. Julia Gillard unwittingly forces the Labor caucus to consider, once again, its most uncomfortable dilemma—likely destruction at the polls, or a gamble on Kevin Rudd as leader.'

Michelle Grattan, *Age*: 'Julia Gillard should consider falling on her sword for the good of the Labor Party, because she can no longer present an even slightly credible face at the election. Her spectacular U-turn on everything she'd said before on Craig Thomson and Peter Slipper has left her looking nakedly expedient, and further exposed the state of crisis within the government.'

Richo of course weighed in with another prediction that Gillard wouldn't last a month, and former Liberal PM John Howard also predicted her demise. Given how authoritative his comments were made to sound, you'd have been forgiven for thinking he'd sat in on many Labor caucus meetings and regularly hobnobbed with Labor decision-makers. All this hissy fitting, dummy spitting, conjecture and rage was underpinned, as usual, by Newspoll figures: Labor's primary vote was under 30 per cent. But the election was . . . hmm—a good sixteen months away, if the parliament went full term.

Polls are at best a feeble snapshot of erratic voter sentiment at any given point, heavily influenced by the presentation in the media of the government and its leader's performance. Labor's figures were indeed tracking poorly, but the public was seeing little of the real stuff of government and Gillard's deft steerage of the minority parliament. What they were being fed was chaos, stuff-ups and a woman who had little capacity to govern and no political nous. And polls sixteen months out from an election have little relevance to the way voters will think at the actual election time.

Gillard did stumble badly by backing Thomson, but she wasn't the one who re-endorsed him in 2010 for his seat of Dobell—that was the decision of the funsters at New South Wales headquarters and his pre-selectors. And she wasn't the only one involved in promoting Slipper to the Speaker's chair—that was a collegiate decision by Labor's strategy team. If Gillard's political smarts were so weak, how had she outsmarted her stalker so comprehensively just eight weeks before the disasters of Thomson and Slipper collided so brutally in awful April?

The month concluded on a classy high note when former adviser to John Howard, Grahame Morris, a political lobbyist and right-wing political commentator on Sky News, declared on the channel's *Afternoon Agenda* program that Gillard should be 'kicked to death'. It didn't cause a ripple in mainstream medialand, but the Twitterverse lit up with indignation on Gillard's behalf.

The merry month of May started the way it finished: with leadership speculation drowning out worthier subjects. The media mindset, which lumbers Gillard with sole responsibility for the sins of Thomson and Slipper, took hold as the dubious duo sustained their headline acts day in, day out.

The *Australian* set the tone early, on 2 May, when it gave Gillard only 'a few weeks' before caucus acted. 'Senior members of the faction that blocked a Rudd return and ridiculed his failed leadership bid in February [the very chatty New South Wales right wing] now concede that he is a plausible leadership alternative and that sentiment is strongly shifting in his favour,' wrote Sid Maher and former Rudd staffer Troy Bramston. 'The shift came as numerous Labor figures told *The Australian* they believed it was "inevitable" that Labor would dump the Prime Minister, but predicted the dispirited caucus would not act for several weeks amid faint hopes that next Tuesday's federal budget would restore Labor's fortunes.' Graham Richardson backed it up the following day in the same newspaper in a scathing critique of the PM's personality and performance, concluding: 'Gillard is one move away from checkmate.'

The *Australian Financial Review* gave Gillard a bit more time. On 3 May Gemma Daley, channelling Team Rudd, allowed the PM until the end of June to single-handedly lift Labor's stocks from the poll doldrums. On 7 May, the *Herald-Sun*'s Phillip Hudson gave Gillard a new, very Melbourne-centric deadline: she had 'until the AFL football finals in September' to lift her game and Labor's polling figures or she'd be booted out of The Lodge by her colleagues.

Readers of these newspapers must wonder if there are any brave, collegiate souls left in the Labor caucus; this is the party that prides itself on shared responsibility and team work, yet it seems as far as the current Labor Party is concerned, the press believes the leader must carry the government and party entirely on her own while limp ministers and backbenchers sit on their haunches and watch.

The 2012 budget was quintessential Labor and received mild applause from the commentariat, but Gillard couldn't hold a press conference on it, or on any other policy matter, without being swamped by leadership questions. The momentum that Team Rudd so loved to generate as its chief weapon of war against the Prime Minister was again in play thanks to over-heated media concentration on what were perceived as deep prime ministerial flaws.

By month's end, News Ltd's Samantha Maiden has the Ruddites back counting numbers—led by chief whip Joel Fitzgibbon, who is again suspected of throwing his swag down at Team Rudd headquarters. Fitzgibbon publicly denied the report, tweeting: 'I thank my colleagues for the publicity but no one does more to support the PM and the government than me!' As he hails from the New South Wales Right, this was surely confirmation that he was helping Team Rudd muster forces for another crack by their boy at Gillard.

Then there was June and the second anniversary of Gillard's succession, and a pasting by the press and a stealth attack by one of her former ministers. No wonder she chose to go overseas on government business instead of spending the weekend of her second anniversary as prime minister wading through the usual news treacle of leadership speculation.

NO REST FOR THE WICKED
July–December 2012

On her second anniversary as prime minister, we left the redhead strapped to the railway tracks as the Rudd engine hurtled down the line, Captain Kevin cheerily yelling 'Choo-choo!' Meanwhile a gaggle of journalists and Team Ruddsters were furiously shovelling coal into the furnace. And now they are joined in their exuberant efforts by Kev's media-savvy family.

Therese Rein makes another of her regular interventions into Kevin's world when she coyly suggests, in a soft interview with Fairfax journalist Deborah Snow early in July, that her husband would be prepared to serve again. Only for the national good, of course. Because leadership isn't about yourself. It's the second time in a month that Therese has opined about Kevin, The Lodge, the past and the future. 'Is it [supporting him in that role again] something I would do?' she appears to think out loud to Snow. 'I don't know. But if I ever agreed to do that, it would be on the proviso that it was completely about the country, the national good, Australia's place in the world and the people who have, over many years now, told me, "Look, we're vulnerable on this or we're hurting on that, and things need to be better".'

Such bon mots from Team Rudd are sprinkled like droplets of acid rain at all the right times. Gillard is making a mess of it and we need Kevin back to clean up the mess is the message. Greens leader Christine Milne suggests: 'This is Team Rudd letting everybody know that Kevin is ready to be begged to take it on.'

A week later another Rudd joins in the merriment, bless his cotton socks. Come on down—brother, Greg! Eyeing off a career for himself in the Senate, Kevin's older brother joins the conga line of crystal-ball-gazers. The clairvoyant tells us that the Labor Party will make the decision over Christmas to return his brother to the prime ministership. 'It is very much still in internal discussion mode, but it is ramping up.' So we noticed.

But that isn't the surprising bit. In a refreshingly frank assessment of his sibling, he says Kevin will not forgive those who plotted against him. 'Hell hath no fury,' he confides. Hallelujah! Someone who knows Rudd outside the political context is giving us a glimpse into his world.

Next up is daughter, Jessica—telegenic, smart and, like her dad, in love with the media limelight. She gave birth to daughter Josephine in May, and pics of the happy extended family are now beaming out from newspapers. There's also a joyful splash in the *Women's Weekly*, where proud new grandpa Kevin speaks coyly about his ambitions—sorry, about the newest member of the Rudd clan. 'I suppose what I'm saying through all that is: when you see this little possum . . . you think of where she'll be beyond that and what sort of Australia and what sort of world she lives in.' And what does this mean for you, Kev? 'Without wanting to sound too sort of pious about it all, you just have a keen eye to where will the country be in half a century's time when this little one's contemplating grandchildren.' Pass the bloody tissues! Gillard's loyal colleagues are now on red alert: Rudd the pursuer is running a little faster.

Then there's Rudd's wider political family, doggedly doing its bit for the patriarch. Joel Fitzgibbon—still sweating and smarting over his demoted stature within the government—idly speculates that any leader (that's you, Julia) suffering poor polling for an extended period is in for the chop if the poll numbers don't improve. 'No matter what political party you're talking about, if leaders remain unpopular long enough they'll inevitably stop leading the party,' he says on the ABC's *Q&A* on 16 July. He goes on to emphasise the message in an ABC radio interview the following morning, despite having received a hostile reaction from some of his ministerial colleagues to his artlessly freewheeling commentary. 'I was just speaking the truth and stating the obvious!' he wails innocently. 'No political leader can stay on low polling numbers forever!' Yes they can—if you keep talking them down, they can do it easily.

And then there's that other venomous grumbler, Robert McClelland—like Fitzgibbon, forever looking back with vengeful pining to his glory days. On 14 July he re-stokes the fire under the old Australian Workers Union (AWU) affair in an interview with the *Australian*'s chief investigative head-kicker, Hedley Thomas. Archived documents have miraculously fallen into Thomas's lap. His story, which takes up most of page 3, is provocatively headlined 'How Robert McClelland led pursuit in union funds scandal' and is sprinkled with documents detailing McClelland's historical advice. They reveal his role as a solicitor in the 1990s, when he was pitted against Gillard in a legal saga involving her then boyfriend Bruce Wilson. But the allegations of misappropriation of union funds against Wilson never progressed to charges. Wilson has always vigorously denied any wrongdoing and Gillard has also vehemently denied she had any knowledge of Wilson's financial circumstances. Both denials are contained in the story, although the thrust of Thomas's narrative ignores that.

Creeps on the internet, such as Larry Pickering, have been spewing bile about Gillard and the AWU for months. They have gathered supporters and spawned similarly disturbing websites, sprouting outrageously misogynistic and defamatory allegations against the PM, usually showcasing sickening anti-Gillard cartoons.

Oh, and the carbon pricing scheme has now been part of Australians' lives for a month. Nobody seems to have noticed except maybe Tony Abbott, whose face is coated in egg-wash.

In a 20 July article on The Drum, the ABC's online opinion and analysis portal, *Insiders* host Barrie Cassidy identifies a strange, infectious disease gripping the Canberra media, writing that at least 80 per cent of the Canberra press gallery would at this point predict Gillard wouldn't last until year's end: 'But that kind of mind set has a self-fulfilling prophecy to it. The journalists don't want to be wrong, whether they make the predictions in public or in private conversations among their peers. They become willing participants in what to many of them is the only game in town . . . The fear is that if you don't support the concept of a challenge, then you will miss the story.'

There's a common theme to the mantra being chanted by the leading opinion-shapers in the media: Gillard is on borrowed time, yet Rudd won't challenge and he wants the job handed back to him. But this is actually the Team Rudd manifesto; its strategy is to destabilise, undermine and wreck Gillard's leadership and drive the government's polling numbers down until panicky caucus members flock to the former prime minister.

Before February's challenge, the message had been that the caucus numbers were gathering in ever-increasing numbers for Rudd; of course, he wanted the prime ministership gifted back to him, but he was also prepared to get it back by challenging if he had the support to win. But in the phase we're now in, there's a subtly tweaked difference; Kevin must be seen as being absolutely oblivious to the activities and even the existence of the Restore Rudd Movement. Incredibly, the pretence is that the movement is operating entirely under its own momentum while its principal sits humming to himself in the eye of the storm, as a kind of human embodiment of the three wise monkeys—hearing no evil, speaking no evil and seeing no evil. Ultimately, the script goes, Kevin the reluctant saviour will be prevailed upon to step in and rescue the government—because the PM is lacking authority, she's hopeless, and the government is chaotic and lacking purpose.

Matthew Franklin in the *Australian* succinctly outlines the strategy on 24 July: 'With Julia Gillard having promised a recovery in opinion polls from the horrific 30 per cent level after the intro-duction of the carbon tax at the start of this month, Rudd supporters insist that, when there is no recovery, the Prime Minister must fall on her sword "for the good of the party". Then, so goes the grand plan, the party can prevail upon the former leader, who has vowed not to challenge Gillard, to take over and prevent the embarrassing rout that Labor is facing.'

By the end of the month the *Australian*'s oracle, Paul Kelly, has decided that 'public destabilisation of Julia Gillard's leader-ship is institutionalised'. But the last word for the month must go to Malcolm Turnbull, himself a victim of a leadership putsch by

Tony Abbott in 2009. Turnbull muses on his blog on 28 July: 'We have fewer reporters than we used to, at least in the Canberra press gallery, but for all one would know there is just one revolving, recycling, never-ending story—and that, of course, is Rudd v. Gillard . . . Is the obsession with this story preventing our hard working political writers from pursuing other issues?'

Sometimes the polls don't run to script. On 7 August, a Newspoll finds Labor's numbers have climbed five percentage points to a six-month high of 33 per cent. It's easy to see why—Matthew Franklin tells us the PM has been on holidays, and Aussies are focused on the London Olympics. Further into the story, he mentions that something did happen politically. What was it now? Oh yes, during the previous week the Prime Minister convinced five states to join with the Commonwealth in a trial of the National Disability Insurance Scheme—a policy that, when it was originally announced as a concept, received wide acclaim.

This significant achievement by Gillard rates a mere one-line mention and yet it was a formidable feat, given that she clinched agreements with the conservative governments of New South Wales and Victoria. Much more important for the *Australian* is that: 'The Newspoll comes amid ongoing tension over the Labor leadership, with critics of the Prime Minister within the Labor caucus pressing colleagues to accept that she will never lift the vote out of the doldrums and urging them to draft former leader Kevin Rudd to save their seats before the next election, due in the second half of next year.' But surely she has just lifted the vote out of the doldrums? My mistake—it was *the Olympics* that did that.

But for once it's not the polling that's getting the journalists at the *Australian* all hot and bothered. Hedley Thomas is back on the

AWU trail and over the next three weeks he pens eight prominent yarns—slithering and sliding every which way, hinting at the possible complicity of Gillard in the allegedly nefarious financial transactions of her former union boyfriend. On 18 and 19 August, in its weekend edition and on *Australian Agenda*—the newspaper's own one-hour Sunday morning program on Sky News, fronted by its key journalists, including Paul Kelly—the paper's attack intensifies. 'I did nothing wrong Paul, have you got an allegation to put to me? If you do not, why are we discussing this?' Gillard robustly challenges Kelly. And then on 23 August, after suffering a few days of reprimand from the *Australian*, from other journalists and from some Opposition MPs for having the temerity to confront the Oracle, she fronts a press conference in Canberra. After initially discussing asylum seekers, she then turns to the AWU.

'For a number of months now, there has been a smear campaign circulating on the internet relating to events seventeen years ago,' she starts. 'Much of the material in circulation is highly sexist. I've taken the view over time that I will not dignify this campaign with a response either. However, this morning something changed on that. The *Australian* newspaper republished a false and highly defamatory claim about my conduct in relation to these matters seventeen years ago. In these circumstances, where I am seeing, recycled again, false and defamatory material attacking my character, I have determined that I will deal with these issues. I'm therefore happy to take questions on these matters. I am going to do that today . . . This will be the only occasion on which I deal with this matter. I am not going to dignify it by ongoing answering of questions.'

For close to an hour, she answers every question put to her. Traversing the history of her relationship with her old legal firm

Slater & Gordon, she deals with prickly personal questions about her relationship with Wilson, his financial affairs, and her personal business. She reflects on modern politics: 'It does worry me that that's where politics has got to, that things that are demonstrably untrue, indeed absurd, are circulated and recirculated and recirculated and somehow, at least in some section of the population, manage to worm their way in to become the orthodoxy.'

As for the mainstream media: 'I've been on my feet now for, what? I can't quite recall—fifty minutes, something like that—taking every question that the journalist elite of this country have got for me. If that doesn't end the matter, then with respect I don't know what would.' Her loyal cabinet colleagues are delighted: she took command, she was authoritative, and she's laid it to rest.

But not by a long shot has she laid Kevin to rest. He's firing now on all leadership comeback cylinders. With the polls currently turning her way, Team Rudd is stepping up its efforts to drive the numbers down.

In Sydney on 28 August, ostensibly launching a new book about Gough Whitlam, Rudd speaks feelingly of the termination of Whitlam's prime ministership as 'absolute political brutality', 'a simple, naked lunge for political power when the opportunity presented itself'. A person doesn't need to be an expert in irony or allegory to get his drift. For thirty torturously long minutes he pays tribute to the achievements of the Gough and Rudd governments—lauding, amongst other single-handed achievements, his government's apology to Indigenous people, his signing of the Kyoto Protocol, and the so-called education and health revolutions. But he offers one miserable line on Julia's achievements: 'The government under Prime Minister Gillard continues to implement a program of reform today, including a National

Disability Insurance Scheme of far-reaching importance for our people.' Gushing is not a word that springs to mind.

On Saturday morning 8 September, Gillard's beloved dad, John, dies after a short illness. His daughter is at the APEC summit in Russia. She rushes back to the family home in Adelaide, arriving tear-stained and visibly shaken late the following afternoon in order to spend the week mourning the loss of her 'inspiration'—a humble Welshman born in a coal mining village, who left school at age fourteen. Three days after she retreats to the bosom of her family, Rudd bobs up on the ABC's *7.30* in his first major interview since his failed February challenge. Provocatively, he talks about the stark choices facing the electorate at the upcoming election, and insists that he won't be silenced and will speak up on a myriad of issues.

Three times he is pressed by presenter Leigh Sales to refer to Gillard by name, after chanting how he supports 'the Prime Minister'. This showy chest-puffing, at a time when the woman whose job he craves is behind the curtains mourning her adored father, does not go unnoticed by his colleagues. Remarks one in disgusted tones in a private conversation with me: 'Kevin is the Kim Kardashian of politics.'

But just as the wheels on the Rudd Express start chugging a bit faster, along comes another opinion poll showing Gillard with another big rise. Bloody hell—fair suck of the sauce bottle! In a Newspoll published on 17 September, approval for Labor has risen another three percentage points to 36 per cent while the Coalition has crashed, and Gillard has passed Abbott as preferred prime minister. This is almost becoming a trend—Labor's poll numbers have improved for the last two months. Dennis Shanahan is so flustered he's dropped Rudd like a hot potato and declared that: 'The timing, the results and the context have virtually delivered Gillard with a pass to lead Labor to the next election.'

But Shanahan's so not a happy camper on another level. He writes indignantly that his old pal Abbott has only slipped behind because of a 'relentless and unfair attack on his character' and the government is only ahead because 'in the past few weeks, Gillard has demonstrated a ruthless political brutality that has undermined all claims to be driven by policy and the national interest, and disclosed an intent to win at all costs'. Shanahan is referring to a brazen political tactic by Labor women in parliament—Gillard, Tanya Plibersek, Nicola Roxon and others—to capitalise on a *Quarterly Essay* by noted Fairfax journalist David Marr, who revealed accusations about Abbott's allegedly anti-female, violent university past.

Over at Fairfax, a Nielsen poll has found the bounce to be a bit less impressive—Labor has only lifted to a 34 per cent primary vote. An ungracious Michelle Grattan in the *Age* manages to link Gillard's revived fortunes with her recent loss: 'Labor's primary vote has increased 2 points to 34 per cent in the poll of 1400 taken Thursday to Saturday, in the wake of Ms Gillard's absence from the public stage after the death of her father.'

But Kevin is up for a bit of chit-chat with the media today. It's strange how he pops up much more frequently whenever Gillard's not around—this time she's in Perth for another funeral, for Aussie Sapper James Martin, killed in Afghanistan. Rudd tweets to gallery reporters that he's in Parliament's Mural Hall, and they flock to his 'impromptu' doorstop. His momentous news grab? 'I think it's great that the government is doing well. I think it's great that the government is doing better.'

Then the leadership questions start up. Are you down for the count, now that Gillard's polling is up? Would you be better as PM? No, he cries, as he starts trotting back to his office. There's only one PM, and her name is Julia Gillard! And off he zips, leaving a trail of question marks wafting in the air. What was that all about?

2GB's Alan Jones doesn't like Julia Gillard. He's been reminding his 150,000 Sydney listeners of his poor opinion of the woman for two years. She's a liar and a witch. Can't govern, can't lead. Bring on The Abbott. But surely even his strongest supporters blanch when they pick up the *Sunday Telegraph* on 30 September.

One of its reporters has recorded an after-dinner speech Jones made last Saturday to a gathering of gormless Sydney University Liberal Clubbers, in which he declared that Gillard's father recently 'died of shame'. 'To think that he had a daughter who told lies every time she stood for parliament!' The daughter's tears of grief earned her a spike in the opinion polls, he sneered; and she's been let off lightly by the Opposition because she's a woman. To cement his credentials as a decent human being, he'd personally signed a jacket made out of a chaffbag—the club organisers thinking this is an amusing reminder of the time Jones told his radio audience Gillard should be bundled into such a bag and tossed out to sea.

Gillard is so outraged and insulted that she goes to ground as a media and public firestorm mushrooms around Jones. She gathers some unlikely supporters, among them Mark Latham, who is caustic on Sky's *Australian Agenda*. 'The campaign against her in recent times has been a disgrace,' he fumes. 2GB programming was 'one long hate session' against Gillard and Labor, and the vituperation from the media the worst he's ever seen. 'It is a trend in our body politic that is most regrettable and is dragging down Australian democracy; no attention on the issues, no attention on the battle of ideas. It's the politics of hate, it's directed at Gillard, and it's disgraceful.'

The brushfire turns into a bushfire, burning into October. For once in his opinionated life, Jones is being subjected to a cacophony of harsh judgments and, even worse, his advertisers are deserting him. The verdict is in: he's a bully and misogynist. And for once in her prime ministerial life, the cards are playing in Gillard's favour. She and a clutch of her female ministry buddies have been successfully out and about for weeks talking up Abbott's Problem with Women.

It's hard, effective politics, and it's the sort of game Abbott has been playing against Gillard since she became prime minister; it's just the themes that are different. He has misrepresented her position on the carbon pricing regime; he has constantly attacked her honesty and integrity, muttering 'liar' to her in parliament whenever he can get away with it, and liar in public when he can't; he has vociferously distorted her position on asylum seeker policy.

Anyone who knows Abbott knows he's no misogynist, even if many of his old student comrades claim his behaviour and attitude towards women in those-days were deplorable. These days, the modern Abbott is respectful. He wears his conservative political beliefs on his sleeve, but Gillard and other Labor figures have misrepresented him on a range of women's issues. But karma's a bitch sometimes, and the fact that he was slow to condemn the Jones remarks was a remarkable, exploitable political mistake.

Gillard is denting Abbott, and it's not just the Opposition feeling bruised. Rudd again raises his head above the parapet. On 8 October he is in the New South Wales Blue Mountains, planting trees to honour former prime ministers (something of a theme for the Ruddster in the last few weeks). The task of leadership is to 'unite, not divide', he says pointedly, to be 'positive, not negative'. Nobody in parliament pays the slightest attention.

On 9 October, when Peter Slipper's speakership is ebbing away on a tide of lurid reporting about the unvarnished minutiae of his relationship with his former staffer James Ashby, Abbott taunts Gillard in parliament by moving a motion to have Slipper removed from the chair for misogyny. At the centre of the storm is a text message from Slipper to Ashby that has just come to light, in which he describes female genitalia as being like shell-less mussels.

This has sent the political and media world into paroxysms of moral outrage. In truth, it is a hypocritical hoot. Sexist and often distressing words and phrases about women and their bodies are constants in robust exchanges among the political and media fraternity. And in comparison to some of the electronic vulgarity that buzzes from office to office, the mussels reference could almost pass as polite society chat.

Gillard is not defending Slipper's schoolboy confidences with his staffer; she is supporting his retention in the chair as a matter of principle. She believes his fate should rest with the courts, not parliament's kangaroo court. The colour rises in Gillard's cheeks as she gets to her feet; she fixes Abbott with a steely gaze and lets rip with a withering speech about how she will not be lectured to by a misogynistic man about misogyny. Abbott's chin drops, his colour fades, his face collapses. It is riveting, unexpected, thrilling theatre. This is Gillard at her politically artful and oratorical best.

Journalists, particularly those in the press gallery's cabal of indignant middle-aged men, see it very differently. The *Australian*'s Shanahan denounces Gillard for defending Slipper. The *Sydney*

Morning Herald's Peter Hartcher takes the same tack as Shanahan: 'She showed she was prepared to defend even the denigration of women if it would help her keep power. If Gillard will not defend respect for women, what will she defend?' Peter, you are such a tosser! She actually defended women, but she was not prepared to hang a bloke out to dry on a smutty reference to women's genitalia (and maybe Slipper's description was pretty accurate, anyhow).

Geoff Kitney in the *Australian Financial Review* declares she's failed the leadership test: '. . . yesterday Gillard made a terrible error: she made a passionate and angry speech attacking Abbott for double standards on sexism and misogyny. But then she offered a weak and dissembling explanation as to why it was not the time to take any action to deal with Slipper despite his appalling language . . .' Peter van Onselen thunders: 'Is it possible for a political party and a prime minister to have more egg on their collective faces than Labor and Julia Gillard do right now?' The *Sydney Morning Herald*'s Paul Sheehan let forth with one of the ugliest attacks on Gillard seen in print, accusing her of being the real driver of hate in Australian politics. Michelle Grattan was also unimpressed: 'The Prime Minister threw everything into her argument, which revolved around trying to pin the "misogynist" label on the Opposition Leader. It was perhaps the only weapon available to her, but it sounded more desperate than convincing.'

But meanwhile, back in the real world and beyond the bubble on the Hill, Gillard's speech had immediately gone viral. Rolling thunderclaps of applause could be heard on social media across Australia and internationally, as far afield as the United States, with popular American women's website, Jezebel, calling her 'one badass motherfucker'. Even the website of the British conservative magazine, *The Spectator*, put its gloved hands together for a polite clap: 'Anyone who admires the cut and thrust of parliamentary theatre and debate will enjoy these 15 minutes. Mr Abbott does not look best amused. But then he's just been carved to pieces so he wouldn't, would he?'

The only Australian print journalist to concede the gallery might have missed the point and the impact of Gillard's fiery speech entirely is the *Sydney Morning Herald*'s Jacqueline Maley. She starts a column on 11 October with the frank assessment: 'The bubble of the Canberra press gallery has been decisively popped this week.'

Team Rudd hasn't paid enough attention to the home-grown and global wave of praise for Gillard, either. It floats the line on 11 October, via the *Herald-Sun*'s Phillip Hudson, that the Slipper affair has been 'a fiasco' for Gillard, and the caucus should turn to Rudd. Yawn.

Rudd's new rallying cry is that we must all accentuate the positive. So he makes a direct crack at the Gillard misogyny incursion on 17 October on ABC's *Lateline*: 'This sort of stuff frankly doesn't add up to a row of beans and the sooner we get past the deeply personal attacks on both sides of politics the better,' he lectures. Leadership was required of all of us, he tuts.

He's just spent the day campaigning in Sydney's Hurstville with Daryl Melham, who last week resigned as caucus secretary after eight years. The Ruddsters had spun the decision to the media as a 'massive vote of no-confidence' in Gillard. Rudd has also taken a pot-shot at Gillard and Swan over an announced expected short-fall in the mining tax. The next day he's on ABC radio Brisbane, commenting—upper lip stiff, back strong—that his removal in 2010 was a 'traumatic event'. And golly gosh, isn't the pace of reform under the current mob just a teensy bit slow?

At 7.53 pm, the *Sydney Morning Herald*'s Phillip Coorey posts a piece on his newspaper's website stating that Team Rudd is back counting numbers. 'His supporters freely admit the former prime minister is repositioning himself for the leadership, but insist there will be no challenge and the caucus must come to realise it needs him to win the next election.' When the cat's away, the vengeful mouse will play—Gillard's been in Bali, Afghanistan and India all week. But another good Newspoll at the end of the month again sends Team Rudd into a mid-game huddle. What to do, what to do? The message from Gillard's backers—like from most of the caucus—is simple: the political killing season is here so, boys, why don't you give it your best shot?

With polls for Gillard in the ascendancy, leadership chatter in the media abates. Instead, spookily, attention returns to matters damaging for her. Only two months ago, the PM believed she had laid to rest the seventeen-year-old AWU matter. But it appears the *Australian* wasn't satisfied and still has her in its sights, even though it has not and still does not offer one shred of evidence of Gillard's complicity in any corrupt or illegal dealings. On 26 November—after more than two dozen stories on this matter have appeared in the *Australian* and in other newspapers and countless news stories have been aired on radio and TV, and as parliament prepares to sit for the last week of the year—Gillard holds another press conference. The *Australian*'s journalists are gathered in a pack, barking questions at her to the point where she asks one of them, Sid Maher, to stop hectoring her.

After all questions have again been exhausted, she concludes: 'And out of all of this—all of these questions; the last marathon press conference; the times I've taken questions in Melbourne, in Brisbane; all of the peddling of this right back to Phil Gude [a former Victorian Liberal MP] in 1995; across all of those years in between—there is not one person who is able to come forward and clearly say I did something wrong.'

On 12 December Justice Steven Rares in the Federal Court throws out the Peter Slipper sexual harassment case, explosively concluding that the action launched by Ashby was a planned attack carried out in order to seriously damage the former Speaker's reputation. A battered and bruised Slipper, whose mental state has caused great anxiety within Labor's ranks, says simply that he feels vindicated and that he believes the action was always about destroying him and bringing down the Gillard government.

The roll call of those entangled in this conspiracy includes News Ltd journalist Steve Lewis, former Slipper staffer Karen Doane, and former Howard minister Mal Brough, who fought and won a bitter Liberal National Party pre-selection for Slipper's Queensland seat in July, just three months before the alleged improprieties exploded in the *Daily Telegraph*. All three had been in regular contact. News Ltd paid for Ashby's hotel accommodation in Sydney when he filed the action on 20 April, and Lewis had texted Ashby earlier that month boasting 'We will get him!'. The judge didn't buy Lewis' explanation that these words referred to getting a hire-car driver. 'That is not how the text messages read. In my opinion the reference is clearly to Mr Ashby and Mr Lewis "getting" Mr Slipper, not to Mr Lewis finding a driver.' Tony Abbott, who has relentlessly hounded his old friend (he attended Slipper's wedding) onto the backbench, will no doubt rise above the very public exposure of this win-at-all-costs episode and, like Lewis and, Brough, simply sail on to his next adventure.

Sensing that the end game may be slipping from his grasp, the Kevin Express is trying to fire up the engine again. On 18 December, he alights at one of his favourite stations, *Sunrise*. He's on the Channel Seven brekky program to announce the winner of a T-shirt competition he launched in October to raise campaign funds for his re-election in the Queensland seat of Griffith. Pre-recorded four days ago, Kev is having a great time with his old mates on the program that made him a household name. He's even engaging in a spot of Gangnam-style dancing. The winning T-shirt is a sartorially splendid little number with the words 'It's Our Ruddy Future' emblazoned on its front. Its back sports a hit list of what he considers his signature solo achievements as PM— 'signed Kyoto', 'withdrew Australian troops from Iraq', 'abolished WorkChoices', 'apologised to Indigenous Australians', 'kept Australia out of the global recession'—all contained within a map of Australia. Right through the middle of the map runs the slogan: 'It just makes Ruddy sense'. Weird, though: the T-shirt is intended to help re-elect Rudd in his seat, but the designer has forgotten to mention his electorate. Curiouser and curiouser is that *none* of the six designs selected by Rudd as a finalist has included the name of his electorate; they are all focussed on Kevin the PM, Kevin the national leader—maybe even Kevin the could-be-again prime minister.

Asked on *Sunrise* if he wants his old job back, Kev belts out his familiar theme song: 'I'm very happy being the federal member for Griffith, and I'm very happy being able to have a campaign with, I think, a very good T-shirt!' But what about your personal popularity? 'It's better than the alternative, which is to be whacked about the head every day, all the time,' he muses.

Surely he's not referring to the redhead? After all, out of sight is out of mind. By a stroke of lucky coincidence, the PM has been on leave for less than a day when this *Sunrise* segment goes to air. There is no rest for the wicked, though: she is entering a period of R&R yet again peering over her shoulder at those who will do her harm.

THE COUNTDOWN BEGINS
Early 2013

Happy new year, Julia Gillard. And here's a special 2013 surprise for you: after this political festive season hiatus concludes at the end of January, Kevin will be back on *Sunrise* as a regular weekly guest. The program's producers have bumped Environment minister Tony Burke in favour of their old mate. But Kevin is devoutly loyal to his prime minister, of course—he's not trying to build a higher profile for himself with his media mates. And he is most definitely—wash your mouths out!—not trying to build momentum for his return to the prime ministership.

The trouble for Rudd is that he's just not getting enough traction. And then on 14 January the she-devil surpasses his 935 days in office. He congratulates Gillard without managing to utter her name. At the same time, with a kaleidoscope of interpretations, he expresses his devout support for the government's re-election. 'I congratulate the Prime Minister on achieving this important milestone. For 2013, I will be giving my all to support the government's re-election,' he states. Patrick Lion heroically (for

News Ltd) concludes in the *Daily Telegraph*: 'So as 2013 unfolds, Gillard appears to have put the leadership genie back in the bottle.'

The following morning brings another burst of promising news for Gillard, from an unlikely source in an unlikely newspaper: Labor's primary support, according to the *Australian*'s Newspoll, has jumped to 38 per cent, its highest since the last election. While polls this far out from an election should be treated with a grain of salt, Team Rudd relies on poor polling figures for Gillard and her government to keep driving their momentum. It is most inconvenient to their narrative that Gillard's numbers appear to be modestly but consistently rising.

There's another hiccup in the form of a glowing report from BlackRock—one of the world's largest buyers of government bonds, which invests US$3.7 trillion worldwide—when it pronounces that Australia's economic position is 'exceedingly strong', and strengthening. 'The plain fact is, compared to the rest of the world—and this is what we are doing—Australia's public debt position is very, very strong,' says BlackRock's Australian head of fixed income, Steve Miller. 'Whether you are looking at budget balance or public debt to gross domestic product, whichever way we look at it, Australia comes out exceedingly strong.' This highly favourable assessment gets scant media attention.

Nevertheless, feeling and looking confident, on 30 January at Canberra's National Press Club Gillard gives a refreshingly frank address about the economic and other challenges facing the government. Towards the end of her speech, she announces the election will be held on 14 September. Making public the date in this way will enable 'individuals and business, investors and consumers, to plan their year'. 'But the benefit of fixing the date now is not just the end of speculation about election timing. It gives shape and order to the year and enables it to be one not of fevered campaigning, but of cool and reasoned deliberation,' she says, emphasising that she's not firing the shotgun on an eight-month campaign. She doesn't remind her audience, but the agreement she signed on 7 September 2010 with Tony Windsor and Rob Oakeshott to form minority government provided that 'this Parliament should serve its full term and the next election will be held on a date to be agreed in September or October 2013'. Given that there are realistically only a few dates in those months on which the election could be held, her announcement could hardly be described as earth-shattering (the agreement is a public document that can be googled by anyone interested).

At 1.15 pm the following day, five burly coppers turn up at Craig Thomson's New South Wales Central Coast electorate office to arrest him on a single charge of fraud and to frogmarch him to the local copshop for more charges to be laid. TV cameras, obviously tipped off by either the New South Wales police or people within the New South Wales Liberal government, are on the spot to record the ambush of a startled Thomson.

Neither he nor his lawyer, Chris McArdle, was given the usual courtesy of advance notice. 'It's unbelievable that the rule of law has been supplanted by reality TV and a circus,' fumes McArdle, who just happens to be appearing on Sky News at the very time Thomson is being bundled off to the police station. Berating 'unintelligent politicians', he pleads: 'I call upon the circus performers to honour the rule of law'. Good luck with that one, Chris. The timing couldn't be worse for Gillard: a day after she's announced the election date and slap-bang in the middle of an appearance by Abbott before the press club, allowing him a perfect opportunity to lambast her again.

The immediate media reaction to her announcement of the timing of the federal poll was mixed, but the overlay of the Thomson arrest begins to turn the coverage from reasonably balanced to negative. Gillard was again verging on a crisis! Two days later, on Saturday 2 February, she calls a press conference to announce that senior cabinet ministers Senator Chris Evans and Nicola Roxon won't be recontesting the forthcoming election. They will step down from the ministry forthwith in order to allow for a rejuvenation in the lead-up to the election; Gillard has long discussed this with the pair, and they all collegiately agreed this was the optimum time. The press conference is appropriately dignified, but relaxed; it is at times funny, at times emotional. Evans and Roxon pay generous tribute to Gillard's abilities as a prime minister and leader.

But the media instantly decide the resignations mean Gillard has inflicted yet another crisis on her government. It reckons the election campaign that she plainly stated was not yet in motion is actually in full swing. Josh Whittington and Simon Benson on News Ltd online immediately cry that the resignations have plunged Gillard's 'stuttering election campaign into further disarray' (apologies for channelling another redhead, but . . . please explain!) and prompted 'Opposition speculation of more Labor resignations'. (Liberal MPs would know, of course). They extensively quote Liberal Christopher Pyne, as though he has become an instant expert on Labor's internal workings.

The *West Australian* decrees that 'Julia Gillard's leadership has been rocked' by the resignations, even though Gillard, Evans and Roxon all made it plain that the resignations were orderly and planned. Mark Kenny and Jessica Wright on the *Sydney Morning Herald* website decide that the Gillard government's 'turbulent start to the new parliamentary year continues'. On Sky News immediately after the press conference, chief political reporter David Speers has Bruce Hawker—the campaign manager for Rudd's 2012 challenge—sagely pontificating about how really odd the resignations are. The *Financial Review*'s Phillip Coorey, and Fairfax's Mark Kenny, pop on to the show for a chat, too. Everyone agrees that the resignations are nothing less than a bloody shambles.

Former roving scribe for Fairfax, the ever-incisive David Marr, appears on the ABC *Insiders* panel the next morning. He expresses frustration and amazement at the reporting of the resignations; much of it is 'political campaigning', he says. Perhaps he has been looking at Fairfax's *Sun-Herald* or its *Brisbane Times* online, which this morning under the headline 'Labor in crisis: Gillard on back foot after ministers quit' reckons that Gillard 'capped the third day of her election campaign with the resignation of two frontbenchers, leaving her to fend off accusations Labor was spinning out of control'. Or perhaps he is referring to Michelle Grattan's effort in the *Age*, where she tells us that the danger to Gillard is that the reshuffle will be seen as ministers 'deserting a sinking ship', and that the resignations added to an 'impression' of chaos, 'which can be used to fuel doubt about her judgment'.

But this impression has been created solely by an opportunistic Opposition and a journalist at Gillard's press conference, who asked whether her government was in chaos, to which Gillard responded in exasperation: 'Well, why on earth would anybody say that?' Equally as absurdly, the introduction on Seven's *National News* tonight begins: 'As she tries to breathe new life into her election campaign . . .'

So thank God for some comic relief. Rudd has today despatched to his one-million-plus Twitter followers a homesy photo of himself lying on the family couch with grand-daughter Josephine sitting on his stomach. 'She's already delightfully wicked, just like her mum at the same age!' he tweets. To my mind she looks like she's about to either throw up on him, or to hit him with her rattle. Maybe I'm having a bad Sunday. Nah—Conductor Rudd is back, toot toot!

Two days later, on 5 February, Mark Kenny in the *Sydney Morning Herald* tells us Rudd has 45 votes in a caucus of 102 (caucus has been reduced by one vote, as Thomson is no longer in the ALP). The story spreads like a virus across other media outlets.

Following a slump for Labor in the Nielsen, Galaxy and News polls because of the impression that Gillard is again in crisis, full-blown leadership speculation is now rampant. The public takes a dim view of governments and leaders seen to be losing control, and Team Rudd relies on outbreaks of widespread media criticism about Gillard to stir up another wave of leadership agitation. It's like bloating yeast. Journalists are naive if they think their reports don't influence events. Members of Team Rudd become more active when the collective press gallery judgment is that Gillard has stuffed up, yet again. The bad coverage for the PM affects her standing in the public eye and her polls slump, prompting another round of damaging criticism and prophesies of doom for her government. It's a never-ending, vicious cycle. Now Team Rudd is out and about again, capitalising on the latest media tornado.

This time, they're busy as bees telling journalists that they don't want to be seen moving around the hive. Simon Benson tells us on 14 February that Rudd has been 'privately counselled by some of his key backers to pull back from his public campaign for fear it could spark another showdown before they are ready . . . one Rudd supporter yesterday admitted that the issue was coming to a head but wanted to give the appearance that "nothing was going on".'

On 21 February in the *Australian*, Graham Richardson, who apparently has lots of idle phone chats with Rudd loyalist Joel Fitzgibbon, orders Gillard to run up the white flag, give Rudd 'a big hug' and resign for the good of the party. Fairfax's Katharine Murphy tells us the next day that Gillard may not survive. On it goes.

Emerging from this pack mentality is one brave soul—the *Courier-Mail*'s Dennis Atkins, a journalist of three-plus decades, who has previously worked for Queensland state and federal Labor. On 26 February he belts out an opinion piece: 'For the sake of sanity all round, let's declare a ban on talking about Rudd until he actually does something. The usual Kevin stuff is what we're familiar with—self-serving, attention-seeking, social media stunts or some tricked up school visit where he incites the crowd to scream and wave. His television appearances are increasingly strange . . . and his radio interviews include extreme narcissism. The import of all this is close to zip. There has been no great movement of caucus votes. In fact, despite increasing depression and despondency, most of Rudd's parliamentary colleagues find his behaviour annoying and counterproductive. The usual response from exasperated MPs is: "Why won't he just shut up?"'

He can't, and he won't, is the short answer. Liberals who have offices in the parliamentary corridor inhabited by the former PM whisper privately about a recent massive increase of traffic into his modest backbench office. Media, caucus colleagues, outsiders—they're wearing a groove in the carpet leading up to Kevin's door, the snoops confide. One can just imagine him in there, doodling away on a grid. It's the way he does his political business: like a field marshal, he puts people and groups critical to his goals on a grid; then he timelines them and methodically duchesses 'each and every one', to borrow a favourite Rudd expression.

February has long been forgotten, as has Gillard's rocky week-long roadshow to western Sydney, which Rudd supporters mocked behind the scenes, some of them while standing beside her. The Ides of March—another media deadline for her prime minister-ship (for two years now)—is rapidly approaching. Team Rudd is getting antsy: their desperation is reflected in media reporting that the Prime Minister's gig will be up during the coming fortnight's sittings, which will be the last before the long April–early May break, after which caucus will not reconvene until the Budget session starting on 14 May. Their lines *de jour* are that 'something must give' and 'something has to be done'.

Then along comes the gift of the media reform package, rushed into cabinet on 12 March by Communications minister Stephen Conroy, who wants it introduced, debated and passed by the time parliament rises on 21 March. News Ltd launches a vicious attack across all its mastheads on key proposals, particularly the idea of a Public Interest Media Advocate to regulate existing industry-based self-regulating bodies such as the Australian Press Council. Tastefully, the *Tele* runs a tricked-up picture of Conroy as Joseph Stalin.

Some members of Team Rudd, such as cabinet minister Chris Bowen, pretend continuing allegiance to Gillard while at the same time Rudd's forces are marshalling for a major attack. 'This matter was resolved last February,' Bowen tells ABC Radio National disingenuously on 12 March. 'We've all said that we had our votes in February and that was where the matter was resolved.' How do these guys sleep at night?

At times such as these, rumours within parliament can spark

a feeding frenzy. And so it is on the afternoon of Thursday 14 March. A wall of cameras and hysterical reporters are parked in corridors linking to the PM's office after wild speculation sweeps the building via social media that Gillard is about to be told by Simon Crean that it is time she shoved off in the interests of the party and the government. The Twitterverse is in meltdown; journalists and staffers are tweeting a rumour a second. Fairfax's Stephanie Peatling, while blogging parliamentary proceedings live, vents about the '24-second media cycle'. '3:54pm: Sometimes all one can say is "Oh for goodness sake".'

But it is all hot air. 'Silly' is the verdict of the PM. Even Rudd backers, alarmed that events are moving too fast, dissed the reports. Besides, nobody had bothered to check with Crean. It turns out he wasn't even in the building; he wasn't even in Canberra. News Ltd pumps a story out online about the fact that there was no story; Peter Hartcher and Dennis Shanahan front up on Sky News *Agenda* to talk about the shoulder-tapping that didn't happen. Says Hartcher: 'Above and beyond everything in specific, it's like a barometric pressure reading of the mood in parliament house. The components are speculative tweets, half-imagined movements of people in the building, and half-heard conversations.' Always a basis for good journalism.

'There is no doubt that the ALP caucus is a tinderbox', adds Shanahan. 'They are ready to go off at the smallest spark—likewise the press gallery. Everyone is ready for something to happen. It's the Ides of March ... there are deadlines coming and going. It is as Peter said, it's febrile and it doesn't take much at all to set things off.' Even tweets planting the idea of a spill, apparently. Some people around the parliament have sourced the origin of the mayhem to Liberal Party staffers.

On the night of the real Ides of March, Rudd addresses a Brisbane St Patrick's Day dinner. His speech includes a laughing, teasing announcement that he is about to turn off the 'cold shower', emerge from the 'ice bath' and the 'cryogenic tank' (all lines he's previously used to dismiss his leadership ambitions) and, he tells his audience: he will challenge! After a moment's silence and the sound of the proverbial single pin dropping, Rudd continues that he will challenge '. . . any of the Liberal politicians here present to demonstrate that they have any more Irish heritage than I have.' Hahahaha! Kev the Comic! More likely it is a serious warm-up act to what he hopes will unfold sometime soon.

Two days later at a social cricket game with press gallery journalists, Rudd numbers man Alan Griffin openly talks about the possibility of a leadership challenge. Other politicians tell me they believe Rudd and his forces will move this week. A businessman with Foreign department links tells me the challenge is planned for Tuesday's caucus meeting. Another from outside the rarefied atmosphere of parliament says Thursday is the day for Julia's denouement. It seems to be an open secret in many circles outside the press gallery, and assuredly even more well-known within it. Some of Gillard's senior supporters are so dismayed at the momentum now gathering, they concede privately to me on Monday that anything could happen: they feel helpless to stop the media and Team Rudd tornado.

Against this backdrop, the stories that appear are almost coy. On ABC Radio's *AM* on Monday, Alexandra Kirk understates: 'One Rudd backer warns it will be a torrid week for the Prime Minister.' Phillip Coorey in the *Australian Financial Review* knows what Rudd is thinking and writing: 'Kevin Rudd has told those close to him that if the leadership transition cannot be effected this week, then he's really not that interested in waiting any longer because Labor's prospects were fast becoming a hopeless cause.'

Rudd's media mate Peter Hartcher doesn't change his tune of the last two years, even affirming his support for the comments of that great Labor bloke, former Victorian Liberal powerbroker Michael Kroger, who's prophesied the death of Labor unless Rudd is returned. Lectures Hartcher: 'Labor might yet change drivers, and it will be very sharply focused on this question this week, the last practical opportunity before the budget in May. But if it can't overcome its reluctance to undo the mistake it made in deposing Rudd in 2010, it seems that Kroger will get a vivid slow-motion demonstration of mass political suicide at work.' This isn't journalism, or reasoned commentary; it is zealous advocacy for Rudd's return in an attempt to influence events.

For good measure, the *Herald* publishes a Nielsen poll. Besides the usual two-party polling that finds Gillard and her government are cactus, it has conducted a leadership poll in which Bob Carr has been thrown into the mix—even though Carr is in the wrong house in parliament to be the leader. Talk about *déjà vu*. This is a re-run of my old *Sun-Herald* days, when we put Carr into a Labor leadership poll when he wasn't even in federal parliament. The silliness knows no bounds.

On Tuesday 19 March, Hartcher, wearing an ill-fitting journalist's hat, co-writes with Mark Kenny a sweeping front-page story in the *Sydney Morning Herald* titled, 'Ministers turn on PM'. In it, they assert: 'Senior ministers in the Gillard government are reconsidering their support for the Prime Minister, a sign of collapsing confidence at a critical moment.' The Fairfax duo state that cabinet minister Mark Butler is 'reconsidering' his position, and Bob Carr long ago lost faith in Gillard. 'Their changing positions are a sign of a loss of confidence in Ms Gillard within the government, and evidence of a gathering momentum to restore Mr Rudd to the leadership.' Three cheers for Momentum, the star of the last few years! The article states that Carr was unavailable for comment.

Within hours both ministers claim they have not defected from Gillard, and Carr furiously denies he was unavailable for comment, saying no comment was sought from him or his staff. He adds: 'She has my support and I think the media's in a frenzy of speculation—speculation feeding on itself that generates these stories . . . I am not going to feed speculation that feeds on itself and goes very, very silly. I made it very clear . . . that I am a strong supporter of the Prime Minster and that what you read is media speculation feeding on itself endlessly.' But the damage has been done. The dogs are barking and Team Rudd is seriously on the move.

On Wednesday night, Joel Fitzgibbon says on Sky News it's 'silly' to suggest nothing is going on. There's one thing for which Fitzgibbon can be relied upon: he follows instructions. The momentum is building nicely. Team Rudd is even more satisfied with its work on Thursday morning, when News Ltd's Simon Benson and Phillip Hudson write: 'Julia Gillard faces the most crucial 24 hours of her leadership as it emerged Labor polling taken on the eve of Kevin Rudd's political assassination revealed a rebound for the overthrown PM. The polling, which suggested Labor could still have won an election in 2010 under Mr Rudd's leadership, was kept a secret from him, most senior ministers and the majority of the Labor caucus for fear it could have unravelled plans for the coup already under way.'

The poll that was concealed? It revealed that Rudd was personally more popular than Abbott in the marginal South Australian seat of Kingston, and there was 'only a 0.5 per cent swing against the Government in that marginal seat'. Huge! Any similarity to a deliberately planted story designed to damage Gillard at a critical moment is purely coincidental, as were similar stories of polling allegedly kept secret by Gillard which emerged prior to Rudd's failed February 2012 challenge.

Something, indeed, has to give, and it is Simon Crean who steps up to the plate and demands an end to the damaging speculation and the frenzy. In two fiery, exasperated, often muddled press conferences on Thursday 21 March, he calls for a spill and says, unexpectedly, he'll be supporting Rudd. By the time Gillard walks into Question Time at 2.00 pm, she's set 4.30 pm for a leadership ballot. She must wonder how it could all come to this. Again.

EPILOGUE
The carnival is over

On 21 March 2013, Kevin Rudd stood warm and comfy at the base of a political cliff and watched as his acolytes leapt off into career oblivion. After vowing over a two-year period—which included one humiliating and spectacularly unsuccessful assault on Gillard's leadership in February 2012—that he would one day lead his followers into a promised land of a revitalised Rudd-led government, his vision was finally unmasked for what it had always been: a mirage.

In the hours between the start of Question Time at 2 pm and the time of the leadership showdown, 4.30 pm, the usual parade of Rudd spruikers, pushers, illusionists and snake oil salesmen, along with media seers and pro-Rudd propagandists in the commentariat, had appeared live on TV and radio pumping up their bloke's credentials and pouring scorn on Gillard.

There was the eternal Richo on Sky saying Rudd would win—'and if Julia Gillard wins, she's dead in the water anyway'. Then there was Bruce Hawker, like one of those pests who stand behind reporters on live TV waving and jumping, solemnly delivering his repetitively smooth spin about his man, including the dog-eared line that any MP who 'wants to secure their seat in parliament' would vote for Kevin. And the usual parade of journalists had leapt onto radio and television to declare that Rudd had the numbers to win. The strong whiff of Groundhog Day was suffocating.

At 4.18 pm, just minutes before the big showdown, Rudd appeared in his parliamentary corridor to announce that he had always said he wouldn't challenge the PM and he wasn't going to now. 'I believe in honouring my word . . . others take such commitments lightly, I do not,' he said solemnly, to the shrieks of laughter from the offices of loyal Gillard MPs. 'I have been very plain about that for a long period of time . . . I have given that word. I gave it solemnly in that room after the last ballot and I will adhere to that word today.'

Once more with feeling, Kevin! 'I'm not prepared to dishonour my word, which I gave solemnly. I will, therefore, adhere to that word as I have said before. Excuse me, I'm going to caucus.' And with that, he zipped. *Gotta go, folks!* Off he trotted to his party room, to not vote for himself in a ballot he and his supporters had plotted to bring on for thirteen months.

Rudd's announcement was an act of mammoth self-serving political bastardry, and an exercise in deluded spin and nonsense. Over the following twenty-four hours Rudd went on to contradict himself; he unmasked his key plotters and the plot, and he gave us a glimpse of the confused and dangerous world of Kevin.

The day after the greatest piece of theatre of the absurd ever to play in Parliament House, Rudd, looking breezy and unaffected, held a press conference in Brisbane to say he would never, ever seek the leadership of the Labor Party again. As if that's believable, given that what Rudd says and what he does are polar opposites. He then let us in on an open secret—he hadn't challenged because he didn't have the numbers—and, strangely, he named all his chief lieutenants. Here was the backbone of Team Rudd, the men who'd either gone to him or spoken to him on the phone before the caucus meeting to tell him he had 'zero' chance of gaining a majority in caucus: Chris Bowen, Anthony Albanese, Joel Fitzgibbon, Richard Marles, Alan Griffin and Kim Carr. The decision the day before by party elder Simon Crean to call for the spill had been a 'spontaneous combustion', he declared.

Bullshit, responded Crean, in so many words, when it came his turn to spill the beans. Crean said he had discussed the leadership with Rudd on the Monday and Tuesday before the Thursday fiasco, down to who would serve as what. Crean wanted to be deputy PM, but Rudd wanted Leader of the House Anthony Albanese. What's more, Crean told Sydney radio's loudmouth Alan Jones, Chris Bowen had been appointed by Rudd to discuss the leadership issue with him.

'Him not running was never part of the discussions we had,' Crean said indignantly. He told Canberra reporters, 'He reneged on our deal, it was gutless'. Team Rudd knew exactly what it was doing. Bowen had told Crean it was time to 'go harder', which is why Crean precipitated the ballot. 'At no stage did they say to me that Rudd wouldn't run if he didn't have the numbers.' He told the Australian: 'This argument that he [Rudd] had said he wouldn't challenge, in my view is a nonsense.'

Rudd and his Team damned themselves with their own words; it was an exposé of their own duplicity, straight from the mouths of the principal protagonists. And while all the publicly named frontbench members of Team Rudd (bar Albanese) fell on their swords (joined by long-serving minister Martin Ferguson), Rudd trotted off, for all the world a man who believed his integrity was intact. Because he'd honoured his word.

Rudd's inability to grasp the enormity of the wreckage he had left strewn across the political battlefield after the civil war he'd incited was revealed in a scary few paragraphs by Phillip Coorey in the *Australian Financial Review* the morning after the carnage: 'Mr Rudd believes that the government's plight is a result of self-induced errors by Ms Gillard. He believes the government will continue to struggle and momentum may yet gather for him to be drafted.' If the Rudd heart still fluttered with leadership yearning after the many wounds he inflicted on his colleagues, his party and the government, he has serious issues to address.

Behavioural therapist Maryanne Campbell has watched Rudd with amazement and concern for years, and has a few ideas about his personality that can go a little way towards explaining the complexity of a man his colleague Labor MP Steve Gibbons described in a tweet before Rudd's humiliating 2012 ballot defeat as a 'psychopath with a giant ego'. Campbell emphasises that her comments are based on her observations and study of his public persona, not through any personal interaction. She tells me she believes Rudd's feeling of superiority camouflages deep insecurity and a multifarious contradictory personality.

He has an unshakeable faith in himself that is 'close to delusional', Campbell says. 'One of the things that happens with these types of people is they get much further than one would expect because they just drive themselves. And they get further away from their real core at the same time. Then when it falls apart, they can't face that reality; deep down they deny that it's happened.' In Rudd's own mind, if life was fair he'd still be prime minister, she says, but he won't or can't accept that life isn't always fair. And:

'He strongly relates to pain, especially his own. That's why we see moments of real compassion from him, but many more moments of rage and anger.'

Rudd is not a wise person, Campbell concludes: 'When people really have wisdom, everything is in perspective.' It has been obvious throughout his political career that Rudd is not a team player and, she says, 'he shouldn't be in politics'. Campbell's observations of Rudd in the context of his relationship with Gillard lead her to believe that he hasn't known how to move on from June 2010. 'I find the extremities in his character daunting. He is the best-ever friend, and the worst-ever enemy. He's in constant denial that he's not PM, and he's constantly searching for a way back in. That is denial; it isn't wisdom.'

How on earth did it happen—*again*? The result of the February 2012 ballot, when Rudd was whopped by Gillard seventy-one to thirty-one, was a strong message from an overwhelming majority of his caucus colleagues that his hopes were a delusion; nonetheless, Svengali Rudd had continued to keep his followers loyal and his destructive dream alive. Now this farcical no-show challenge and its sequel—the unedifying spectacle of eight front benchers nose-diving to their career deaths in the following twenty-four hours—unmasked the Great Rudd Delusion. But it also dramatically put on public display the Rudd whom many in the government and bureaucracy knew all too well, the man who always had to be the chaotic centre of attention, and whose needs and ambitions inevitably took priority over the interests of the government and the Labor Party, or his loyalty to colleagues.

The destabilisation of Gillard's government since 2010 by Team Rudd and its media mouthpieces was a shadowy exercise in political marketing that spectacularly misfired. It was led by a commander-in-chief who had no workable strategy, only a goal to bring the PM down and return himself to the top job. Team Rudd's primary weapon was white-anting, by claiming that Gillard was inadequate in her handling of her cabinet, in her policy-making, in her leadership of the party. Rudd's team reinforced this message by feeding time limits for the end of Gillard's leadership to compliant journalists.

The longevity of her prime ministership was constantly threatened by a never-ending succession of deadlines: *Tick, tick, tick*, whispered Team Rudd, *you're on notice, Julia. Tick, tick, tick*, echoed journalists and headline writers. Buried towards the bottom of many of the Team Rudd–inspired stories published in the lead-up to the 2012 challenge and the 2013 phantom resurrection was the fact that Rudd didn't have sufficient support to mount a challenge.

No matter. Every month, Rudd had more and more numbers in caucus—well, at least he did according to many in the media and the biased mystics in the radio and tabloid commentariat. Every month he was about to challenge. And every month he didn't— because he didn't have the numbers. The basic political truth is that if you have the numbers you use them; and if you don't have them, you use the media to build momentum to get them.

When another deadline came and went, journalists and Team Rudd simply set another one. She'll be gone by Easter! Very definitely, she'll be gone before parliament breaks for winter! Still there, is she? Then her Waterloo will be before the end of the footy season. What, still bloody hanging on? Well, the traditional political killing season in November and December will definitely take her out! That was the script, running endlessly on a loop, for nearly two years.

When one deadline fails to eventuate, it should be an embarrassment for a gullible media; when dozens and dozens fail to materialise over two years, it's been a massive, humiliating con. Very few in the media were prepared to give as much weight to the reality—that Gillard had the overwhelming support of her caucus—as they gave to the spurious claims of Team Rudd. We in the fourth estate have much to answer for.

As the ABC's political editor at *7.30*, Chris Uhlmann, remarked frankly after the day of high farce: 'The media has played a role in this, and it's for others I guess to parse how well or how badly the media has done. There's not a shadow of a doubt that the media has been used to help build momentum, to help build a sense of chaos, particularly this week. And anytime it looked like it was falling off, there was someone else [from Team Rudd] out and about . . . There is absolutely no doubt the Rudd forces have been using the media quite cleverly for some time now.'

The press gallery can be a beast that feeds on itself. Apart from attending the occasional press conference, Question Time or ministerial interview, gallery journalists are shackled to their desks. Their company is each other; their sounding boards are each other; their judgements about the political angle of the day are formed out of exchanges with each other. But the competition is fierce for the headline story—to be the agenda-setting pundit, or to be the first online to report a whisper. The added dimension for journalists nowadays is the voracious appetite for novelty that the twenty-four-hour online story beast demands. Coupled with the sacking by newspapers of experienced sub-editors and fact-checkers, journalists find themselves in a dangerous new space of unvetted reporting.

In this climate, the anonymous quote—once used only to protect legitimate deep throats or to give nuance to a story—became the most popular bedrock for Gillard–Rudd leadership stories that dominated news headlines and threatened to derail the PM and her government. Every rule in the handbook of good journalism was broken. The international news agency Reuters provides this guidance to its reporters: 'Anonymous sources are the weakest sources.' Rule 5:5 of the ABC's editorial principles states: 'Where a source seeks anonymity, do not agree without first considering the source's motive and any alternative attributable sources.' Despite this, two of Aunty's most respected political journalists were said to be privy to the inside running on Rudd's battle plan for his February 2012 challenge weeks before the leadership ballot, yet they chose to keep this to themselves.

What now of journalists such as the *Sydney Morning Herald*'s Peter Hartcher, who promoted Rudd's cause month after month? I emailed him questions about the ethics of his reportage and his commentary on the leadership issues, given his robust advocacy for Rudd. He responded that he 'utterly' rejected my premise that he had advocated for Rudd 'and, therefore, the questions predicated on it'.

What of others who gave daily credence to anonymous backgrounders, thus lending regular credibility to Team Rudd's inflated and fanciful claims? Gallery journalists were complicit in presenting to the public a picture of a government paralysed by leadership instability, when the forces that created this destabilisation relied on just such media coverage to drive their number-gathering.

Rudd did gather caucus followers as his journey progressed after the February 2012 challenge, but his ambition to kill off Gillard would not have gathered pace if the media had treated it as the dull background noise it deserved instead of the daily thunder crack

Rudd's supporters needed and received. To continue to write, month after month, that Rudd was gaining on Gillard and was poised to mow her down was enabling journalism. As members of Team Rudd told journalists, in the same breath as they acknowledged they didn't have the numbers, 'It's all about the momentum'. And that's what a tidal wave of media coverage gave them: the gift of daily coverage, poisoning the public opinion of the government and relegating any substantive scrutiny of policies to secondary status.

Over the last few years there have been serious reporting mistakes, gross errors of judgement, biased commentary and empowering of Team Rudd's agenda. When the house of cards collapsed—twice—those journalists have remained at their desks. And they pull handsome salaries; they are paid more than a back-bencher in many cases, and among the upper echelons as much as ministers. But while ministers are forced into abject *mea culpa*s and apologies for mistakes, we in the fourth estate simply waltz on to the next project without acknowledging our errors.

The media hold politicians up to the highest possible standards of behaviour. Not even human error or a slight slip of the tongue escapes our harsh judgement; the echo of ridicule about Gillard's mispronunciation in April 2011 of 'hyperbole', for instance, still reverberates. Something has to give.

Journalist and media scholar Dr Helen Ester believes the answer lies in removing the press gallery from parliament house, for the good of the profession and the good of democracy. She explains that the gallery was never supposed to remain in the parliamentary building; it was a temporary arrangement seventy years ago, when the federal parliament moved to Canberra. Ministers weren't supposed to have their offices in parliament, either—they were to be located in their departments. But the temporary became permanent, and over the decades housing the executive and press together led to a closeness that was abused by both sides. 'It proved positive for the executive to have the press gallery there, for it to be easily manipulated,' Ester says. 'But that intimate problematic relationship between the executive and the press gallery got mightily confused with the hung parliament. Everything was fine when Rudd was there, because the press basically wrote his views of the world. The press didn't like it when the game changed.'

Most in the gallery also failed to grasp the dramatically different way the parliament operated. It was no longer a two-horse race, yet the reporting continued to be focused on the personality fights of the good old days. Gillard has earned high praise from the cross benchers for her deft handling of the minority parliament, her negotiating skills, her integrity, good humour and hard work ethic. By the time the day of debacle arrived on 21 March 2013, the parliament had passed a record 480 or so pieces of legislation, but the public knows little of these and other accomplishments of Gillard's government because the two attempted political assassinations of the PM knocked out most reasoned reporting about them.

There is no better example of the media's failure to inform the public of important matters than the reportage during the week leading up to, and on the day of, the resurrection-that-wasn't. The Canberra media was utterly consumed by the theatre of a drama they had helped to create. Many in the gallery and wider commentariat had a stake in the outcome of Rudd vs Gillard; reputations were on the line, and one senior pro-Rudd media spruiker's glittering future career options depended on his bloke returning to The Lodge. The result was that the real stuff, the stuff that affects peoples' lives, slipped into insignificance.

During that week, important legislation passed through parliament and there were other political events of relevance to the public, but these were either ignored in the mainstream press or lost under the weight of media clairvoyance about the leadership. Pensioners and welfare beneficiaries, for example, began to receive their carbon pricing scheme compensation, plus half-yearly pension bonuses. The ground-breaking National Disability Insurance Scheme passed through parliament, to start on 1 July in South Australia, Tasmania, the Barwon region of Victoria and the Hunter in New South Wales. The Sex Discrimination Act was extended to ensure gays, lesbians and transgenders could not be discriminated against. Workers were given the right to request more flexible working arrangements, including extensions of their unpaid parental leave.

On the very day Labor's Ruddites were busy detonating their bomb belts in self-indulgent glory, their Prime Minister made an eloquent, impassioned, historic apology to those affected by forced adoptions, to an audience of thousands who sobbed away decades of grief. It was a day many had waited a lifetime for, and had battled years for parliament to acknowledge.

In July 2012, I randomly sampled across the *Sydney Morning Herald*, the *Australian*, the *Daily Telegraph* and the *Age*, plus a smattering of ABC news and current affairs programs, new stories that contained these three taglines: 'Rudd', 'Gillard' and 'leadership'. Barely a story was written or aired that didn't touch on published opinion polls. The fortnightly Newspoll published in the *Australian*, the monthly AC Nielsen poll published in Fairfax newspapers, and the *ad hoc* Galaxy polls published in News Ltd tabloids are treated by journalists as more important when assessing the government's performance than its achievements or policies. Yet these polls are at best arbitrary snapshots of the public mood, tiny random samples of a voter's reflexive reaction to events of the day—reactions that are strongly influenced by the media's portrayal of the way the government is faring. And the way the media interprets the polls influences the next poll—constant cries that the government is wretched and doomed, is led by a wretched and doomed leader, affects the perception the voting public has of the government and its prime minister.

Journalists who habitually ply statistics to promote the case that a government or its leader is terminal when there are months, even years, before an election are engaging in fraudulent misrepresentation. They are conning the public. Paul Keating was a goner six months out from the 1993 election, the polls predicted; Beazley was supposed to be a winner in 2001; Mark Latham looked like he could get there in 2004, according to the polls eight months out; and in 2010 Labor's lead seemed healthy.

These days the regular published newspaper polls concentrate on voting intentions alone, and reporters simply look back at the political events of the previous fortnight and draw conclusions about the issues that have affected the public mood—even if there is no proven connection. Then they peer into their crystal balls and declare that, based on their deductions and the numbers in front of them, it spells doom or success at an election that can be the political equivalent of light years away. Yet the future is full of events, circumstances, people, twists and turns that will affect and maybe change voters' opinions of their elected representatives.

Because the headline results are circulated the night before, so as to maximise a particular newspaper's bang for its bucks, the polls are absorbed and spat out by television and radio from dawn the next day. The conclusions of those journalists and commentators who interpret the polls frame the political discourse for the day, sometimes for forty-eight hours, and are echoed in the news analyses from other media outlets. Independent polling analyst Andrew Catsaras is appalled at how the polls are often interpreted, and that the interpretation is then mimicked elsewhere. Even polls that show no change, or changes that are within the 3 per cent margin of error, are splashed around by the commissioning news organisation. The *Australian*, for one, is brilliant at prominently running reams of copy on polls that haven't shifted, or only shifted slightly, setting an artificial news agenda for the day.

'The papers that spend money on these polls need to make news stories out of them, even if there's nothing to report,' Catsaras tells me. 'The interpretation is often distorted—if they want to promote a particular leadership story, they can do it. What is a statistical variation can be interpreted or spun around something that has occurred in the political world in the previous fortnight, even if there is no connection at all.'

Former political editor of the *Australian*, Glenn Milne, revealed in a candid article in *IPA Review* in November 2010 that both he and his newspaper used the fortnightly poll to gain valuable political capital: 'You were aware that the poll was expensive,' he wrote. 'Therefore you had better make good use of it. A headline that said "Newspoll Results: Not Very Much" would not cut it with any editor. There was therefore an unspoken demand to dramatise the numbers within reason. To make Newspoll count was to make the *Australian* count.' He was also frank about his own role: 'Yes, there was ego involved as well. As the political editor of the *Australian*, your importance as a player in Canberra was magnified by your role interpreting Newspoll. Any one of my successors that tells you differently is kidding themselves.'

Note the unabashed use of the word 'player'. The reality the newspapers don't tell you is that outside of an election cycle polls are only good for use as weapons against political opponents; as a propaganda tool by whatever party or party leader is in the ascendancy; as a marketing tool by the newspapers that publish them; and as a barometer for lazy journalists to judge a government's performance

Many senior politicians privately anguish over the influence Newspoll and the *Australian* have on power plays and the standing and conduct of governments and opposition, but they feel helpless to take on what is now treated as an omniscient part of the political infrastructure. There's also the need to keep News Ltd onside; over the years the *Australian*'s editors, using its polls as its principal weapon, have worked deftly to erode the standing of governments or leaders they don't like or don't deem fit to govern.

It's not as if the *Australian*'s editors hide their political aims: when the Greens assumed control of the Senate in July 2011, for instance, the newspaper editorialised that it would do all in its power to drive the party into the wilderness. And the paper hasn't hidden a dislike for Gillard or Treasurer Swan. Neither has the *Daily Telegraph*, whose newest recruit to Canberra, Gemma Jones, is the anti-carbon price correspondent. One of her better efforts, in April 2013, was an attempt to link Swan's announcements with the works of Karl Marx.

Politicians also play their part in demeaning their own currency and deceiving the public. The art of political communication is now for many what you can get away with saying, rather than reasoned analysis and responses: Stop the Boats, Ditch the Tax (or the Witch, as the case may be), Moving Forward, Working Families. Voters are treated like fools, instead of thinking human beings.

Much of the effort of many parliamentarians is dedicated to vaudeville. Every day parliament sits the prime minister, ministers and the Opposition's key strategists carefully plan the twenty-four-hour news cycle. John Howard pioneered a daily routine in which he'd give an early morning radio or TV interview to a non-Canberra program that needed to be recorded in its network's Canberra press gallery studio. Press gallery television crews would film the interview while journalists from other news outlets would sit in the studio recording it. Within hours, Howard's strategically crafted line or message of the day would dominate every media outlet without qualification, context or balance.

Today, strategists for both major parties distribute key messages on the issue of the day to the backbenchers rostered onto 'doors'. The cant is recited on breakfast TV and radio. The Prime Minister and the leader of the Opposition don silly hats and fluoro vests in early morning or lunchtime media stunts staged in Canberra's industrial environs or some unlucky suburban primary school, trotting out rehearsed lines aimed at discrediting their opponent. An obliging press corps duly records the mock outrage and rehearsed one-liners, knowing it's all theatre and pantomime with no relevance to policy, performance or the public interest. These sound bites end up as centrepieces on television and radio news broadcasts, providing the audio and the images for the political issue of the day. It is a brainless ritual that is contemptuous of the voting public.

When parliament isn't sitting, the same stage-managed performances are acted out daily in marginal electorates across the country in exercises that do little to advance the well-being and quality of life of everyday Australians. Our politicians lock voters into a twilight zone of perpetual campaigning, and the media plays along with the game. No wonder large numbers of Australians are pissed off at, and feel disenfranchised by, their elected representatives and let down by traditional media.

Because of the pre-occupation with Gillard's alleged failings, flaws and fuck-ups, Abbott's team has become the most under-scrutinised Opposition in recent political history, conning its way into credibility. Its lack of proper costings and consistent talk about the terrible state of the Australian economy (the evidence suggests otherwise), the catastrophic consequences of the carbon pricing scheme (ditto) and Gillard's ineptitude as a prime minister (ditto again) have become part of the narrative about, and public view of, the government. Abbott has been given the easiest ride of any Opposition leader I witnessed during the twenty-five years I reported from the press gallery except, perhaps, One K. Rudd, and that didn't end well at all.

Three years on from when she was asked to take over the prime ministership, Gillard has battled the venal Rudd rump, significant members of the press gallery, influential capital city shock jocks and commentators, and internet conspiracists and misogynists. She has defied the biased reporting and the sexism, and has kept bouncing back like a rubber ducky on a stormy sea.

Postscript: As we go to print, the ghost of phantom leadership challenges past is again wafting through the corridors of parliament. And again, One K. Rudd is in his favourite spot, at the heart and centre of fevered speculation. Unbelievably, the script hasn't changed. On 5 June Rudd pops his head up in a rare appearance on parliament's doors to tell his colleagues to stop talking about leadership: 'I think

it's time everyone, and I mean everyone, just pulled their heads in.'
Not everyone, though; not him. A little more than twenty-four
hours later, he does a high-profile interview on ABC's *7.30* before
setting off on a manic round of electoral campaigning bathed in the
glow of TV cameras, playing word games about the ever-burning
leadership ambitions he professes to no longer nurture.

Just as occurred before the February 2012 leadership challenge
and the no-show March 2013 challenge, leaks of alleged internal
secret ALP polling and research catastrophic for Gillard stalk
her in the national media. From 4 to 15 June, seven separate stories
are planted. One alleges a wipeout in key Queensland seats, including Treasurer Swan's seat of Lilley. Another suggests Labor has
given up hope in three Victorian seats, including Corangamite
where Rudd descends two days later in a visit to Geelong. Another
supposedly reveals that voters haven't got over Rudd's dumping,
while another, published on 13 June in the *West Australian*, claims
Labor will be massacred in that state. Gillard just happens to be
campaigning in Perth that day.

At the same time, a charming menu at a Liberal fundraiser
offers a fried quail dish named after Gillard: 'Small breasts, huge
thighs and a big red box'; and West Australian shock jock Howard
Sattler quizzes Gillard if her partner, Tim Matthieson, is gay.
Politics is in the gutter.

It's Tuesday 18 June, and in the second-last caucus meeting of
the 43rd parliament Gillard has not been challenged for the leadership. As ever, her stalkers remain in the shadows, assessing the
right time to strike. For days Rudd has been all over the news,
intoning about how he will do everything he 'physically can to stop
Tony Abbott', at the same time somberly stating that his position
on the leadership 'hasn't changed'. What position is that, Kevin?

Your statement on 22 February 2012: 'There is no way, no way I would ever be party to a stealth attack on a sitting prime minister elected by the people'? Or your pledge on 27 February, after suffering a humiliating 71–31 rebuff in a party room challenge, that you would henceforth put your 'every effort into securing Julia Gillard's re-election as Labor Prime Minister at the next election'? No? Perhaps you mean your unequivocal commitment after the aborted putsch of 21 March 2013, when you stated there would be 'no circumstances' under which you would ever lead Labor again?

Then why is the media yet again full of stories from your sources, chock-a-block full of anonymous briefings about the conditions you would place on your return; about momentum gathering for you to take back the prime ministership (that momentum waltz again); about a falling-away in numbers for Gillard; about unions such as the AWU deserting her (which is denied)?

The body count Rudd will leave behind if he does this time steamroll his way back to the leader's chair, despite the loathing of the majority of his caucus, will be huge: the frontbench lemmings who he led off the cliff in March; ministers such as Swan, Emerson, Garrett, Macklin, Wong and Plibersek, who will go; and the federal parliamentary party, which will be the biggest carcass. It will have collectively surrendered its principles and its fate to one of the great wreckers in modern Labor. And all Labor supporters across the country have been able to do for three years is sit and watch in horror as a once-great party has been devoured alive from the inside.

APPENDIX

Time's up, Julia!

Assessments made mainly by Canberra-based journalists and commentators, including statements made by Team Rudd quoted in media stories. The list doesn't include most non-Canberra commercial TV and radio predictions.

2010
December 16   Andrew Bolt, *Herald-Sun*: Gillard should resign

2011
April 11   Bolt: Gillard is finished as Prime Minister

June 6   Bolt: Gillard will be gone by December

July 7   Phillip Coorey, *Sydney Morning Herald*: Gillard is down for the count

July 25   Chris Kenny, *Australian*: Rudd is Labor's last chance

September 1   Graham Richardson, 3AW: Government won't
               survive another year under Gillard's leadership
September 1   Andrew Bolt, Steve Price, Melbourne radio:
               Gillard should resign now
September 2   Coorey: Doubts over PM's leadership
September 2   Phillip Hudson, *Herald-Sun*: Tick, tick, tick:
               Gillard's authority lost; time to weigh up whether
               to resign
September 2   Hudson, Simon Benson, *Daily Telegraph*: Gillard
               fights for her leadership
September 2   Peter Hartcher, *Sydney Morning Herald*: Gillard
               government like a house on fire
September 2   Piers Akerman, News Ltd: PM's leadership lost
               at sea
September 2   Steve Price, 3AW: The whiff of prime ministerial
               killing season wafts around Canberra
September 3   Hartcher: Is Labor prepared to forgo its only
               realistic leadership hope—Rudd?
September 6   Philip Adams, ABC: Resign, Julia
September 9   Jeremy Thompson, ABC: Gillard is finished
September 22   Benson: Support for Rudd growing significantly
September 23   Coorey: Rudd nine votes from toppling Gillard
September 23   Hartcher: Gillard government on torture rack;
               Kevin could end the pain

October 1   Dennis Shanahan, *Australian*: Rudd
               gathering numbers
October 7   Richardson: Senior journalists tell me Gillard will
               be gone by Christmas
October 14   Richardson: Talk of a challenge will not go away
October 19   Bernard Keane, Crikey: Barring an improbable
               Gillard recovery, Labor will return to Rudd
October 20   Benson: Support for Gillard collapsing

November 3	Simon Benson, Steve Lewis, *Daily Telegraph*: Labor powerbrokers plot coup for this month
December 4	Samantha Maiden, *Sunday Telegraph*: Rudd to mount a challenge within months

2012

January 29	Cosima Marriner, Fairfax: Rudd a strong chance of returning after the March Queensland election
January 31	Fran Kelly, Radio National: A Rudd challenge now inevitable
January 31	Benson: a showdown in March or April
February 1	Shanahan: All the signs of a leadership challenge there
February 2	Coorey: Gillard in danger after Queensland election, before budget
February 3	Emma Griffiths, Sabra Lane, ABC: Gillard's tenure terminal
February 3	ABC online: Gillard in deep trouble, challenge before Queensland election
February 6	Benson: Momentum swinging towards Rudd
February 6	Hartcher: Doomsday clock for Gillard set in motion
February 18	Shanahan: Rudd will strike in the final March parliamentary sittings
February 18	Hartcher: Rudd will again become leader
February 19	Maiden: Gillard should resign now
February 20	Benson: Half the cabinet has switched to Rudd
February 20	Hartcher: Likely Rudd will return to the prime ministership within weeks
February 20	Shanahan: Gillard delusional, in retreat
February 20	Matthew Franklin, *Australian*: Support for Gillard among key cabinet ministers collapsing

February 21	Niki Savva, *Australian*: Too late for Gillard to save herself
February 23	Benson: Assassins are reaping what they sowed
February 23	Hartcher: If Labor wants to be electable, Rudd should return to leadership
February 26	Peter van Onselen, *Sunday Telegraph*: Gillard's chances of recovery very low
February 27	Ben Packham, *Australian*: Rudd leaves door open to being drafted if he loses ballot
February 27	Hartcher: Rising caucus panic will fuel a second Rudd strike in the year ahead
February 27	Hudson: Gillard has six to eight months or she'll be tapped on the shoulder
March 2	Benson: At best she has four months left
March 3	Shanahan: Gillard's leadership was finished if she hadn't appointed Bob Carr
March 26	Gemma Jones, *Daily Telegraph*: Gillard's party is about over
March 26	Richardson, *Daily Telegraph*: Gillard will lose, and lose badly
April 21	Richardson, Sky News: Gillard will be gone by end of May
April 26	John Masanauskas, *Herald-Sun*: Fresh leadership challenge by August
April 30	Michelle Grattan, *The Age*: Gillard should fall on her sword
April 30	van Onselen: Gillard's demise inevitable
April 30	Chris Kenny: Gillard government terminal
April 30	Richardson, Sky News: Gillard won't last another month
April 30	Bolt: Gillard must go
April 30	Akerman: The Gillard government must go

May 1	Savva: Gillard must vacate the leadership
May 1	Hartcher: Even Gillard supporters looking at Rudd
May 2	Sid Maher and Tony Bramston, *Australian*: Inevitable Labor will dump the PM, maybe in a few weeks
May 2	Shanahan: It's only a matter of time for Gillard
May 3	Gemma Daley, *Australian Financial Review*: Gillard's leadership will be reconsidered as early as end June
May 3	Richardson, *Australian*: Gillard one move away from checkmate
May 7	Hudson: Gillard has until AFL finals in September
May 18	Richardson: Gillard and Labor doomed
May 19	Akerman: The party's over for Gillard
May 26	Van Onselen: The only option is to change to Rudd
June 11	Coorey: Gillard will be gone by the end of the week, end of June, late August or December
June 12	Shanahan: Gillard's leadership looking terminal
June 24	Maiden: August strike against Gillard likely
June 25	Shanahan: Gillard will be removed before the end of the year
July 6	Richardson, *Australian*: All Gillard can do is wait for the end
July 17	Simon Cullen, ABC: Gillard for the high jump; only a matter of time
July 21	Mike Carlton, *Sydney Morning Herald*: Gillard must quit, or she'll be tapped on the shoulder, probably in late August

July 23	Leo Shanahan, *Australian*: Gillard in big trouble
July 24	Franklin: If no poll recovery, Gillard should fall on her sword
July 25	Paul Kelly, *Australian*: Gillard's prime ministership being cancelled; it's Rudd or oblivion
July 29	Geoff Kitney, Mark Skully, *Australian Financial Review*: Time is running out for Gillard
August 11	Akerman: Gillard's hold on power slipping
August 20	Neil Mitchell, 3AW: [The AWU saga] is the final straw for Gillard's leadership
August 20	Jennifer Hewett, *Australian Financial Review*: A bad poll tomorrow could see a leadership move
October 9	Geoff Kitney, *Australian Financial Review*: Gillard has failed the leadership test
October 18	Coorey: Rudd back counting numbers
November 5	Hartcher: Gillard is hanging by a thread
November 24	Hartcher: Knives out for Gillard
November 29	Akerman: PM's goose is cooked
November 30	Akerman: Gillard is floundering

2013

January 5	Mark Kenny, *Sydney Morning Herald*: Support for a Rudd challenge getting closer
January 31	Jones: Gillard vulnerable to leadership switch if bad polls ahead
February 2	Mark Kenny, Coorey, Speers: Government in shambles
February 3	Mark Kenny, Jessica Wright, Fairfax: Labor in crisis; Gillard on back foot

February 3	Grattan: Ministers desert Gillard's sinking ship
February 5	Mark Kenny: Rudd within striking distance of Gillard
February 14	Benson: Leadership issue coming to a head
February 14	Grattan: Increased pressure on Gillard's leadership
February 14	Shanahan, Sky: Caucus and press gallery ready to go off at slightest spark
February 19	Mark Kenny: Gillard, beware the knives of March
February 19	Mark Day, Fairfax: Gillard is a dead woman walking
February 19	Benson: Gillard's support base slipping away
February 19	Hewett: Nothing will save the PM
February 19	Packham: Desperate caucus eyes leadership switch
February 19	Tory Shepherd, Fairfax: Gillard gone if next Newspoll bad
February 19	*Age* editorial: Time for a new leader?
February 19	Tony Wright, *The Age*: Rudd's in storage, waiting for sun to shine
February 19	Mark Kenny: Showdown between Gillard and Rudd inevitable
February 19	Coorey: Leadership could come to a head when parliament resumes
February 20	Alan Stokes, Fairfax: Julia, it's time for an exit speech
February 21	Richardson: PM should go for the party's sake
February 22	Richardson, 3AW: PM should go quietly
February 23	Katharine Murphy, Fairfax: Gillard may not recover this time
February 23	van Onselen: Gillard risks her legacy by not ceding to Rudd

March 2	Hartcher: A Rudd leadership could be transformative
March 10	Maiden: Powerbrokers canvas option of asking Gillard to stand aside
March 10	Richardson: The chances are 55-45 leadership change will happen in the next fortnight
March 11	Hartcher: Rudd leadership could transform the election contest
March 12	Mark Kenny: Gillard backers must move against her for the greater good
March 12	Mark Kenny: Momentum growing for leadership change before September election
March 13	Hartcher: Why is Labor not replacing Julia Gillard with Rudd this week?
March 15	Bob Gosford, Crikey: I'll call it now—Gillard will be gone by next Wednesday
March 16	van Onselen: The momentum for change now exists
March 18	Hartcher: Slow motion mass political suicide if Labor won't undo its mistake in deposing Rudd
March 19	Laurie Oakes, Nine network: Move against Gillard, probably on Friday
March 19	Hartcher: Momentum growing for return to Rudd
March 20	Bolt, Twitter: All that's left is the trigger for the switch
March 20	Bolt: Gillard leading Labor to defeat and a legacy of shame
March 21	Malcolm Farr, News Ltd: ALP set to inscribe another fresh page by dumping the first woman to be Prime Minister
March 21	Richardson, 2GB: A slim victory to Rudd
March 21	Richardson, Sky: Gillard will win, but she's dead in the water anyway

ACKNOWLEDGEMENTS

Enormous thanks to the crew at Allen & Unwin, particularly Richard Walsh and Rebecca Kaiser for their steadfast belief in this project. I am eternally grateful to my son Kieran for his patience through the gnashing of teeth times; to my late father Brian, for passing on his love of history and writing; to my mother Trish, for her creative spirit; to my supportive siblings and big extended family. To friends Lou Dodson, Amanda Cavill, Peter Logue and Bill D'Arcy, for their friendship and advice; and a very large bouquet to my steadfast friend since we were seven, Janneke Chudleigh, and the quiet encouragement over decades from Shelly Spees and Tess Crimmins. To other encouraging and supportive friends in politics and the media, who know who you are—thank you. To the late Lew Griffiths, who was looking forward to this book so much, for his great friendship and loyal support over many years. To Priyanka Koci, for her last-minute research assistance; and to my dogs Les and Darcy, for extending silent support from under my desk in the long hours.